PUBLIC LIBRARY
W9-BPE-228

TWENTIETH CENTURY VIEWS

The aim of this series is to present the best in contemporary critical opinion on major authors, providing a twentieth century perspective on their changing status in an era of profound revaluation

Maynard Mack, *Series Editor*
Yale University

VOLTAIRE

VOLTAIRE

A COLLECTION OF CRITICAL ESSAYS

Edited by

William F. Bottiglia

Prentice-Hall, Inc.  *Englewood Cliffs, N. J.*

Library of Congress Catalog Card Number 68-17823. Printed in the United States of America.

Current printing (last number):
10 9 8 7 6 5 4 3 2 1

To Mildred MacDonald Bottiglia

Down, down, down into the darkness of the grave
Gently they go, the beautiful, the tender, the kind;
Quietly they go, the intelligent, the witty, the brave.
I know. But I do not approve. And I am not resigned.

(Edna St. Vincent Millay)

Preface

The critical essays contained in this volume include nine chapters or chapter-sections from books, plus one article, presented in their entirety[1] except for the editor's own contribution ("Candide's Garden"), which alone he has felt free to abridge. They have been selected with the aim of providing for English-speaking teachers and students a fairly broad sampling of the present-day views of specialists on certain basic aspects of Voltaire's life and works. A number of other essays were considered and rejected either for lack of space or because they could not be successfully extracted from their larger context or shorn of their heavy scholarly apparatus.

The editor is in full agreement with most of the judgments expressed by the other specialists represented in this collection, but not with all. In his "Introduction" he offers a number of judgments that differ, partly to show that there continues to be considerable room for disagreement among specialists and partly to encourage independent reflection in the reader.

Unless there is a specific indication to the contrary, explanatory material and translated passages in brackets have been supplied by the editor.

Throughout the volume the abbreviation M. followed by Roman and then Arabic numerals stands for the Moland edition of Voltaire's complete works, the volume number(s), and the page number(s). Similarly, the abbreviation Best. followed by an Arabic numeral or numerals stands for the Besterman edition of Voltaire's correspondence and the number(s) of the letter(s). (For both of these items see the Selected Bibliography at the end.)

[1] This includes the footnotes in all cases but one: namely, Peter Gay's essay on Voltaire's politics, in which they have been abridged and adapted in accordance with the practical needs of this collection.

The editor takes this opportunity to thank those who have granted him permission to reprint the essays which make up this volume (acknowledgments accompany each essay), and to express his special gratitude for permission to reproduce on the dedication page the final stanza of Edna St. Vincent Millay's poem, "Dirge Without Music" (From *Collected Poems,* Harper & Row, Publishers. Copyright 1928, 1955 by Edna St. Vincent Millay and Norma Millay Ellis. By permission of Norma Millay Ellis.)

Contents

Contents

VOLTAIRE

Introduction

by William F. Bottiglia

I

Voltaire's right to membership in any pantheon of illustrious historical figures has often been challenged. By Roman Catholics, for example, who have returned hostility for hostility and denounced him as an agent of the devil or as Satan himself reincarnated. By agnostics and atheists who have found his belief in God no more respectable than the superstitions he so implacably attacked. By moral idealists indignant over his defects of character or his willingness to compromise abstract principle for the sake of small, concrete, practical, impure advances. By political liberals or radicals who have recoiled in horror before his royalism and his distrust of the untutored masses. By philosophers disdainful of his failure to build a system or to develop lines of reasoning with sustained analytical subtlety. By literary critics who have dismissed him as a clever but shallow mimic in the formal genres and, for the rest, a mere journalist consuming his energies in a massive outpouring of ephemera. By academic specialists who have stigmatized him as a popularizing jack-of-all-disciplines bent on spreading himself over an area much too wide for one man's competence and unable to concentrate on any one subject long enough to possess it.

There are cogent answers which can be made to most of these charges, and a number of them will be found in the pages of this volume; but it does not follow that those convinced of Voltaire's greatness have always known how to argue convincingly against his detractors. One could cite Roman Catholics who have tortured the evidence to prove him a loyal son of the Church; agnostics and atheists who have twisted it another way to claim him as one of their own. Occasionally his views have been adapted to modern political biases, and he has been transformed into a democrat at heart or in tendency. A few scholars have tidied up, subtilized, and systematized his thinking in an attempt to rework it into a master philosophy. In some instances judgment has yielded to idolatry, his faults have been extenuated or even made over into virtues, and one critic at least has suggested that Voltaire's formal works, particularly his plays, are held in low esteem today because tastes have changed, not because they are deficient in intrinsic artistic merit.

The fact is that Voltaire constitutes an extraordinarily difficult specialty. There are several reasons why. The Moland edition of his works runs to more than thirty massive volumes, if we exclude the correspondence, and Besterman's monumental edition of the latter totals 107 volumes. Voltaire's production is not only immense, it is extremely diversified, for it includes various types of plays, poems, histories, encyclopaedia articles, philosophic tales, letters, and miscellanea. Around it during the past two centuries there has developed a bibliography of staggering proportions. There may be scholars who have read everything written by Voltaire, but no scholar could possibly read everything that has been written about him throughout the world in numerous tongues. This is not all. Voltaire's works are almost completely rooted in circumstance. Accordingly, a true understanding of what he means frequently depends on accurate, detailed knowledge of such factors as time, place, mood, aim, topical allusions, intended audience, degree of seriousness, and degree of indirection. Those who read him without adequate background preparation will be ill-equipped to determine on a given occasion whether he is speaking in earnest or in fun, whether he is saying what he really means or veiling his meaning in one of a number of possible ways, whether he is setting down a lively first impression or a sober second thought, expressing a momentary caprice or the conviction of a lifetime, slanting his ideas for purposes of propaganda or attempting a balanced historical evaluation.

There are still other complicating factors. A command of the facts is not enough to guarantee sound value-judgments. No less important is critical attitude or approach. In matters of religion Voltaire has always been explosively controversial. Even today, after almost two centuries, it is impossible for many to view this fire-breathing polemicist in a non-polemical perspective and to try to see him as he really was in his complex totality, instead of squinting at him through lenses which yield a simplified and distorted image. Then there is the issue of his moral conduct. The self-styled "friends of Voltaire" strain hard to explain away his notorious defects of character and consequent behavior, often vulgar, sometimes malicious; while his adversaries methodically impute to sordid motives his generous impulses, his campaigns in behalf of the oppressed, his humanitarian enterprises at Ferney, and his crusades for social reform. In addition to these black-or-white attitudes, Voltaire criticism has long suffered and continues to suffer from methods based on approaches that are either inappropriate or reductive. Conventional historians, intellectual historians, and philosophers are conspicuously prone to drain the blood from his literary works, strip off their flesh, and rearrange the dry bones in abstract patterns of ideas. Not seldom they even lapse into the incredibly naïve error of taking literally his satirical deformations and crying out against their "unfairness," unaware that he expects them to savor the artistic license and then make the common-sense adjustment to his true meanings. Specialists, in desperate search of the one key that will magically unlock every door of Voltaire's vast imperial residence and permit access to its most secret vaults and chambers, from time to time announce that they have found it in the form of his bourgeois ambition, or his vanity, or his passion for justice, in the pamphlets, or the correspondence, or the marginalia. But there is no grand master key, and many parts of the palace will remain forever impenetrable to the narrow skills of such locksmiths.

The truth is that the real Voltaire is nothing less than the whole Voltaire, and the whole Voltaire is more, much more than any one individual can fully and finally seize, fix, and define. To dip into Voltaire is to experience the delightful illusion that he is a glittering, limpid, comfortably shallow lake, occasionally ruffled by gentle breezes or stiff winds, but characteristically calm and smiling. To explore him methodically is to discover a broad expanse of ocean, many-laughing yet restless, often tossed by squalls and gales, often agitated by powerful undercurrents, with surprising depths and ever-receding horizons. To explore him methodically is to learn that no method or combination of methods will ever succeed in capturing and controlling the tumultuous vitality of his life or the overwhelming exuberance of his works. Concentration on Voltaire, when unmarred by the fallacy of reduction or by blind predilection or prejudice, leads to the realization that he is inexhaustible, and so teaches a lesson in intellectual humility.

II

There can be no question, then, of saying the last word on Voltaire. One can only, after many years of sustained application and consequently with much hesitation, offer a few suggestions on attitude, approach, method, and evaluation, and a few conclusions which seem to follow, as a guide for the less experienced and as a contribution to the never-ending dialogue with professional colleagues.

The matter of attitude is fundamental. With almost any other famous figure so long dead it would be an affront to lecture our highly sophisticated age of criticism on the need for a liberal stance. With Voltaire it remains necessary. Yet surely the time has come to rise above the wrangle, to suspend belief or disbelief, to accord him the intuitive sympathy one owes any fellow human, and to try to understand him as fully as possible before judging him. It is not true, of course, that to understand everything is to forgive everything; but a sincere attempt, however inadequate, to comprehend the total individual with his many strengths and weaknesses is alone likely to produce an evaluation which has a chance of being sober, sensible, solid, and balanced.

The liberal attitude leads inevitably to an approach focused on Voltaire's period rather than on ours. What Voltaire has to say to our age is a question one should ask at the end, not at the beginning. The approach to an understanding of the man demands a strenuous effort of the historical, as well as of the psychological, imagination, for he cannot be understood save in interaction with his time. Obviously, no one can escape his time. Still, if an individual rises high enough within it, he will turn out to have something of great significance, though not necessarily of topical interest, to say to all ages.

The attitude and the approach just sketched are best realized through a multiplicity of methods. Given the complexity of Voltaire, of the Enlightenment, and of the relationships between them, the wisest recourse is the practice of critical pluralism. Biographical, psychological, historical, aesthetic, and other techniques of analysis can be fruitful—each within limits, to be sure, for no single method has unrestricted applicability. The judicious critic will know how to profit from all without being the dupe of any.

Even so, a multiplicity of methods, no matter how judiciously applied, will come short of the goal. It is especially important to bear down heavily on this point because the typical Voltaire scholar views the world through spectacles ground to a rationalistic prescription. Now methods are systematic procedures which organize and interpret bodies of data through the agency of reason. They impose definitions and categories upon sections of reality. They quantify whatever they investigate. But the living reality of Voltaire interacting with his era over a period of eighty-four years ends by eluding all the artifices of dispassionate intellectual inquiry. It is a living reality of ceaseless flux, of dissolving views, of growth and modification and fluctuation, of irregular, undulating rhythms. Amid this expanse of ocean the illusion of fixity, conceptual and other, disappears, and methodical criticism proves to be less than adequate. It can at best produce a cerebral approximation, it cannot re-create Voltaire in all his mercurial and explosively dynamic vibrancy. For that we should need the visceral empathy, the informing intuition, and the verbal wizardry of a very great novelist or dramatist.

A cerebral approximation nonetheless has its place and can contribute considerably to understanding and appreciation. It can, and should, also conduce to broadly based and carefully pondered evaluation. As already stated, a sympathetic attitude must not be interpreted to imply that all things are permissible. If this were so, the critic would be one who simply classifies, describes, and analyzes without evaluating. He would be a bureaucratic clerk, not a judge. He would, moreover, be a pyrrhonist, not a true skeptic. T. S. Eliot perceptively defines skepticism as "the habit of examining evidence and the capacity for delayed decision"; and he adds: "we need not only the strength to defer a decision, but the strength to make one."[1] The liberal critic is the penultimate skeptic. He defers a decision until he has, by a sympathetic and imaginative examination of the pertinent evidence, arrived at the fullest possible understanding and appreciation—then follows through by passing judgment.

Judgment, of course, is unavoidably subjective; but if the attitude, approach, and method outlined are conscientiously and intelligently applied, the resultant evaluation may seem sound enough to win the approval of others—in which case it will rise at least to the intersubjective level. Beyond the task of judging Voltaire against his own time there lies the final and most delicate effort of all: that of estimating his achievement by reference to enduring civilized values. The critic in search of such an estimate must ultimately ask himself how broad, how deep, how inspiring, etc. he finds Voltaire to be, in other words how great is his achievement. The answer to questions of this kind flow from a set of assumptions about man and the

[1] *Notes towards the Definition of Culture* (New York: 1949), p. 28.

universe; they imply a philosophy of life. And it is precisely here, in the attempt at a grand perspective from a particular point of view, that the subjective factor becomes most conspicuous.

The liberal critic has no reason to feel embarrassed about the subjectivity of his judgments. The execution of his total task does include the use of certain scientific tools of analysis, but he is after all a humanist, not a scientist, and as such entitled to evaluate a writer's life and works by his own standards. If he has begun with an intuitively sympathetic attitude in order to be liberally fair, if he has given Voltaire a chance to live and breathe on his own terms in his own time, if he has sought to understand and appreciate as fully as possible both the virtues and the faults of this exceptionally complex human being, he has earned the right and will naturally want to complete his task by expressing judgments which he hopes some of his readers will be able to share, or at least to respect.

III[2]

Any scholar who follows through on these principles must sooner or later renounce all easy generalizations, all simple conclusions as to the character and the thought of Voltaire. By turns irascible and sentimental, elated and depressed, earnest and buffoonish, sincere and disingenuous, magnanimous and ignoble, methodical and capricious, forever shifting moods, sometimes with vertiginous rapidity, he displayed all the vagaries of a mercurial temperament that rendered him "the glory, jest, and riddle" of his age. His life was long and full, and he reacted with seismographic sensitivity to every vibration of a period prone to frequent tremors and occasional climactic temblors. He made it a habit to record his every reaction, whether trivial or solemn, and so did many who were in his presence, often in conflicting versions; while those not there but in on the hearsay busily wrought their own embroidery. No wonder, then, if his words and actions became the stuff of which legends are made, to the delight of gossips, dilettantes, and artists, but to the despair of researchers and critics. It is difficult enough for the latter to feel their way through the enveloping fog of anecdotal chitchat and inflated or distorted reports to the character of the man as he really was. It is more than difficult, it is impossible, having lived with

[2] Some of the material in this section is an adaptation of ideas previously treated in the editor's book, *Voltaire's "Candide": Analysis of a Classic,* 2nd ed. (Genève: Institut et Musée Voltaire, 1964), pp. 17-62, 292-93.

him a long time in the re-creative imagination, to communicate in analytical prose his sustained vitality, the innumerable contradictions of detail playing over his basic consistency, and the confounding intricacy of his many-sided nature as he went skittering and dodging through the century.

The man as he really was simply cannot be accounted for in neat, clear, precise formulas that will satisfy our rational expectations. He was a bourgeois who grew into an intellectual, and even a social, aristocrat, while retaining intact or modified many middle-class traits. He was an astonishing combination of the writer and the businessman, who succeeded spectacularly in both domains. He hobnobbed with kings and noblemen, yet was passionately concerned to make jobs for the poor and to defend the honor of the oppressed. His insatiable vanity drove him to acts of vindictiveness against his opponents which no explanation can palliate; but in his finest hours he campaigned for social justice with a sublime fervor. One could easily add to this list of paradoxes, contradictions, and complications. Taken together, they create a surface impression of chaos. The impression is misleading. Voltaire's character has a unity that is more psychological than logical. Beneath the apparent confusion and turmoil it is possible to discern a lifelong consistency in his drive toward such goals as fame and fortune, security and freedom, beauty and enlightenment and reform. Circumstances often forced him to pause, backtrack, or detour in his pursuit of these ends, but he persevered, and his persistence gave coherence to his character and meaning to his life.

The unity of Voltaire's thought is likewise more psychological than logical. He was neither a subtle dialectician nor a builder of systems. He was not, in other words, a professional philosopher. He was both a literary artist and a practical moralist deeply concerned with every aspect of the human condition—in sum, a creatively gifted intellectual. It was his destiny to live during a time of turbulent transition from a society of status dominated by traditional Christian values to a society of contract which would be increasingly impregnated with the values of scientific humanism. In this war between ages he fought on the side of the future, but his tactics were those of attrition, not of devastation, of practical gradualism, not of doctrinaire violence. It is true that he fought with a fanatical zeal, yet his ends were moderate. He believed in small steps rather than great leaps forward because he understood the difficulties and the risks of social change and did not want a whole way of life to be suddenly engulfed in a diluvial disaster. This practical gradualism of his kept him in close and vital contact with the concrete realities of his time. It made possible an organic correspondence between his thought and his environment as "the old order change[d], yielding place to new." On the other hand, it has always been the despair of those who would liberate thought from the entanglements of historical process and shape it into abstractly coherent patterns.

The propagandist thrust of Voltaire's gradualism impelled him to use every conceivable trick of persuasion, direct and indirect. He exhorted, pleaded, preached, mocked, rebuked, and fulminated. Above all, he mocked, always with a view to discomfiting the enemy and inching forward toward the new order; and he wielded the weapons of mockery with such mastery that he became one of the greatest satirists in history. There is no type of satire that cannot be found in his arsenal. Burlesque; invective; irony through overstatement, understatement, repetition, surprise, contrast, absurdity—he knew and exploited them all. What is more, in a spirit of experimentation he adapted them to forms which reflected the temper of the times: for example, the letter, the medley, the dialogue, the philosophic tale, the mock sermon or decree, the encyclopaedia article. And with very few exceptions he intended his simplifications, exaggerations, and distortions to stimulate laughter, reflection, and, in men of good will, the resolve to help promote reforms. He did not intend that they be accepted at face value, but that they be relished as literary devices and sensibly interpreted to accord with his sensible implications.

Since Voltaire was a man acutely sensitive to political realities as well as social needs, hence acutely aware of practical possibilities, he frequently adopted a double standard of truth, one for leaders and potential leaders, whom he hoped to persuade by appealing to their reason, another for the untutored masses, whom he hoped to keep under control by preaching publicly useful doctrines which were the equivalent of Plato's royal lies. Thus he made a show of believing in a God who rewards and punishes in an afterlife. His sense of the practical did not, however, lead him in all cases to assume purely pragmatic positions for restraining the multitude. To cite but one contrary instance, in arguing for constitutional absolutism and against the *parlements,* he advocated the one realistic solution for the France of his time, and he did so with open sincerity.[3]

[3] See below, the essay "Voltaire's Politics: France and Constitutional Absolutism" by Peter Gay, pp. 112-30.

Everything which has been said suggests a Voltaire deeply committed to civilized values, recognizing the necessity of order as a warrant of security, enjoyment, self-fulfillment, and social productivity, but at the same time acknowledging the inevitability and the advisability of certain changes, and so feeling his way from concrete situation to concrete situation in a period of transition roiled by all the tensions that build up out of hope and fear. To this must be added the genuine perplexities which Voltaire experienced in wrestling with the great perennial problems of man's destiny. It was in the semidarkness spread across his perspective by the Copernican revolution that he was forced to grope for solutions. The solutions he found for these, as for more earthbound, problems reflect his circumspect moderation, and especially his conviction that enlightenment, like social progress, should come gradually, lest some cataclysm brought on by extremists abruptly shatter the complex and delicate structure of Western civilization.

If, then, one bears in mind the character of the man, the nature of his milieu, and the dynamic interaction between them, his thought takes on a special interest and impressiveness, not for its architectonic, but for its organic quality, not as a feat of the ivory-tower intellect, but as a manifold of ideas incorporated into the active life. The précis of some of Voltaire's basic views which follows is, of course, a mere cerebral—and static—approximation. It cannot convey the drama of his mind at work on issues of the highest practical importance to him and to his society, a drama filled with twists and turns and extending over many decades.

In his vigorous reaction against the coherence overstress of recent philosophers such as Descartes and Spinoza, Voltaire tended at times toward a somewhat unimaginative empiricism, or what might be termed a correspondence overstress in his quest for sure knowledge. On the whole, however, he favored a genuinely scientific approach based on the mathematics and physics of his day, an approach which observed, experimented, and hypothesized, blending a respect for the data of experience with care in the application of logical controls.

In his even more vigorous reaction against organized religion, its dogmas, rituals, otherworldliness, fanaticism, persecutions, immorality, and temporal power, he became a freethinker, but not an agnostic or atheist. Voltaire was a sincere and ardent deist. He believed in a God who, having set up a universe regulated by "natural" law, kept the whole running smoothly without intervening capriciously to perform miracles or answer prayers. But where unbelievers saw nothing but nature, he saw art, and art presupposes a Master Artificer. The trouble was that this art had palpable flaws. Imperfections and evils were there for all to see and suffer from. Voltaire never ceased to worry over this problem, and in the latter part of his life he seemed to be edging toward the idea of a limited God coeternal with a not always tractable matter, who had organized the world as best He could under the circumstances, and who could therefore not be held responsible for its flaws. It is true that Voltaire was propagating a royal lie for the edification of the masses when he preached a God who rewards and punishes, but it is definitely not true that he was in his heart of hearts an agnostic or atheist. His God was for him—and sooner or later, he hoped, for all leaders of society—the very real ground both of the order which the scientist discovers and of the forms which the artist creates.

He was also the ground of the deistic ethic. Voltaire rejected innate ideas. It was his contention that God endows all men with certain instincts which can be developed by proper training into moral principles. God sows the seeds; it is up to men to make them grow into healthy plants. From the seed of gregariousness carefully cultivated springs the supreme virtue, active love of neighbor or "beneficence." It is the supreme virtue because with it civilization will flourish, without it society will quickly deteriorate into a jungle. Virtue is in any case public, not private. It involves relations between human beings; it has nothing to do with a man's purely personal behavior. But why strive to be virtuous? Voltaire's answer to the untutored we have already seen: so that you will receive your reward in the afterlife. To the élite, however, many of whom shared his unbelief in a retributive hereafter, he said: so that you may achieve maximum self-realization on this earth as normal, healthy, civilized individuals.

There remained the correlative question: are men free to make meaningful moral choices? Although Voltaire began by defending the traditional conception of free will, his acceptance of a block universe rigorously governed by the law of causality finally forced him to go over to the deterministic position. He came to believe that if men will an action and are able to perform it, they are free, but that whatever they will is the result of an antecedent cause. By traditional standards Voltaire's notion of freedom is a mockery, since it eliminates true moral agency and converts men into puppets. There is no doubt that he was disturbed by the difficulties implicit in his stand. Nevertheless, he combatted fatalism because it destroys moral initiative—which means that he was an *active* determinist, convinced that men could and should struggle to better their lot and that of their fellow humans. Characteristically, he made his most effective statement on the subject, not as a philosopher weaving a web of dialectical subtleties, but as a practical moralist concerned with the needs of action, when he affirmed that, regardless of theory, men would always behave as if they were genuinely free.

Voltaire's faith in science, his humanism, his deistic ethic, and his reformist gradualism combined to give him a melioristic outlook. Intellectually, he had never been an optimist in the sense of maintaining that "whatever is, is right"; but he had shown a certain complacency with respect to the needs of action against remediable evils, and it took the Lisbon disaster to engage his emotions and, along with other crucial events such as the Seven Years' War and the battle over publication of the *Encyclopaedia,* to arouse his fighting spirit. Earnest attempts have been made to prove that as he grew older, he turned into a pessimist. What is involved here is the academic fallacy of stacking quotations without properly evaluating them in the light of the whole. Voltaire suffered frequently in his old age from passing moods of depression variously caused by illness, fatigue, disappointment, frustration, etc. Yet all the while he went on composing an overwhelming succession of works short and long in a grand campaign for the enlightenment and betterment of mankind. It should be added that one could just as easily pile up quotations which show him in a gay or confident or aggressive mood. The key to the matter is his way of life. No pessimist could have done what he did at Les Délices and Ferney. Not that his meliorism was a simple, uncomplicated faith. He took it for granted that with hard work and good luck men could move forward, but he was only too well aware that there was no such thing as automatic progress. Men had to earn anew every day their title to civilization. If they relaxed their efforts or if some great disaster struck, all would be lost: the jungle would overrun the garden. Voltaire knew too much about the past to have any illusions about the future on that score.

It has already been pointed out that Voltaire supported constitutional absolutism as the only realistic solution to the problems bedeviling the French government of his day. Since this position is liable to misinterpretation, it must be further pointed out that he was interested in practical alternatives, not in utopian postures, that he was unalterably opposed to both the tyranny of the one and the tyranny of the many, and that he extolled and promoted the rule of law rather than a given form of government. The form that best befitted the French tradition and the French temperament was the monarchy. Provided the law was supreme and everyone equal before it, Voltaire was content to be as royalist as the king. Direct democracy he felt to be, for the most part, beyond mortal capacity, for he had little trust in the will of a popular majority. But whether the people were or were not competent to govern was less important than the fact that they were human and should be treated humanely. All things considered, Voltaire was a political moderate who pressed for liberal reforms while trying to conserve enough of the old régime to ensure a bloodless passage to the morrow. Thus he advocated equality before God and the law, but he was no believer in either social or economic equality. In his judgment any civilized society would naturally develop hierarchical or class distinctions. As for the organization of the economy, he warmly embraced the capitalism of his era, amassing great wealth through shrewd and sometimes sharp practices; yet he was munificent in his donations to the actors of his plays in Paris, as well as in his provision of work for the poor with his ambitious farming, construction, and manufacturing projects at Ferney.

It is clear enough, even from this brief and incomplete summary of Voltaire's thought, that living through a time of troubles, he was not content with a spectator's role, could not look on serenely from an Olympian perch while elaborating some grandiose speculative construction. But in engaging himself he was forced to conceive, express, and communicate ideas which were topically pertinent, which took into account the irrational, not just the reasonable, aspects of the human psyche, and which therefore had a fair chance of surviving amid the rough-and-tumble of public life. Furthermore, he was most anxious about the extreme conclusions that certain of his contemporaries were drawing from the new situation of man implied by the Copernican theory. Pushed too far, relativism could eventuate in abandon and anarchy. As a responsible, civilized individual, he deemed it his duty to help guide institutions and events toward a society of contract permeated by scientific humanism, but with a decent respect for what deserved preservation and as little injury as possible to the great mass of human beings involved. This is why his thought, while unified by its general aims—order, security, freedom, justice, "beneficence," social productivity, reform, enlightenment, beauty, cultural taste, refined enjoyment—is at the same time asymmetrical, elastic, untidy, and soiled with the grime of concrete circumstance.

IV

It is common knowledge that in his time Voltaire was a towering figure, with a reputation built upon his plays, his poems—especially his epic, his histories, his all-around ability as a writer and a thinker, his broad contacts among the social and intellectual aristocracy, and in later years his hospitality, his philanthropy, his defense of the victims of oppression, and his reformist propaganda. In the judgment of his contemporaries he was above all a great dramatist, formal poet, and philosopher. Today there is general agreement that he was none of these. The discriminating critic would look in vain through Voltaire's many works for a philosophical synthesis or a poetic or dramatic masterpiece of sustained power and lofty inspiration. In his old age he wrote: "I have done a bit of good; that is my finest work." This may or may not be true, but the good that men do does not live after them in the tangible, uniquely identifying, self-sustaining form which confers perdurability on classic monuments of the intellect and of the creative imagination. Are we, then, to conclude that, aside from a few productions in minor genres, Voltaire is to be regarded as nothing more than a human period piece? Certain critics have in fact so concluded. Their evaluation, however, is subject to challenge, though on other grounds than that of Voltaire's contemporaries. More of this in a moment.

Another, currently popular criterion of judgment finds expression in the question: what does Voltaire have to say to our age? This is a question which, narrowly interpreted, seems to presuppose that our age is characterized by uniformity of standards throughout the globe and represents the ultimate in standards, also that Voltaire's life and works can be abstracted from their historical context, transferred to ours, and still be understood without serious deformation. Since these propositions are false, any honest answer to the question in its obvious meaning must be hedged round with so many qualifications that it inevitably turns out to be a mere game of conjecture. In his time Voltaire was a royalist, a capitalist, an aristocrat, a polymath, and a humanist with a deistic metaphysic and ethic but an over-all scientific bias. In his time he was on the whole moving toward ours. This is the reality of Voltaire. But to argue by analogy from his time to ours, to assert or estimate what positions he would take on the topical issues of our day, is to indulge in fantasy, considering the profound differences between the two periods and the circumstantial character of his thought. The fact is that if Voltaire were alive today, he would not be the Voltaire we know. The Voltaire we know needs the Enlightenment for his ambience. Without it he would be unrecognizable.

Voltaire's contemporaries lacked the requisite perspective for judging the nature and quality of his achievement. Some of today's critics have forfeited their perspective of two centuries by truncating him to fit the Procrustean bed of their topical concerns. As has already been pointed out, there is a sounder way to gain and maintain a genuine perspective. It entails finding an answer to the following question: does Voltaire rise high enough *within his period* to have something of great significance to communicate *to all periods,* our own included, and if so, what is its nature and quality? Any honest answer to *this* question will be admittedly subjective, but the critic who has faithfully followed through on the liberal attitude, approach, and method is entitled to suggest an evaluation of Voltaire's achievement for the consideration of others, it being understood that a suggestion is not to be mistaken for an ex-cathedra pronouncement.

The suggestion offered here is that Voltaire, viewed against the ambience of the Enlightenment, looms great enough in several domains to command the sincere admiration and the unremitting study of all generations. These are the domains:

1. He was one of the world's most irresistibly exciting personalities by reason of his coruscating wit, his extraordinary conversational ability, his grace and elegance as a host, his business and social and intellectual relations with countless contemporaries of every station, and his knack for attracting and holding the attention of the public—not to mention his numerous scrapes and even more numerous displays of temperament. The evidence for this is found in the whole of his voluminous production, but most of all in his marvelous correspondence, as well as in the profusion of reports by those who had contact with him. The assumption on which this claim to greatness rests is that personality has intrinsic worth and can, in exceptional instances, exert a powerful and legitimate fascination on posterity.

2. He was an illustrious practical moralist, first of all by virtue of his active humanitarianism. He not only preached, he practised "beneficence" both in large and in small. Mention has been made of his donations to actors and his provision of employment for the poor at Ferney; but he performed many other charitable deeds, and

he expended incalculable amounts of time, money, and energy in defending victims of injustice such as the Crassy brothers, Jean Calas, the Sirvens, the Chevalier de La Barre, D'Étallonde, and Count Lally. If the good that men do does not live after them in the form which makes distinguished works of art and philosophy immortal, it nonetheless, like personality, has intrinsic worth and can, when sufficiently outstanding, set an inspiring example for future generations.

3. As a practical moralist he was equally illustrious in the realm of propaganda for enlightenment and reform. At once a crusader, a popularizer, and an artist, he exploited his flair for techniques of publicity, his gift for clarification of ideas and issues, and his stylistic virtuosity to transmit the new scientific knowledge, to attack abuses, and to promote justice. In reading through the collected works one finds it difficult to believe that a single individual could with such sustained missionary zeal and skill have produced so many plays, poems, histories, essays, treatises, tales, pamphlets, articles, and letters in a massive campaign for the emancipation of the mind and the amelioration of the social order. The feat remains unexampled, heroic, and awesome.

4. He was an eminent pioneer historian, partly because of the inherent merit of his performance, partly because of his break with traditional approaches and his influence on his successors. Allowances must be made, of course, for certain palpable limitations and flaws: e.g., the underdeveloped state of historical scholarship in his time, his tendency to interpret past epochs in the light of eighteenth-century standards and with an eye on the needs of action, and his attitude of detachment precluding emotional involvement in the spirit of an age or direct penetration into the inner life of individuals or groups. Such allowances made, there remain a number of important strengths. Voltaire's commitment to a scientific view led him to respect the documentary sources and the reliable oral evidence that were available, and to eliminate Providence from history in favor of such natural causes as great men, chance (i.e., seemingly trivial causes), technological inventions, and productive labor. As a liberal humanist, he contributed mightily to broadening the scope of history from a European and Christian to a global perspective, and from the chronicling of reigns and wars to the critical examination of civilization in all of its aspects: political, economic, social, intellectual, artistic, moral, and religious. As a melioristic realist, he was wise enough to believe that progress, while always possible for societies which work at it and are reasonably lucky, is never inevita-

ble; and by working at it he meant moving toward such goals as wealth, comforts and luxuries, economic and political liberty, religious tolerance, and the efflorescence of the arts and sciences. As a writer, he brought to his historical material a highly distinctive and often distinguished style, characterized by clarity, smoothness, analytical precision, intellectual incisiveness, wit, and occasional aphoristic concision. All things considered, his achievement in this domain alone would suffice to commend him to the notice and scrutiny of the ages.

5. He was a brilliantly effective informal poet. In tragedy, in the epic, in the formal ode, despite memorable brief passages or single lines, he toiled under visible strain, attempting a grand manner alien to his natural self. But in his light epistles, stanzas, satires, epigrams, madrigals, and other such familiar forms he managed to express with ease, elegance, charm, wit, and sincerity the various facets of his free-ranging personality. Throwing off the shackles of the heroic alexandrine couplet, he composed in decasyllables, octosyllables, or a mixture of verse-lengths, creating a felicitous effect of rapid and effortless flow, of conversational spontaneity. Early and late, indeed up to the very end of his life, he excelled at light poetry which transformed the topical into the typical by expertly blending autobiographical situations with certain eternally recurring themes: among them love and friendship, praise of virtue, ridicule of vice and folly, epicurean enjoyments, the pleasures of a life of retirement, the melancholy that attends thoughts of transience and death, and the miseries and consolations of old age.

6. Lastly, he was one of the world's supreme masters of literary prose, especially in genres of brief length which display the personality of the author and call for two-dimensional fantasy rather than three-dimensional imagination. His genius in this domain is perfectly exemplified in his philosophic tales, which also show him to be a consummate story-teller; in his dialogues, which reveal in addition an exquisite ear for serious intellectual, as well as for mischievously parodic, conversation; and in his innumerable and multifarious encyclopaedia articles, private letters, and propaganda pamphlets. The pamphlets include, among other types, many burlesques—e.g., ludicrous imitations of homilies, epistles, and edicts—skillfully contrived to arouse laughter, indignation, and a desire for correction of the abuses mocked. As a prose artist specializing in miniatures (even his long works tend to be collections of short pieces), he commanded the entire register of rhetorical and satirical devices and handled them with taste, grace, and point. It is true

that he lacked the novelist's psychological insight, empathy, and re-creative magic; but no prosateur can have everything, and what he uniquely possessed was enough to make him a writer of remarkable individuality, originality, and power.

These claims to greatness should not be allowed to obscure Voltaire's limitations and defects as a writer and as a man. He was larger than life in his shortcomings no less than in his excellencies, and both must be included in a final accounting of what he was and did. It is important to recognize that he was vain, that he could upon occasion be malicious, that he devoted much of his energy to cultivating literary forms ill-suited to his talents, etc. We need to know that we are dealing with the whole Voltaire, that is to say, with a human being, not with a myth. On the other hand, once we have made an honest attempt to understand him in his totality, it becomes appropriate to distinguish between the chaff and the grain, between what merely serves to fill out the mortal record and what compels not only the study but the admiration of posterity.

A careful examination of Voltaire's life and works based on liberal principles yields a rich harvest of grain. The six domains in which he achieved genuine greatness betoken an astounding versatility. "He multiplied himself among mankind,/The Proteus of their talents." There are very few individuals who have shown themselves capable of doing so many things so well in such quantities over so long a period of time. Voltaire was like the Olympic master of the decathlon, surpassed by specialists in most, if not all, of the events involved, yet scoring well enough to win the gold medal by virtue of his multiple and varied skills. It is the many-sidedness of his genius which, perhaps more than anything else, fully entitles him to membership in *any* pantheon of illustrious historical figures.

Sg9
106,838

Duplicity and Protective Lying

by Norman L. Torrey

With regard to the [philosophic] party, Voltaire thought that Rousseau's charges might ruin the whole campaign for enlightenment. In the same letter in which he announced Rousseau's attack to Damilaville, he told of police activities in Paris: "Omer is working on a requisition for the *Dictionnaire philosophique*. People continue to attribute that work to me who have no part in it. I think my nephew, who is a councilor in parliament, will prevent him from designating me" (M. XLIII, 418). Such designation, he said, "would take from me the freedom of being useful" (M. XLIII, 318). For he considered this dictionary his most useful project. He had been working on it since 1752, when he submitted the first articles to Frederick II, the original sponsor. It was packed both with scholarly criticism and mocking ridicule of what he considered the absurdities of Christian theology and tradition and was permeated throughout with his guiding principle, the "crushing of infamy" in behalf of tolerance.

To add to his discomfiture at this critical moment, a pirated edition of his works was printed abroad by Rousseau's publisher, so he thought, and his name had treacherously been put on the volumes. The time and energy he spent in denying his own works was prodigious. He was a constant double dealer, he lied and believed in lying that he might live to lie again another day. In this way alone, he believed, he could be useful and work for humanity. It was not only his best works that faced two ways, through his skillful use of irony and innuendo, but also the very method of his attack. Nothing appeared to him so foolhardy as Rousseau's in-

"Duplicity and Protective Lying." From *The Spirit of Voltaire,* The Marston Press, Oxford, by Norman L. Torrey (an unaltered reprint of the original edition published in 1938 by the Columbia University Press, New York). The pages reprinted here reproduce the final section of the chapter entitled "Pride and Prejudice."

sistence upon signing his works. Much earlier in the century Montesquieu was admitted to the French Academy on his reputation for the very bold *Lettres persanes,* which had been published anonymously and which could not be officially mentioned as his. Rousseau's foolhardiness, in Voltaire's eyes, was exemplified by the effectiveness with which he was silenced after the various condemnations of his books and his person. Diderot, with a still different method, kept his most original works in manuscript and left them to posterity. Such policies would not do for such an active fighter as Voltaire, who lived and wrote most intensely in the present. Censorship, repression, and religious persecution are not, of course, keenly felt by people whose ideas are traditional; to men like Voltaire, with radical and reforming ideas, they were forces which had to be met in very practical ways. The absolute moralists will ever condemn him as a liar and a hypocrite, on the principle that the end never justifies the means. The relativists reply that it is again a question of what end and what means, that in our feeble attempts to weigh human values we cannot be dogmatic, that the smashing of the political and persecuting power of religion was Voltaire's greatest gift to humanity, and that it was far better for the world that he should lie and live.

His violent outbursts against his enemies were often entirely contrary to his most cherished principles; his lying and hypocrisy, on the contrary, constituted an accepted systematic, reasoned method. The necessity of such duplicity was early impressed upon him by his many exiles and flights from justice, by two sojourns in the Bastille, and by the bitter enmities he had made in the opposing camp. Threatened with a *lettre de cachet* and imprisonment (at least) for his *Lettres philosophiques,* he denied roundly that he had France or the French in mind when he wrote these intimate letters from England to his friend Thieriot. As a matter of fact these letters on the English nation have no point or value unless they are read with reference to France and her needed reforms, and they were written for the most part with that sole end in view three to four years after Voltaire's return to France.

The issue of hypocrisy was squarely met, too, when Voltaire was a candidate (for many years unsuccessful) for membership in the French Academy. To his enemy Boyer, bishop of Mirepoix, he affirmed that he was a true Catholic—officially to be sure, he was never anything else; he promised Père de la Tour that he would tear up any page of his works that was hostile to the Church and would live and die in her bosom (M. XXXVI, 428-30); and he "kissed the pope's slipper" in the dedication of his tragedy *Mahomet.* At the same time, he wrote to D'Argenson on the subject of Boyer: "He is certainly playing a wicked rôle, and he is doing more harm than he thinks. He ought to know that it is a sad business making hypocrites" (M. XXXVI, 221). And to Thieriot, too, he wrote: "Virtue should not be obliged to render homage to fanaticism and hypocrisy" (M. XXXVI, 297). The philosophical tale *Zadig* is a beautiful example of a work that faces two ways; it is not only full of ironical expressions, but the whole work is an ironical review of Voltaire's years at court. The religious party received it, much to Voltaire's surprise, as on the whole orthodox, preaching resignation to Providence.[1] Voltaire's friends read in it the opposite and more typically Voltairean view. Resignation to destiny, yes, but not until after the fight; and as for interpreting the history of human folly and ignorance as the unfolding of God's will, this was the very principle which he attacked so thoroughly that he has acquired the reputation of being the first modern historian. He hated the self-appointed or traditionally appointed agents of God's will, those who assassinated tolerant kings in the name of God and those who merited heaven through the slaughter of the natives as did the Spaniards in Peru.[2] *Zadig* was written for his enlightened friends and was personally presented to them. If the general public believed it an orthodox work, so much the safer. "I am as harmless as a dove, and want to be as wise as a serpent," he wrote later, quoting the instructions of Jesus to his disciples.[3]

During his stay at Colmar, in 1754, he was being closely watched by the Jesuits, who were doing everything in their power to prevent his settling in their proximity. At this juncture he decided it was distinctly better for his health, or at least for the repose of his mind and his body, to receive communion. Perhaps with some exaggeration, one of his secretaries, Colini, described the grimaces he made when presented with the Host. In a letter to his old friend and comforter at Potsdam, the Marquis d'Argens, Voltaire wrote: "I can see how a devil goes to mass when he is in papal territory, like Nancy or Colmar; but you have a right to groan when a child of Beelzebub goes to mass through hypocrisy or vanity" (M. XXXVIII, 199).

[1] *Zadig,* ed. G. Ascoli, Paris, 1929, I, xiii-xvii.

[2] See W. R. Price, *The Symbolism of Voltaire's Novels,* Columbia Univ. Press, 1911, p. 238ff.

[3] M. XLV, 331. (Matt. x. 16).

> On the subject of that hatred that he vowed to intolerant and fanatical priests [wrote his secretary Wagnière] I asked him one day what he would have done if he had been born in Spain? "I would have had," he said, "a great chaplet, I would have gone to mass every day, I would have kissed the monks' sleeves, and I would have tried to have all their monasteries set on fire. I was not made to live in Spain, nor even in France." [4]

The celebrated *Dîner du Comte de Boulainvilliers,* one of the most witty and effective of the anti-religious works, will serve as an example of Voltaire's methods. It was published under the name of Saint-Hyacinthe. To Panckoucke, his projected editor, he denied roundly that he himself had written it:

> The more you prove to me your friendship, the less I understand how you can apply to me for the infamous work entitled *Le Dîner du Comte de Boulainvilliers.* I had by chance a copy, but I threw it in the fire. It is a tissue of bitter mockery and atrocious invective against our religion. This unworthy work has been known for forty years; but it appeared in Holland only a few months ago, with a hundred other works of the same nature. If I were not spending all the last days of my life on a new edition of the *Siècle de Louis XIV,* enlarged by almost a half; if I were not using up the little strength I have left in erecting this monument to the glory of my country, I would refute all those books that are daily written against religion (M. XLV, 513).

The borderline between irony, propaganda, and plain lying is but vaguely drawn in this letter; only the certain knowledge of the degree of understanding at this moment between Voltaire and Panckoucke would permit the classification of this quotation. Four days later, he wrote to Damilaville, from whom he withheld no secrets: "My desert is becoming more precious to me than ever. I would be obliged to quit it, if calumny imputed to me Saint-Hyacinthe's little book" (M. XLV, 516-18). Damilaville, thus warned, was to oppose this "calumny" in Paris. In a letter to a Parisian admirer, Mme. de Saint-Julien, Voltaire's tone is entirely serious:

> You do me great honor, madame, and mortally grieve me in attributing to me Saint-Hyacinthe's work, printed forty years ago. Suspicions on such a serious matter would be enough to ruin me on earth, in an old age overwhelmed with maladies, which does not permit me to transplant myself. My last days would be most fatally poisoned (M. XLV, 519).

[4] *Mémoires sur Voltaire,* I, 45.

As for Saint-Hyacinthe, Voltaire had had some little unpleasantness with him some forty years before; but he was now dead: "No harm is being done to Saint-Hyacinthe's memory," he wrote to M. Saurin in self-defense, "in attributing to him a joke written forty years ago. What do the dead care about calumny! But the living might die of it." So Voltaire sought Saurin's aid, too, on the ground that the wise must help each other or they will be too severely persecuted by the fools (M. XLV, 518-19).

Such phrases, which are plainly ironical when he is writing to his friends, are mendacious and hypocritical when he is addressing neutrals and enemies. One of his favorite methods was to quote, word for word, some of the more absurd theological discussions of the age. No comment was necessary; the fact that Voltaire was quoting them gave them all the intended comic effect. The duplicity of his conduct, his works, and his letters is thus partly an ethical, partly an aesthetic, consideration.

His protective lying varied, of course, in direct proportion to the danger and intensity of the activities in which he was engaged. The most marked period follows 1762, when he determined to make the *Extrait des sentiments de Jean Meslier* the first of an endless series in the clandestine trade of anonymous publications. During the same year his activity increased in behalf of the Calas family, and he followed it shortly thereafter by his defense of the Sirven family and finally, in 1766, by his efforts to avenge the Chevalier de la Barre. It was during this period, as we have seen, that after many years of patience and restraint, he blazed forth against Rousseau, who seemed to be jeopardizing, both by his conduct and by his attacks, the sacred cause of philosophy. The aftermath of the Chevalier de la Barre execution brought him sadness and worry. His own *Dictionnaire philosophique* was found in the young martyr's possession, and many people would have liked to avenge themselves on the master as well as on the disciple. His letters were strictly watched and intercepted, and he was obliged to adopt all sorts of subterfuges and pseudonyms in order to keep in touch with his brothers. His taking of communion in the spring of 1768 was a purely defensive measure, but he was nevertheless forced to excuse himself to the "brothers." To D'Argental, his "guardian angel," he gave the following nine reasons for the apparently hypocritical act:

1. It is a duty that I have fulfilled with Mme. Denis once or twice, if I remember correctly.
2. It is not the same with a poor farmer as with your Parisian

nobles, who can escape with a noonday walk in the Tuileries. I have to render the blessed bread in person in my parish; I am alone of my band against two hundred and fifty timorous consciences; and, when it costs no more than a ceremony prescribed by law to edify them, there is no use making two hundred and fifty enemies.

3. I am situated between two bishops who date from the fourteenth century, and I must howl with these holy wolves.

4. I must be on good terms with my curate, were he an imbecile or a rascal, and there is no precaution that I should not take, after Attorney Caze's letter.

5. Rest assured that if I see a procession of Capuchins passing, I will go to meet them with bared head, during the heaviest downpour. [La Barre had omitted this deference and had been condemned for sacrilege.]

6. M. Hennin, official resident at Geneva, found a chaplain already in office; he is weak enough to keep him. This priest is one of the most detestable and most insolent rascals of the tonsured rabble. He becomes the spy of the bishops of Orleans, Annecy, and Saint-Claude. Since the resident hasn't the courage to discharge him, I must have the courage to silence him.

7. Since people obstinately attribute to me the works of Saint-Hyacinthe, of the ex-Capuchin Maubert, of the ex-Mathurin du Laurens, of Squire Robinet [Voltairean pseudonyms], all people who do not take the sacrament, I am obliged to take it; if I were at Abbeville [where La Barre was condemned], I would take it every two weeks.

8. I cannot be reproached for hypocrisy, since I make no pretense.

9. I ask you please to burn up my reasons, after having approved or condemned them. I much prefer being burned by you than at the foot of the great stairway [of the Hall of Justice] (M. XLVI, 23-24).

The distance from Paris to Ferney had again caused a slight misunderstanding between Voltaire and his friends. But he was as explicit here as he dared to be; the very intolerant bishop of Annecy had indeed written a letter of complaint to the court and asked for the strict application of the Revocation of the Edict of Nantes; so Voltaire, in order to give the Church party no hold on him, obeyed the very letter of the law: "The king wants people to fulfill their Christian duties," he wrote the following year; "not only do I acquit myself of my duties, but I send my Catholic servants regularly to church and my Protestant servants regularly to the temple; I pension a schoolmaster to teach the catechism to the children" (M. XLVI, 335). And again, to D'Alembert: "However, that rascally bishop, whom I failed to tip, still swears like a devil that he will have me burned in this world and in the other. I lay all that at the feet of my crucifix; and to escape being burned, I am putting in a provision of holy water" (M. XLVI, 337).

There is, of course, a great deal of truth in his statement that he was no hypocrite in taking communion because he made no pretense of piety. Only a few of the more fanatical wanted to burn him; the others in authority were very glad to have him obey the letter of the law, take the sacrament, and deny the authorship of his books. In this way he prevented what would have been a very unpleasant persecution for all concerned; for he still had crowned heads up his sleeve (M. XLVI, 335).

Protective lying and hypocrisy, irony and poetical exaggeration, these traits do not tell the complete story. Much more serious are the lies that can be classed only as willful calumny and libel. It is, of course, easy for a student, two hundred years after the battle, to sit quietly with copies of all the essential documents and convict Voltaire of gross manipulation of facts and texts. He was himself an outstanding victim of calumny and libel; generous souls such as Vauvenargues, men of integrity such as Stanislas, father of Queen Marie, were shocked and disgusted at the Voltariana which made Voltaire's residence in Paris morally impossible (M. XXXVI, 446, 558); enemies such as the publisher Jore repented later of their share in the calumniation, and Jore received Voltaire's blessing and financial aid (M. XXXVI, 134; XLVIII, 446). If he had really believed in an eye for an eye and a tooth for a tooth, no inconsistency could have been discovered; but he professed faith in the Silver Rule of Confucius, "Do not unto others what you do not wish them to do unto you," as much more ancient and much less selfish than the Golden Rule. Again he may be said to have observed this rule in great measure; he was never the first to attack, he would have liked to live at peace and without jealousy in the fraternity of men of letters; yet when others wronged him, he returned the compliment in full measure—fuller, perhaps, because of the sting of his mocking genius. There was a trace of maliciousness in his nature which he admitted early and late: "By my stars a bit inclined to malice."[5] Nor is there any doubt but that he enjoyed the battle. On sending his play *Les Scythes* to Cardinal de Bernis, he gave an account of his activities during the busy year of 1766:

> As for my puny self, I make war up to the last moment, Jansenists, Molinists, Frérons, Pompignons, to the right, to the left, and preachers,

[5] *Grande revue,* CXXXV, 450. Cf. M. XXXIII, 29, 34.

and J.-J. Rousseau. I receive a hundred thrusts and give back two hundred, and I laugh. I see at my door Geneva in combustion over trifling quarrels, and I laugh again; and God be praised, I look upon the whole world as a farce which sometimes becomes tragic. All is the same at the end of the day, and all is still more the same at the end of days (M. XLIV, 550).

Reviewing his life during his eightieth year and speaking of Piron, he wrote to the Abbé Duvernet, his future biographer: "My friends have always assured me that in the only good play that he wrote he made me play a very ridiculous rôle. I could very well have returned the compliment; I was as malicious as he, but I was busier" (M. XLIL, 537). Piron, he thought, had wasted his talents in frivolity and useless endeavor; his own maliciousness had on the contrary always been set to the service of reason, and he could therefore die more happily (Ibid.).

Tolerance is, like democracy, a virtue which should not be considered in the abstract. In discussing Voltaire's acts of intolerance, his persecutions of his enemies, and his libels against them, it is clear at the start that distinctions must be made: that he never contributed to the execution of any man for religious or intellectual differences and that he would have done all in his power to save even Rousseau from the clutches of the Inquisition. It is also generally accepted that more than any other one man he contributed to that measure of tolerance which the world enjoys today. To the Protestants of Geneva, whom he constantly reminded of the burning of Servetus, and to the Catholics of France, who were still persecuting Protestants, he said: "If you want to imitate Jesus Christ, be martyrs and not executioners!"; and he was fond of repeating that Christ had never had anyone burned for his religious views (M. XXXIX, 334). His savage attacks on authority were attacks on men who wielded authority unjustly or inhumanely; he was in a sense a Don Quixote in the fight for justice, but he wasted little time on windmills. As Frances Newman put it, "He had the advantage of a literary début which encouraged his cynical view of his fellow men in the personally injurious way that is so much more effective than any amount of impersonal imbecility."[6] He is often accused by friends and by enemies of having killed the learned Maupertuis, not with the sword, but with the pen, which is mightier than the sword, and of being thus both diabolically clever and an assassin. Again it will not do to exaggerate. Maupertuis was of a jealous, domineering nature. He had tried to settle an argument by

[6] F. Newman, *The Short Story's Mutations,* New York, 1926, pp. 41-2.

the force of his authority as president of the Berlin Academy and had unjustly treated another noted mathematician and philosopher, Koenig; he had written a foolish book, thus presenting a fair target for Voltaire's shafts; he was already afflicted with his mortal malady —"But I am sick, too," said Voltaire, "and half in the grave"; yet he survived by some seven years the personal ridicule of the *Diatribe du docteur Akakia.* None of Rousseau's physical or moral sufferings can be laid at Voltaire's door; and Fréron died in comparative poverty, not because he was ruined by Voltaire's *Anecdotes sur Fréron,* but because he spent as rapidly as he earned the relatively large sums of money with which he was rewarded for being Voltaire's wittiest and most insidious opponent at Paris.

It is nevertheless true that Voltaire often besieged the authorities with requests to suppress parodies and libels written against him or against the philosophic group. Here he gives us help in understanding his motives. He was much interested in problems of crime and punishment, preached even more effectively than Montesquieu that the punishment should be proportionate to the crime, and won his most signal victories in the improvement of justice and the abolition of torture. He maintained, however, that justice is based on law and that it is the business of law to punish criminals. "There are insulting books which ought to be burned," he wrote, "because an insult is a civil offense; while the *Contrat social,* being only illogical, ought to be refuted, not suppressed." [7] In 1739 the libellous *Voltairomanie* cut him to the quick:

> If the Abbé Desfontaines and those of his temper who persecute me [he wrote to Frederick] were content with defamatory libels, well and good; but there are no devices they do not set in action to ruin me. Now they circulate scandalous writings and charge me with them; now anonymous letters to government officials, stories forged at will by Rousseau and consummated by Desfontaines. The religious hypocrites join them and hide under religious zeal their furious desire to wound me. Every week I am afraid of losing my freedom or my life; and languishing in solitude, powerless to defend myself, I am abandoned by those very people whom I have helped the most and who think that it is in their interest to betray me (M. XXXV, 192).

In appealing to civil justice he had to contend with the hostility of the pious group who surrounded the Queen and often supported his enemies and with hostile courts whose Jansenist members could

[7] Kingsley Martin, *French Liberal Thought in the 18th Century,* London, 1929, pp. 137-38. Cf. M. XXXVI, 431-32; XLV, 363.

not forgive his defense of the Jesuits against Pascal. Often he was obliged to secure the Queen's permission before taking the case to court (M. XXXVI, 431-32, 531). Parodies, too, were written with the direct purpose of ruining his plays and his reputation; laws protecting authors against piracy and parody were nonexistent or ineffective; his struggle for protection was thus again inspired by his desire for essential justice.

> The Queen had Mme. Luynes write me that parodies were customary [he complained to D'Argental] and that Virgil had been travestied. I reply that it was not a compatriot of Virgil who wrote the *Enéide travestie* [sic], that the Romans were incapable of it; that if a burlesqued *Enéide* had been recited to Augustus or Octavia, Virgil would have been indignant; that this folly has been reserved for our long unpolished and ever frivolous nation; that the Queen was deceived when she was told that parodies were still customary; that they have been forbidden for five years; that the French theater is part of the education of all the princes of Europe, and that Gilles and Pierrot are not fit to form the minds of the descendants of Saint Louis (M. XXXVI, 539).

When, in 1767, his efforts to rehabilitate the Sirven family, persecuted for Protestantism, struck a snag, he suspected again his calumniators, especially La Beaumelle, who had so atrociously beleaguered him at Frederick's court.

> I am sending you, my dear Huguenot philosopher [he wrote to pastor Vernes] a little philippic that I was obliged to write. Friend La Beaumelle is maltreated. The ruler of the province threatened him somewhat, by order of the king, with the cell that he deserves. I am very tolerant, but not with calumniators. I have to defend innocence with one hand, and crush crime with the other (M. XLV, 362-63).

For his most intimate views on tolerance, it is well to avoid the *Traité sur la tolérance,* a work that admittedly "faced two ways" and was carefully designed for its effect on the public, and to quote from a letter written to D'Alembert a passage which explains in some measure this essay. The author worked, he declared, only with the advice of two very learned men:

> It was long debated, in composing this work, whether we should limit it simply to the preaching of indulgence and charity, or whether we ought to be unafraid of inspiring indifference. It was unanimously agreed that we were forced to say things which would lead, against the author's will, to that fatal indifference, because

> it can never be brought about that men will be indulgent in fanaticism and because they must be taught to despise, to look even with horror on the opinions which they now uphold.
>
> You cannot stop being a persecutor until you have first stopped being absurd. I can assure you that the book has made a great impression on all who have read it and has converted some. I know well enough they say that the philosophers ask for tolerance for themselves; but it is very foolish and silly to say that "when they have accomplished this, they will tolerate no other religion but their own"; as if the philosophers could ever persecute or be in a position to persecute! They will certainly not destroy the Christian religion; but Christianity will not destroy them, and their number will ever increase; young men destined to high places will learn from them, religion will become less barbaric, and society more refined. They will prevent priests from corrupting reason and manners. They will make an abomination of fanatics, and a laughingstock of the superstitious. Philosophers, in short, cannot help being useful to kings, laws, and citizens. . . . Such is our present situation that we are the execration of the human race if we do not have noble-minded people on our side; we must have them at any price; work then in the vineyard, crush infamy. What can you not do without compromising yourself? Do not leave such a handsome candle as yours under the bushel (M. XLIII, 127).

Voltaire thus saw very clearly that it would not be for the philosophers to persecute. The champions of justice in human affairs are still relatively few in each generation: they realize that the goal can never be attained in any absolute sense, and that it must be fought for anew with each succeeding generation. Yet since he lived and wrote, many abuses have been definitely eliminated, and the battle has not always been so arduous. Only after serious efforts of understanding, then, should his lukewarm followers attempt to criticize his methods.

Voltaire looked on libels and calumny as very practical legal matters and on intentionally vicious parodies as matters that the law should consider in any civilized country in which literature was to be held in esteem. Tolerance itself was an entirely practical matter, signifying the abolition of persecution; intolerance on the part of philosophers was thus a purely academic question, for how could they be intolerant unless they had an army, a police force, and courts to allow them to persecute? Intellectual intolerance is another thing, or rather is a phrase without meaning, for if a man has an intellect he will naturally agree or disagree with expressed opinions; the whole question is whether he could be friendly to those with whom he disagreed. Voltaire was very capable of this sort of tolerance. "There are as many opinions as there are heads," he wrote to M. de Pomaret two years before he died: "And I, sir, who agree with you on questions of morality, am unfortunately very far from the sentiments that you are obliged to profess [belief in certain doctrines of Christianity]; but that is for me only one more reason to be attached to you, and to be with all my heart, sir, your . . ." (M. L, 52).

It is hard to deny, however, that, in his *Sentiment des citoyens* against Rousseau, as well as in his *Anecdotes sur Fréron,* he took unjust advantage of his anonymity. Both pamphlets contain vicious untruths, some of which at least, we may assume, Voltaire knew to be untrue. The anecdotes were furnished on request by his Parisian friend, Thieriot, and published as anecdotes. They may fairly be compared with the *Voltariana* from which Voltaire had himself suffered so grievously. Fréron was the successor and eulogizer of the Abbé Desfontaines—to Voltaire the pamphlet was pure retaliation, not persecution; the difference was that Fréron was well supported by civil and religious authorities in his regularly insidious criticisms of Voltaire, while the latter deemed himself defenseless against the calumnies heaped upon him (M. XXXIV, 18). He could and did pardon his enemies when they were in trouble and needed his help: "I have heard," he wrote, "that the Abbé Desfontaines is wretched; I pardoned him at once"; twice Voltaire rescued him from prison, and once he intervened to save him from execution on conviction of homosexuality; his reward had been black ingratitude. The attack on Rousseau in the *Sentiment des citoyens* fits in very ill with Voltaire's general nature and principles, especially the admonition there expressed that blasphemers should be dealt with by the law. That opinion was indeed held by many of the citizens, but it was not at all Voltaire's. Either this work is a flagrant abuse of anonymity and a very black mark on Voltaire's record, or some details are still missing from the picture; it was not included in his printed works until fifty years after his death, and the best evidence of its authenticity is the testimony, nearly thirty years after it appeared, of his secretary, Wagnière, usually trustworthy. We know that Voltaire was not responsible[8] for all of it; whether he gave his sanction to it in its final form, that perhaps we shall never know. In any case, it was an exceptional rather than a typical act.

In the interests of truth it is unfortunate that prejudice and

[8] Cf. P. Chaponnière, *Voltaire chez les Calvinistes,* Genève, 1932, p. 127.

malice, often omitting necessary distinctions and extenuating circumstances, have made so much of a few incidents of this nature. For as a general rule Voltaire practiced and preached the virtues of justice and tolerance which are recognized as fundamental to the civilized human state. He could have purchased complete personal integrity only at the price of martyrdom.

The Real Voltaire Through His Letters

by Theodore Besterman

(to Jean Pommier)

First a word of explanation and even of apology. I fear you are going to find the tone of these lectures altogether too personal. You see that I have already uttered one "I," if not two. But what can you expect? For forty years I have been a devotee of Voltaire's (I hasten to add that I was very young when I began—it is at the age of ten that I purchased my first edition of Voltaire), for twenty years I have been spending my every day in his company, for six years I have been living in his house, I have been sleeping in his bedroom; in his library I have been reading his letters, opening his mail, exploring his most intimate secrets; I have in some modest measure, *longo intervallo,* become Voltaire. Under these conditions it would be mere hypocrisy or affectation to speak to you about the great man in a distant and impersonal tone. You have doubtless understood all that, I know, and if I stress it, it is because I nonetheless have one immense advantage over Voltaire: *he* was never invited to the Collège de France. I would not for anything in the world want you to think me capable of abusing this honor with a display of egotism. If I speak of Voltaire as though he were an intimate friend, it is quite simply because he is.

It is not easy, moreover, to compress within the limits of two lectures all that I should have liked to say. I have, rather, been obliged to cast them in the form of a single address arbitrarily divided into two parts, and to adopt a very compact scheme, with somewhat abrupt transitions. So permit me to offer you a brief analysis of what you are going to hear. I shall begin with a few very

"The Real Voltaire Through His Letters." From *Studies on Voltaire and the Eighteenth Century,* ed. Theodore Besterman, Volume X (Genève, 1959), by Theodore Besterman. This selection comprises two lectures given at the Collège de France, 23 and 25 February 1959.

general remarks on Voltaire. They will be followed by a few considerations on the art and the history of the epistolary genre. Next we shall see how our great man fits into this framework, and the unique role of his correspondence, whose scope, dispersion, and transformations I shall then very briefly indicate. To this will be added a few words on the new contributions of my edition; and finally we shall focus our attention on a single day in the great man's life. This last section, in the course of which I shall have the honor of presenting to you some rather remarkable unpublished letters, occupies the most space in the second part of my address.

I

Almost two centuries after his death Voltaire is as alive as ever: adored by some, reviled by others, but commanding the attention of all, amazing even those who detest him. The name of Voltaire invariably provokes a reaction in any company and in almost every country—a reaction more or less favorable, more or less informed, but always attesting a living influence. This year 1959, which sees the bicentenary of *Candide,* will also see the publication (to my knowledge) of some thirty volumes devoted to its author; and the requests for information which I receive in connection therewith come from every continent. All are agreed that *Candide* and the other tales are masterpieces, and the *Dictionnaire philosophique* has not yet been forgotten, nor that extraordinary universal history which can be compared only to an eagle's flight, nor the monument which Voltaire erected to the glory of an age, nor many other writings in every genre and on every subject. However, there is only one part of his so vast and varied production that is admired by all without reservation, and that part, by an irony of fate, is only a by-product of the *philosophe*'s inexhaustible verve, a *parergon* which, moreover, he had a horror of seeing in print. What would he have said if he had ever suspected that someday we should set about publishing his slightest notes, his most intimate letters?—for, as you have guessed, that by-product is in fact his correspondence—surely on that day his mail would have been enriched by some lively bursts of fury and indignation.

As a matter of fact, Voltaire did not hesitate to describe a certain publication of his letters as an offense to the public and a violation of all the rights of society; I almost dare not add that he likewise judged the publisher's notes to be worthy of the stake. But Scaliger, although he called the eminent bibliographer François Grudé de La Croix Du Maine crazy because he "had a room completely filled with various persons' letters stuffed in wardrobes, *in nidis,*" was obliged to add: "Such people are scholars' porters, who collect everything for us. This is very useful to us; there have to be such people." In effect, the quest for truth is its own justification: the editor blushes, proudly accepts the title of "scholars' porter," plucks up courage, and carries on.

II

The Neoplatonist Proclus, in his learned work Περὶ ἐπιστολιμαίον χαρακτῆρος, established forty-one categories of letters. The effort was praiseworthy, but after all, civilization, as we are told every day, has made immense progress since the age of innocence. And indeed one would be a bit cramped for space today with so few pigeonholes. How, for example, should one classify certain pastoral letters, or the denunciatory epistles of such and such a statesman, or Brigitte Bardot's fan-mail? Then, too, a category such as that of love-letters, for instance, really offers nothing more than a very abstract homogeneity. There are as many types of letters as there are of love. We have material enough to build an ample system of decimal or even duodecimal classification. And it is certainly not the difficulty of the thing which makes me forgo a more scientifically detailed and finely shaded structure than that of the Constantinopolitan grammarian, in order to propose to you instead a rigorous simplification. The reason is quite different. Actually, when I contemplate the vast stream of letters which has been flowing uninterruptedly since the invention of writing up to now, I give up all methodical classification, for I realize that there exist for me only two categories of letters: those of Voltaire and the rest. Why, yes, when you concentrate on that marvelous figure, you find yourself drawn irresistibly toward such affirmations, which sound very much like vainglorious boasting—but which are not, for the simple reason that they are true.

III

Cicero, Erasmus, Madame de Sévigné, Horace Walpole, Voltaire, Bernard Shaw: these are the great names of the epistolary genre, and their mere enumeration suffices to show how incomparable Voltaire is. Cicero approaches Voltaire's stylistic elegance, but the relatively small number of his letters with which we are acquainted reflects very inadequately the orator's universality. Erasmus depicts a whole epoch in his letters, but his correspondents are few, and his letters, written in an almost barbarous language, are accessible, if at all, only to Latinists. One may dearly love all the grace, all the charm, all that is truly *literary* in Madame de Sévigné's letters, without harboring any illusions as to the narrowness of her knowledge and her preoccupations. As for Horace Walpole, he is a very little great man: never has anyone more lengthily and deeply explored the surface of things. Fortunately, no judgment on the epistolary art of Bernard Shaw is yet possible, since his letters are known only fragmentarily—what a treasure already! But, for all that, how superior Voltaire is to Cicero in style, to Erasmus in range if not depth of knowledge, to Madame de Sévigné in grace and friendships, to Walpole in universality of interests and number and variety of correspondents!

IV

A few months before Renan's death (yes, Renan, whose name it may be indiscreet to mention in this establishment), a journalist questioned the old writer on the evolution of literature, and received a reply which held surprises for the inquirer: "Literary fashions . . . ," he said, "are childish, infantile. They are simply not interesting. . . ." And he went on: "Literature itself, you see, is a mediocre preoccupation. . . ." Then, on second thought, he exclaimed: "I beg your pardon, I take back what I have just said; it's an exaggeration. Racine composed some very beautiful things, and Voltaire! Oh! Voltaire's letters, I must say, are divine; what treasures they contain! They're marvelous. . . ."[1]

In actual fact, there can be no doubt that Voltaire's letters constitute the greatest of all *biblia abiblia,* of literature in spite of itself. There are several reasons for this. Save for one childhood letter signed Zozo, Voltaire's earliest surviving missives date from 1711, when he was at school. There then remained for Louis XIV four somber years of decline which were to be followed by the all-too-brief regency of the Duke of Orléans and the interminable reign of

[1] Jules Huret, *Enquête sur l'évolution littéraire* (Paris, 1891), pp. 420-21. I am indebted for this quotation to Monsieur Henri Guillemin.

Louis XV, dearly beloved in name only; and Voltaire still had a few very active years before him when Louis XVI mounted the throne. In sum, he was born at the high point of the old régime and died only a decade or so before the French Revolution. So his correspondence amply includes sixty vital years, years during which the modern world came into being.

That, of course, does not delimit its complete history in time. Voltaire's so brilliant endowments and personality captivated persons much older than he. As a small boy he so deeply impressed Ninon de Lenclos (born in 1615, eighty years before him) that she included him, not, as is too often repeated, among her bed-partners, but in her will. While still at school, he was treated as an equal by Chaulieu, last of the "libertine" poets, his senior by sixty years. We possess a few of the delightful letters in prose and in verse which they wrote each other. Through a Chaulieu, a Caumartin, a Prince of Vendôme, the lad tuned in on signals issuing from far within the great century.

And in 1718 the unprecedented success of his first play, *Œdipe*, made Voltaire, at the age of twenty-four, after eighteen months of imprisonment and exile, with all that that implies consequentially and symbolically, the recognized leader of French literature. Already people were keeping, buying, stealing his letters, passing them around, yes, and even printing them. In his adolescence he had a fleeting affair with a girl whose mother, a third-rate journalist, hastened to publish the letters he was writing to her daughter. How mortifying! No wonder he always detested seeing his letters in print! One is even surprised that he was ever able to write another one after that.

V

Voltaire's publications so obviously sparkled with genius, even when he handled the most forbidding subjects, that his reputation was extraordinarily widespread in his own country and beyond it. Although he was above all a creative artist, Voltaire was also much more than that: an original historian, a popularizer of science, a social reformer, an adversary of every religion qua superstition, a fighter for freedom and tolerance. That is what gives his works, and even more his correspondence, a scope as remarkable for its content as for its duration. And this is reflected in the astonishing quality, variety, and number of his correspondents. In the first place there are, of course, his peers: Fontenelle, Alembert, Diderot, Helvétius, Vauvenargues, Rousseau, Buffon, Condorcet, Beaumarchais, Pope, Swift, even Lessing, as well as minor figures (at least in comparison with the giants): Algarotti, Goldoni, Maffei, and Spallanzani; Bernouilli and Haller; George Keate, Boswell, and Horace Walpole; Sumarokov; Siscar y Mayáns; Jean Baptiste Rousseau, Maupertuis, Destouches, La Condamine, Moncrif, Voisenon, Prévost d'Exiles, Tressan, Piron, Mairan, Saurin, Marmontel, Delisle de Salles, Madame de Graffigny, La Harpe, Du Pont de Nemours, Madame d'Epinay, Madame Du Deffand, Ximenès, Suard, Sedaine, Palissot, Chambord, Madame Du Bocage, Florian, Duclos, Dorat.

I do not want to insist unduly on this aspect of the correspondence, but I cannot help stressing one small detail which emerges from this enumeration: Fontenelle was born in 1657, Suard and Du Pont de Nemours died 160 years later, in 1817. What is more, in 1769 Voltaire writes to the Duke d'Aumont (in an unpublished letter): "My first patron was your great-grandfather." Now, that great-grandfather had been born in 1632, which represents a bridge of 185 years.

Voltaire also corresponded with a good many of the chief statesmen of Europe, from Dubois, Fleury, the Argensons, Amelot, Bernis, Maurepas, Richelieu, Choiseul, and Turgot, to Bolingbroke and Wilkes; the Austrian Kaunitz; the Swede Bernstorff; the Germans Podewils and Cocceji; the Swiss François Tronchin; the Hungarian Fekete de Galántai; the Spaniard Miranda; the Russians Shuvalov, Vorontsov, and Golitsuin.

He was on friendly, and in some cases even intimate, terms with many of the great ladies of the century, including the Marchioness de Bernières, the Duchesses d'Aiguillon, Madame Dupin, the Duchess Du Maine, the Marchioness de Pompadour, the Duchess de Choiseul, Madame Necker, Madame de Saint-Julien, Countess Bentinck, and above all the learned, scintillating, dearly beloved Emilie Du Châtelet, whose correspondence I have just had the honor of publishing.

As for rulers to whom he wrote as an equal, although at the time they still partook of the divinity which invested the throne, Voltaire was the preferred correspondent of two of the most remarkable monarchs of all times, Frederick II, King of Prussia, and Catherine II, Empress of all the Russias: Frederick, his disciple, his dear friend, or rather his beloved enemy; Catherine, perhaps because they never met, quite simply his disciple. A complete list of the other reigning princes who corresponded with Voltaire would be boring: I shall mention, along with the Kings of England and France, and the Queens of Prussia, only Ulrica of Sweden; Christian VII of Denmark; Wilhelmina, Margravine of Bayreuth; Charles Theodore, Elector Palatine; Louise Dorothea, Duchess of Saxe-Gotha; Caroline Louise, Margravine of Baden-Durlach; Prince de Ligne; Stanislas Leszczynsky and Stanislas Poniatowsky, Kings of Poland; Charles Eugene and Louis Eugene, Dukes of Wurtemberg; and many others, as well as princes of the Church such as Popes Benedict XIV and Clement XIII, and numerous cardinals and bishops, including Tencin, Passionei, and Quirini, leaving aside such exotic figures as, for example, Gabriel Podosky, Prince-Archbishop of Poland and Lithuania, and Biord, Prince-Archbishop of Geneva.

These listings are far from covering the entire range of Voltaire's correspondence—obviously, since there were in all 1,200 correspondents. I have said nothing of the letters, some of them among the most exciting, to actors and actresses; nor of those written to artists, doctors, publishers, financiers, bankers; nor of those addressed to the numerous academies of which he was a member in several countries. I have said nothing of his letters to his family; and I can but briefly refer to the lengthy and profoundly interesting series of letters to friends of his youth, permanent friends: Argental, Cideville, Thieriot. And there is a very remarkable fact to be noted in this connection, a fact which should suffice per se to prove false the image formed by so many people of a Voltaire who is a grumbler impossible to get along with. I have just mentioned the names of only three friends; but here is what is impressive, it's that in the list of his correspondents one finds about thirty-five names of persons with whom Voltaire carried on a sustained correspondence for twenty years, and a score of uninterrupted exchanges, not counting his family, which lasted more than thirty years. Who among us could say as much—even those who have lived beyond eighty like Voltaire?

Let us note in passing that Voltaire's correspondence, though naturally written for the most part in French, also includes a good many letters in English and Italian, and one finds in them even Latin, German, and Spanish.

VI

All this is extraordinary, in fact it is unparalleled. A correspondence of such duration and of such vast interest would in any case be historically important, without having for all that to be literature. That, however, is the unique character of Voltaire's letters. What turns a simple document into a piece of literature is the author's personality, the quality of what he expresses and the way in which he expresses it. There is a fine but appreciable distinction here. There are men who generally write well, and even supremely well, and who are nonetheless incapable of writing a good letter. Baudelaire's correspondence is proof of this, among so many others. On the other hand, there are those who write very good letters, although they are utterly incapable of composing, for instance, a novel or a tale, which nevertheless appear to be elaborations of letters; we all know examples among our acquaintances. There is no question here of style. Even writers whose style is extremely artificial—such as Henry James, Proust, James Joyce—have written admirable letters, as have some—such as Flaubert—who have gone to enormous pains to achieve simple, flowing effects. I think the essential is, rather, psychological. The writer composes for the public—that this public may even be very limited makes no difference; the letter-writer addresses a private individual.

Enough has been said to show that this calls for very precise qualities, some of them perhaps surprising. The main thing is obviously a capacity for establishing a rapport with the person addressed. Voltaire possessed this gift to an almost miraculous degree. To see him describe the same event, express the same thought to an old friend, a fellow-member of an academy, a woman, a young protégé, a country neighbor, is a whole education in itself. Not that he necessarily seeks to please—there are countless letters far removed from such a preoccupation—but to affect, to involve each individual by that aspect of the subject which corresponds to his own interests, inclinations, beliefs. "Accuse me, if you will, of exceeding vanity," Madame Du Deffand said to him one day (1 March 1769), "but you say nothing which I do not believe I have thought myself." Could one better define a good letter? And Voltaire replied (15 March 1769): "One can easily adopt the manner of those to whom one speaks; it's not the same thing when one writes. It's plain luck if one hits it right." Plain luck! A strange kind of luck which favored Voltaire every time he took pen in hand!

Much generosity of mind, and generosity, period, are also necessary for a great man to write good letters. Consider that Bernard Shaw received astronomical fees for everything he published, and that his slightest letter had become a precious commodity—that did not prevent him from replying very frequently and very lengthily to young writers and actors who sought his advice and his support. This was not exactly the case with Voltaire, since he never derived a penny from his writings; but think of the man's occupations: village lord, administrator of justice for both capital crimes and misdemeanors, farmer, builder, businessman, householder, and even, in his spare time, author of a few thousand writings under 150 pseudonyms. All that did *not* prevent him from writing letters to an Helvétius or a Chabanon commenting at length on their writings; to a Damilaville or an Argence for the purpose of encouraging them to crush *l'infâme;* to Madame Du Deffand in order to console her for her ill nature and her blindness; to Frederick to dissuade him from suicide; to Catherine in order to encourage her to free the serfs or to crush Mustafa; to everyone to solicit subscriptions for Mademoiselle Corneille, to rouse public opinion in favor of Calas, Sirven, and so many others; to his bankers, his business agents on money matters; to his publishers and printers to complain of their work, their delays, misprints, the use of poor type, margins too wide or too narrow; countless letters of simple friendship, neighborliness, or consolation.

Nowadays it is *de rigueur* to say that the art of letter-writing is quite simply a function of distance, that one does not write what one can say, that speed of communications, and above all the telephone, permit us to say everything, and that consequently the art in question is dead. It seems to me perfectly obvious that this commonplace, like so many others, is false. I have already cited Bernard Shaw; one could add many other cases. What about the letters of Proust? And the Gide-Claudel correspondence? And the letters of D. H. Lawrence? And that extraordinary volume which has just appeared with a selection of Thomas Wolfe's epistolary eruptions? It is not even true that one writes less—we shall see this in a moment. All that is true is that certain very limited types of letters are no longer written, or are written far less often. A very large proportion of Voltaire's charming notes to his Genevan publisher would certainly have been replaced by very frequent telephone calls. That would have been a great pity, but after all it hardly justifies the overall pessimism habitually displayed by historians and anthologists.

It is true that formerly the arrival and the departure of the mail was a great event; preparations were made for sending and receiving letters, so pains were taken to write them, all the more because it was normally the addressee who paid the postage, which was often very expensive. But what letters have lost in this sense, have they not perhaps gained in naturalness? Alas, the transformations of social and family life have also produced a contrary result: the fear of letting oneself go. Many are the persons in our time who are haunted, even in writing the most intimate letters, by the fear of hearing them quoted someday in the course of a trial. But enough of that.

Besides, one must not imagine that the absence of the telephone and the difficulty of travel automatically brought on the production of good letters. Actually, even in the French eighteenth century, that peak of polite civilization, we must frankly acknowledge that hardly any but a few letters of Jean Jacques Rousseau, Diderot, Frederick II, Madame Du Deffand, Mademoiselle de Lespinasse, Madame Du Châtelet, and Catherine II have entered French literature alongside the immense mass of Voltaire's—and it is not unimportant to note that this short list includes the names of a Swiss, a Prussian, and a German-born Russian. Precisely in this does the Voltaire miracle consist, that among so many letters, one must look long and hard to find any that are boring.

VII

For after all, though a letter can, strictly speaking, be interesting even if poorly written, it will nevertheless not resist the wear and tear of time: *a fortiori* a correspondence composed of twenty, a hundred, five hundred, indeed twenty thousand letters. To survive, that is, to become literature, a letter must, for all that, have literary qualities. And it is in this, of course, that Voltaire triumphs. He had an instinctive feeling for the word and the sentence, a feeling so refined by unremitting discipline that it was impossible for him to write a banal line or to dictate one—for he wrote as he spoke and spoke as he wrote: no difference, or scarcely any, between a dictated and a handwritten letter. Little difference likewise between the young man's and the old man's letters. The former are perhaps more poetic, but in general it is the same vocabulary, constantly enriched with the passing of time, but retaining the same manner, a vocabulary in which echoes of the Latin of Louis-le-Grand and reminiscences of readings in the old French poets and modern English thinkers mingle so felicitously with technical expressions drawn from jurisprudence and the arts and crafts, with the dialects of Burgundy and Geneva. Everywhere one finds the same flowing grace, the same passion, the same sincerity, the same seriousness, the same reasoning sensibility, the same spontaneity, the same love of antithesis, the same wit: in short, the same style. His slightest business memoranda, even the most ordinary ones, invariably evoke a smile or a grimace of sympathy.

And what a course in epistolary style! How to complain to one's publisher because one has not received any proofs that day: "I am quite dumbfounded at receiving nothing from dear Gabriel. I am not accustomed to such neglect. A day without a proof sheet is a day wasted, and it wasn't worth while to come here and turn into an Alpine chamois only to suffer such reverses. To what, then, are you sacrificing Jeanne, the History, Oreste? It's killing me." (Be it said in passing, the expression "a day wasted" is one of Voltaire's favorite classical allusions: according to Suetonius, the Emperor Titus, having allowed a day to pass by without giving someone a gift, exclaimed: "Amici, diem perdidi.").

How to defend oneself against a forgery: "I have seen," he writes to the Duke of Grafton, "I have seen in the *Whitehall Evening Post* of 7 October 1769, no. 3668, an alleged letter from me to His Majesty the King of Prussia. It's a very stupid letter; nevertheless, I did *not* write it." And he adds his signature.

How to consult one's doctor: "An old man of seventy-six has long been attacked by a scorbutic humor which has always kept him extremely thin, which has taken away almost all his teeth, which sometimes attaches itself to his tonsils, which often causes rumblings in his intestines, spells of insomnia, etc. etc. connected with this disease. He begs Monsieur Bouvard to be good enough to indicate at the bottom of this note whether he thinks that goat's milk might bring some relief. It is perhaps ridiculous to hope for a cure at such an age; but since the sick man has some business matters which cannot be settled in less than six months, he takes the liberty of asking whether goat's milk might keep him going until then. He asks whether it is known from experience that goat's milk, along with a few absolutely indispensable purgations, has done some good in such a case."

Finally, for I obviously can quote you only a few examples, and very brief ones at that, finally, in an entirely different vein, it is in these terms that Voltaire, at the age of eighty-four, only a few days before his death, declined a lady's invitation on a small scrap of paper owned by the Institut et Musée Voltaire: "I know very well what I want, but I do not know what I shall do. I am ill, I am suffering from head to toe. Only my heart remains sound, and that is good for nothing."

And in addition to all that, Voltaire's letters contain some of his most charming occasional verse, with here and there a profounder touch of poetry.

It is true that the altogether special circumstances of Voltaire's life were of considerable help in making him a great letter-writer. From this point of view his life is divided into three rather clearly defined parts. First there is the society period. Voltaire lives in Paris and from there visits his friends as far as Forges and La Rivière Bourdet to the north; Caen toward the west; Richelieu, Ussé, La Source, and Sully farther south—not to mention the residences in the neighborhood of Paris, Sceaux, Maisons, Vaux, and many others. This phase could be called that of the château letters; it is the period which includes the beautiful letters in prose and verse addressed to Chaulieu, Ussé, Brancas, Sully, and many others.

Next comes the period of absence from the capital, of the sojourns in England, then at Cirey, in The Netherlands, in Prussia. Here we find the great philosophical and scientific letters, addressed to Frederick, Maupertuis, Mairan, and a hundred others. It is the period of the reflective letters.

Finally, there is the exile period. Voltaire is completely absent from Paris for a quarter of a century, and it is the phase of the massive correspondence with the entire world, since letters have become almost the sole means of communication with the outside world. He becomes first and foremost the *philosophe*. It is the period of the letters of propaganda and action.

It is obvious that if Voltaire had remained tranquilly at home, his correspondence would have been very different, much more limited, and infinitely less interesting.

VIII

At this point please permit me a simple word of warning. To evaluate a letter of Voltaire's in depth is a most subtle task. His correspondence includes letters of every sort: the mere list of his correspondents is proof of this. Such being the case, it is obvious that all the letters do not equally express the writer's true thoughts and feelings. The utter effusiveness of a letter addressed to an intimate friend in a moment of sorrow or joy reveals the writer with obvious sincerity; but what Voltaire feels often varies, even very rapidly. There is indeed in what he feels a sincerity which may be deep, but which is liable to last but a brief while.

On the other hand, a letter meant to be read by more persons than the addressee, and even to be printed, might on first consideration call for a cautious reading. But that is not always the case, since in such a letter Voltaire often goes to great pains to express with clarity his true thoughts on this or that subject. Even here there are fine distinctions to be made. Voltaire was not unaware that certain of his correspondents, Madame Du Deffand for example, despite their protestations, had his letters read before the habitués of their salons. In such instances Voltaire wrote letters that were intimate, and yet so expressed that they might be seen by other eyes than those of the individual concerned. A delicate problem, and the drafts of his letters to Madame Du Deffand bear witness to the pains he took in order to resolve it.

Then, too, in the most intimate letters, written to an Argental, a Thieriot, a Damilaville, who communicated with him in a sort of secret language, Voltaire very often said the opposite of what his own words literally meant. Once this special language has been learned (it is not a question here of more or less coded letters, for which there is a key to decipher), one easily succeeds in distinguishing the formulas whereby Voltaire disclaims certain works, those which indicate to his Parisian friends that such and such a work was really not by him, or was by him but must absolutely not be acknowledged as his, or was by him and could be tacitly acknowledged, or was by him and must be attributed to someone else, and so on with an almost infinite number of variations. One can imagine how many errors have been committed by commentators unacquainted with these little mysteries.

The error is often made of attributing to writers the opinions which they put into the mouths of the characters they have created; the error is a crude one and is recognized as such. But one who should quote Voltaire's letters without taking into account the frequently very subtle difficulties which I have just but very lightly sketched, would be guilty of an error almost as serious. The most multiple character created by Voltaire is Voltaire himself; he moves that character about like a puppet, one cannot confine him in a strait jacket.

IX

How many letters did Voltaire write? Well, my files, my card-indexes, my chronological and alphabetical lists indicate the presence of twenty thousand letters, nine-tenths of them either in manuscript form or photo-copied—in all, nearly a quarter of a million sheets of paper; for I have in my possession a large number of letters in several, indeed as many as ten, twelve, and even fifteen versions: rough drafts, originals, copies intended for Voltaire's archives, contemporaneous transcripts, editions with variants, variants often composed by Voltaire himself in the letters which he allowed to be printed (but those were public letters or display pieces—never did he publish a personal letter). Certain periods of his life supply us with a great number of letters; but they are rare and brief. For other periods, especially the early ones, we have relatively few; for still others, for example, when Voltaire was actively pursuing a particular goal, we have many, but we know that he wrote still more. Thus, in October 1748 Voltaire made a great effort to prevent a parody of his tragedy *Sémiramis* from being performed. We have the letters he wrote in this connection on the 10th to the Queen of France, the chief of police, and his *angel,* Argental; but he himself tells us—not vaguely that he has written thirty more letters, a purely figurative remark cited over and over again as if it had statistical value—he tells us very precisely that he has also written to Madame de Pompadour, the Duchess d'Aiguillon, Maurepas, the Duke d'Aumont, the Duchess de Villars, the Duke de Fleury, and the Duke de Gèvres—a very ducal correspondence that day. All these letters are lost, or at least have not yet been recovered.

Is it any wonder that he who dives deeply into this ocean often experiences the same sense of the infinite as that expressed by Newton before the universe which he had just unveiled? This sense is incommunicable, one can only symbolize it by means of numbers, themselves scarcely apprehensible. The astronomer expresses his astonishment in light-years; fortunately, we are not at that point. I ask your permission, however, to present to you a few statistics that are every bit as staggering on the human scale. But first I must undeceive you on one detail. It is very often said that Voltaire wrote a huge number of letters. Nothing of the kind. Figure it out for yourselves. I have already told you that I have succeeded in finding 20,000 letters. Now, leaving aside one childhood letter, Voltaire's correspondence spreads over 67 years; 67 years have 3,484 weeks; 3,484 weeks have 24,388 days—not counting leap years. So we arrive at an average of scarcely one letter per day. I think we have, very roughly, half of all the letters written by Voltaire. If so, the average rises to two per day. Absolutely speaking, even relatively speaking, this is a modest figure. For it seems, according to the American newspapers, that ex-President Hoover wrote in the course of a single year, and it was his eighty-fourth, 55,952 letters.[2] *That* is a great many. It is even incredible, since it averages out to 155 letters per day on condition that Mr. Hoover worked 365 days a year. But even if highly exaggerated, this figure throws into the shade the mere 20,000 letters of Voltaire's entire lifetime which I offer in my edition. Actually, what is remarkable is not the number of letters written by Voltaire, but the number which his correspondents insisted on saving from his youth on. Except for archivists out of necessity, and collectors because of the worst characteristics of that type of person, who will ever save a letter of Mr. Hoover's, and how many will be left that are alive after two centuries in those cubic meters which in our time measure the archival acquisitions of all countries?

So in my edition I offer 20,000 letters, twice the number found in preceding editions. These twenty thousand letters are addressed to 1,200 correspondents, 400 of them new, and will compose 80 volumes [*107* volumes, as it turned out—Transl.], 39 of them already published, in a text accompanied by a commentary of about 200,000 notes, some 250 appendices, and several hundred illustrations.

X

Since Voltaire wrote to so many persons in so many countries, and since his letters have been so assiduously collected for two and a half centuries, it is not surprising that they are widely scattered. Manuscripts—for the edition is naturally based on the original texts—have in fact been found in nearly 200 public and private collections located practically everywhere, from Tartu to Naples and from Honolulu to Wisbech. Among the collections which possess Voltaire manuscripts, the Gossoudarstvennaya Biblioteka Poublitchnaya Imyena Saltykoff-Shchedrin at Leningrad necessarily remains incomparable, *facile princeps,* since it contains Voltaire's library,[3] including a large proportion of his archives, not to mention the countless notes in his hand which decorate the margins of the

[2] *Time* (International Edition, 18 August 1958), p. 31.

[3] The Institut et Musée Voltaire has just published the catalogue, set up by Voltaire himself, and under his direction, of his library at Ferney: *Voltaire's Catalogue of His Library at Ferney,* eds. George R. Havens and Norman L. Torrey, *Studies on Voltaire and the Eighteenth Century,* Volume IX (Genève, 1959).

printed works. Leaving aside this marvelous aggregate, the finest collection of Voltaire manuscripts, taking into account both quality and quantity, if I dare take the liberty of saying so with so little discretion, is currently that of the Institut et Musée Voltaire, at Voltaire's Les Délices; second in importance is that of the Bibliothèque Nationale, which is remarkably rich, thanks above all to Cayrol and to Seymour de Ricci; next comes the collection of the Pierpont Morgan Library in New York, largely made up of first-class items; and in fourth place is the private collection of the Queen of The Netherlands, so graciously placed at my disposal. Also remarkable are the collections of the Bibliothèque Historique of the city of Paris, the Bibliothèque Royale of Belgium (thanks to Count de Launoit), and the Bibliothèque Publique et Universitaire of Geneva. To my knowledge, there are manuscripts of Voltaire's letters at the present time in collections located in eighteen countries (though my definition of a country is perhaps too broad): Algeria, Austria, Belgium, Canada, Denmark, Esthonia, Finland, France, Germany, Great Britain, Hawaii, Italy, The Netherlands, Poland, the Soviet Union, Sweden, Switzerland, the United States. As for France, I have found manuscripts in 67 archives, libraries, and private collections.

This is doubtless the finest opportunity I can ever have to thank the numerous archivists, librarians, and private individuals, and the few booksellers, who have so generously granted me their aid and passed their treasures on to me, by means of sale, loan, or photographic reproduction. I whole-heartedly extend to them my public thanks; besides, they are all named in the notes to each letter and in the preface to each volume of my edition. This is likewise the appropriate moment for me to pillory the very few who have refused their coöperation. As for them, I have not yet named them, I am keeping my hopes up, but . . .

XI

One way or another, nine-tenths of the letters of Voltaire which have survived are now known in manuscript form. This figure would be still higher but for the disappearance, during and after the war, of numerous papers from collections that were destroyed or plundered—although some of them are beginning to reappear. For example, King Frederick's letters to Voltaire, which are cautiously, gradually being produced on the autograph market, were stolen from the Prussian archives in Berlin. Caveat emptor!

The examination of so many originals (about 150,000 manuscript pages) has revealed, among other things, the hopelessly defective state of the published correspondence. Already during his lifetime there were thirty brochures and volumes devoted exclusively to Voltaire's letters, for the most part intercepted or stolen, so great was the public's thirst for them. In these publications began the process of corruption. Judicious juxtapositions, careful selections, an ingenious omission or addition here and there, greatly amused the gallery, while Voltaire helplessly fumed. What is not realized is that this process has since gone on without interruption. Beaumarchais and Condorcet, in the great and beautiful Kehl edition, were obliged to respect the susceptibilities of many correspondents, including Catherine and Frederick, who were still alive. There had never been any separate edition of Voltaire's correspondence in its entirety, but in each successive edition of his works (there have been more than fifty, ranging from three volumes in microscopic type to 125 volumes) the text of the letters was subjected to shifts of taste and censorship; and since, as a rule, each publisher modified the text on the basis of the one which came to him from his predecessor, all these changes have been cumulative.

Some of them were merely amusing. Here is one instance, which at the same time allows us to peep under the veil concealing Alembert's personality. As a matter of fact, we do not know the true character of the *philosophe*-mathematician. It is only when one has gained acquaintance with numerous passages and entire letters which up to now have been suppressed, that one becomes aware how foul-mouthed he really was. So here is Alembert revealing to Voltaire the author of the comedy *Les Philosophes,* in which Rousseau, Diderot, and others are ruthlessly attacked. In his letter Alembert calls Palissot a "pimp," and he names several distinguished women as his patronesses, describing them as "official call-girls and honorary prostitutes." The Kehl edition reduced "pimp" to its initial letter, suppressed the names of the ladies, printed "call-girls," but changed "prostitutes" to "call-girls." An editor of the early nineteenth century, the bibliographer Renouard, who for once consulted the manuscript, restored "pimp" and the ladies' names, but, with a cautiously discriminating solicitude, reduced both "call-girls" and "prostitutes" to their initial letters; however, he did it only roughly, for, not being able to give each term its proper initial, since that of "call-girl" would have suggested an even less printable word, he represented both by a "p." There, in miniature, is a whole course in moral relativity, the history of manners, and the transmission of texts.

Since I happen to be talking about Alembert, permit me to quote you another example concerning him, which is at once highly amusing and somewhat serious. Having learned from Voltaire of the fatal events that had taken place in Geneva on 15 February 1770, Alembert replies, with his usual insensitivity: "So they're butchering one another in Geneva, thank God, and it isn't over the consubstantiality or consubstantiability of the Word." To thank God that they're butchering one another in Geneva—that was considered a bit too strong for the tender susceptibilities of Voltaire's readers. Then, too, it was so easy to correct! All one had to do was to shift a tiny conjunction ever so slightly, and the worthy Alembert became perfectly respectable. In every edition, in fact, instead of "So they're butchering one another in Geneva, thank God, and it isn't over," etc., one finds: "So they're butchering one another in Geneva, and, thank God, it isn't over consubstantiality or consubstantiability."

Other changes, however, are much more serious still, for example, passages and even entire letters suppressed, transposed, or so modified as to be made unrecognizable, and the cases in which two, three, and even ten or twelve letters were chopped into pieces and selected fragments were reassembled to form bewildering medleys. All that can be put back into proper order, not without some difficulty, to be sure, whenever the original manuscripts can be found and collated. But there are other difficulties less easy to overcome. Some of them are due to Voltaire himself. The worst is the dating, which is often of the highest importance from the historical and the biographical point of view. Voltaire himself rarely set down the complete date of a letter, frequently he gave only a day and a month, just as often only a day, and very often, too, alas, no date at all.

In this connection, a difficulty arises that is frequently distressing: it is that many of Voltaire's letters bear dates added by other hands, dates which are often erroneous. In the preface to the *Lettres d'amour de Voltaire à sa nièce* I have discussed a disturbing example of this difficulty. Of the 142 unpublished letters presented in that volume there are only three which are completely dated; on most of the others Madame Denis herself added a date. Who was in a better position to do so? Unfortunately, those dates are false, not here and there, but in most cases. The more exact the date she adds, the more it tends to be wrong. That is how it happens that we have one letter which she dated 2 September 1743, and another which bears in her hand the date 12 October 1745. Now, the letter dated 2 September 1743 was actually written in February 1742, and the one assigned to 12 October 1745 can only date from 7 December 1747. I even know another still unpublished letter (of 31 May 1768) from Voltaire to his niece, wherein Madame Denis, in dating it, has made a mistake of thirty years.

All that may help to make clear why fifteen years of spadework were necessary before the publication of the critical edition of Voltaire's correspondence could begin, and why still another ten years will have elapsed before the complete work appears.

XII

Why is the text of Voltaire's letters so incomplete and so defective? The reply to this question is of two orders of roughly equal practical importance: the first philosophical, the second technical. Voltaire has always had an altogether special place in the minds of the French. He was the leader of the *philosophes,* he was even *the philosophe;* this fact, added to his purely literary greatness, made him at the same time the target of all reactions and the victor over all attacks. In the literary sphere we have a striking proof of this affirmation: it is that most editions of the works of the great classicist were published precisely during the years which saw the triumph of romanticism. In the sphere of sensibility, even the most salient trend becomes exclusive only in rare instances. But this kind of intellectual generosity scarcely exists in the sphere of religious and political beliefs. And in fact the unfortunate turn of so many Frenchmen toward extreme opinions in both directions almost completely prevented searching and extensive Voltaire studies for a long period. Already at the end of 1867, a moment when one could dimly foresee a dismal future, Flaubert exclaimed in a letter (Conard edition, V, 344): "If we are morally and politically so debased, it's because, instead of following Monsieur de Voltaire's highroad, i.e., that of Justice and Right, we have taken Rousseau's footpaths, which have brought us back through sentiment to Catholicism. If we had been concerned for Equity and not for Fraternity, we should have made good progress." To appreciate these words at their full value, one must know what Flaubert means by "fraternity"; but even without understanding it one recognizes the words of a man who has grasped what Voltaire represents in our intellectual history. I shall not labor the point. It seems to me that there is a very significant study to be prepared on this subject; but that is a task for a Frenchman.

The technical explanation, to which I have referred, for the deplorable state of the text of Voltaire's letters, and of the entire text of his works, is less delicate. First of all, it is that the eighteenth- and nineteenth-century publishers had their own standards, and that those standards are not ours. They never hesitated to delete a passage which they found uninteresting: it is precisely those passages that interest us the most with the small details of intimate or daily life they contain, which our ancestors regarded as beneath a great man. Then again, if Voltaire described the same incident to several correspondents, the publishers often retained only one of the versions, while for us the variations among the different accounts are significant and frequently fascinating. When Voltaire was extraordinarily engrossed by this or that event—for that matter, he always was—he often wrote a rapid succession of notes to the same correspondent or to different ones. Nothing easier than to blend them into a single "big" letter, sacrificing nothing but the whole flavor, the entire psychological and historical value of the authentic texts.

As for deletions of another kind, here again it is precisely the unpublished material which is likely to be the most interesting. Detailed proof of this statement would take us beyond the limits of a lecture, since it calls for the quoting of many texts, but certain principles are clear. If, for example, in the eighteenth century such and such a reference capable of offending a still-living individual is left out; if, under the Restoration, awkward references to the monarchy are suppressed by the censors in what remains of the text; if, in the nineteenth century, a less visible but all the more effective censorship sweeps away all that is considered to be especially obscene or blasphemous, it goes without saying that the published text represents Voltaire's words only in a very anemic way. It follows, too, that the new Voltaire who will come to be known tomorrow will be an infinitely livelier, subtler, more human person than he is imagined to be today, capable of extraordinary candor, of vigorous language, of Rabelaisian witticisms which spare neither the most hallowed nor the most eminent figures. To be sure, a neutral personality does not frighten the timidity of publishers.

Voltaire has often been accused, I have myself accused him, of being hypersensitive to his critics. The new findings show him to be, in this respect, both better and worse. The non-expurgated texts reveal an even more violent language directed against the hornets of literature, but they also reveal a Voltaire who receives with astonishing patience and docility the well-intentioned criticisms of the very persons who were least qualified to offer them. As for his attitude toward the Desfontaines and the pirate publishers, we must not judge Voltaire by twentieth-century standards. In his time there were no copyright laws, or almost none. Any publisher could reproduce his works riddled with errors, and this was done not two or three times, but with hundreds of Voltaire publications. Anyone could steal his name or his famous initial, and cover therewith the filthiest and most sensational productions. Besides, libel was not yet a legal concept, and one could say and print anything against a man whom one knew to be in disfavor at the Court, and who was spending most of his life far away from Paris. Voltaire, the most famous man in Europe for half a century, was forced to endure all that. And yet people are astonished that from time to time he reacted violently! One must be very insensitive, very ignorant of the world, very ignorant, period, and very much lacking in the experience gained by a man with whom the public is the least bit concerned, to make Voltaire the object of loftily moralizing accusations.

A word or two on a most important component of the unpublished materials which I have succeeded in finding: the letters addressed to Voltaire. All editions offer some of these, but only a few. I add a great many, but I wish I could find many more. It is frequently possible to couple them with the letters by Voltaire to which they reply. There are numerous obscure details which are thereby clarified, and the tone and substance of these letters are often highly significant. On the personal plane one can ascertain how graciously Voltaire replies to the importunities of some poetaster who is asking him to look over his works; how generously he often reacts to solicitations that are addressed to him, requests for money, for intercession, for letters of recommendation, for gift copies of his publications; with what forbearance he endures the indifference, even the incivility of many of his friends and of almost all his protégés; how tolerantly he forgives secretaries who steal his manuscripts; how strong his family feeling is, and how liberally he gives pensions to all, nieces, nephews, grand-nephews, distant cousins. Let me take but a single example among hundreds, a certain unpublished letter from Alembert, who had misunderstood something Voltaire had said, and who wrote him a letter so rude that I prefer not to quote it. Voltaire's reply, likewise unpublished, is remarkable; courteously, amicably, calmly, he replies point by point, and he concludes: "I recommend unity to the brethren, and finally, I love, revere, admire, and miss you." One can see that Voltaire was capable of enduring and forgiving everything, save intolerance, injustice, and malice.

XIII

I have insisted on entering into these few details in order to emphasize that statistical evaluation alone scarcely enables us to judge the new Voltaire who emerges from this edition. Indeed, those who examine only the letters that are entirely new run the risk of making very awkward mistakes. But after all it cannot be denied that what is entirely new interests us the most. How can I give you the slightest idea of what those 10,000 letters represent which I have the very great honor of adding to the Voltaire corpus? Where should I begin? With the 142 love-letters to his niece, discovered too late to take their place in the chronological sequence, and which I was obliged to present in a special volume? Letters so tender, so bawdy that they astonish those who judge Voltaire in accordance with conventionally accepted information. With the hundreds of new letters to other, already known correspondents? For example, the latest edition of Voltaire's works contains about a hundred letters to various members of the Tronchin family, letters printed for the most part in versions which bear only a very remote resemblance to those penned by Voltaire. Now we are acquainted with the manuscripts of 800 letters to the Tronchins, letters which supply us with an immense number of minute particulars on Voltaire's life and activities at Les Délices.

An even more striking contrast is provided by Voltaire's correspondence with his publisher Gabriel Cramer, the man who first and foremost induced him to settle near Lake Geneva. Voltaire's works contain a dozen letters to his "dear Gabriel": I present more than a thousand, letters filled with precious details on the works of our great man, his methods of publication and dissemination, and above all, on their respective dates of composition.

One of the most interesting figures among the newly discovered correspondents is the strangely evanescent one of Charlotte Sophie von Aldenburg, Countess Bentinck, who is scarcely mentioned even in the most detailed biographies of Voltaire. The classic edition of his works does not contain a single letter by her or addressed to her; but recently three hundred of the letters which Voltaire wrote to her have emerged from the archives of various branches of the

Bentinck family, together with some of her replies. They force us to revise completely the years spent by Voltaire in Berlin and Potsdam, at Frederick's Court. It was supposed that he had spent them more or less in solitude, a solitude punctuated above all by the alternating quarrels and reconciliations, by the coquettish behavior which marked his curious relations with the King. But we now know that Voltaire's activities were multiple and varied, although they left him with enough time to see Madame Bentinck almost every day, and to write to her very frequently, if only to request the loan of her carriage, to accept—but more often to decline—an invitation, or to defend himself against her jealousy, in particular, of a mysterious Polish countess.

What else? There is a long series of detailed letters to his grand-nephew D'Hornoy, another very lengthy one to a banker whose very name appears nowhere in the Voltaire literature, numerous letters to Constant d'Hermenches, to his notary Laleu, to Henri Rieu, to Manoël de Végobre, to Labat, a considerable number of letters addressed to Voltaire by Cideville, which reveal in the latter an unknown poet of modest but sure merit. But this enumeration becomes tedious and could only be fragmentary, even if greatly extended, since it would reveal 400 new correspondents. Let us leave these generalities behind to get a closer view of Voltaire the letter-writer, that is to say, of Voltaire.

XIV

There is no question of taking as an illustration a full period of Voltaire's life, or even a year, a month, a week. Rather let us focus our attention on a single day of our great man's life. I have not selected that day from his scintillating youth, or from his middle years at Cirey or in Prussia, or from the period of transformation at Les Délices, a period which saw the birth of what is meant by the Patriarch of Ferney. I have preferred to take one of the saddest, most painful phases of his life. He is seventy-four; already for many years he has been in complete retirement at Ferney, where he pursues a relentless activity, on the one hand destructive of intolerance and religion, that is to say, of superstition, on the other constructive, beneficent, humane. He still has living with him a relative on his mother's side, paralytic and moribund; little Marie Corneille, her spouse Dupuits, their children—it is generally known that Voltaire received into his home the poet's descendant, but it is too often forgotten that he dowered her, married her off, and always kept her under his roof—so then, the Dupuits family; an unfrocked Jesuit; young La Harpe and his wife; the architect Racle; the *philosophe*-lawyer Christin; the faithful secretary Wagnière; the copyist Bigex; fourteen French officers who are blockading Geneva. (They belonged to a regiment whose colonel, says Voltaire in an unpublished letter of March 1768, "is so busy with the King's service that, when he returned to Paris, he didn't even write us a word of thanks." Indeed, Voltaire adds: "That's how three or four hundred Englishmen behaved, whom we received very cordially, and who are so attached to their fatherland that they never remembered us."[4] I have made bold to avenge Voltaire on those three or four hundred compatriots of mine.) As I was saying, some French officers; in the château and its outbuildings 60 servants and farm-workers (that is the figure given by Voltaire in a letter of 4 March 1769); five, twenty, fifty, a hundred guests passing through, who have come to perform plays, spend the night, dine, or quite simply contemplate the most famous man in the world; and finally, the woman we must above all not forget, widow Denis, née Marie Louise Mignot, niece, housekeeper, and mistress of the lord of the estate.

It is Tuesday, 1 March 1768. I could have chosen this or that day for which I have managed to double, triple, or quadruple the number of known letters. That would have been only too easy. I have preferred a more difficult course, but also one that is more revealing. Actually, for this month of March 1768 we were already acquainted with 34 letters, and for this one day of the first of the month, with no less than nine. We thought we were well informed on the events of that period. In reality, our knowledge of it was very poor, we were acquainted only with the surface of things—the essentials had eluded us. It is true that for this month of March 1768 I know only twenty or so letters which cannot be found in previous editions. Quantitatively speaking, this contribution of new letters, not even 60 per cent of those previously known, is of relatively modest size in the Voltairean production, where everything is on a gigantic scale, although they are by no means altogether banal, since among them are communications addressed to Presiding Judge Hénault, the Chevalier de Rochefort, the pastor Moultou, the Russian minister Vorontsov, the pastor Vernes, the publisher Pierre Rousseau, and Alembert, not to mention two letters addressed

[4] Surely a witticism: the English far from forgot Voltaire. See Sir Gavin de Beer, "Voltaire's British Visitors," *Studies on Voltaire and the Eighteenth Century*, IV (Genève, 1957), 7-136.

by the last-mentioned to Voltaire, and other unpublished missives from Madame Bentinck, Erlach von Riggisberg, Bellerive, and others.

But let us return to the first of the month 191 years ago. The strife between Geneva and Paris had somewhat subsided. Voltaire was, so to speak, a link between the two countries; he endeavored to encourage and maintain improved relations, and to do nothing—which was less easy—to arouse fear and suspicion. Now, when he was most deeply troubled and most serious, Voltaire affected to laugh, and this time his laughter took the name of *La Guerre civile de Genève*. This lampoon in verse had been published without Voltaire's knowledge, but he had managed to lock up the most dangerous part, the second canto, which contains a few hundred lines in this vein:

Près d'une église à Pierre consacrée,
Très sale église, et de Pierre abhorrée,
Qui brave Rome, hélas! impunément,
Sur un vieux mur est un vieux monument,
Reste maudit d'une déesse antique,
Du paganisme ouvrage fantastique,
Dont les enfers animaient les accents
Lorsque la terre était sans prédicants,
Dieu quelquefois permet qu'à cette idole
L'esprit malin prête encor sa parole.
Les Genevois consultent ce démon
Quand par malheur ils n'ont point de sermon.
Ce diable antique est nommé l'Inconstance;
Elle a toujours confondu la prudence:
Une girouette exposée à tout vent
Est à la fois son trône et son emblême;
Cent papillons forment son diadème; etc., etc.

["Near a church consecrated to Peter, a church which is very filthy, and abhorred by Peter, which defies Rome with impunity, alas, there is an old monument on an old wall, the accursed remains of an ancient goddess, a fantastic product of paganism, whose accents were animated by Hades at a time when the earth had no preachers. God sometimes permits the Evil One to lend his speech once again to this idol. The Genevans consult this demon whenever they unfortunately are given no sermon. This ancient devil is named Inconstancy; it has always discomfited prudence: a weathervane exposed to every wind is at once its throne and its emblem; a hundred butterflies compose its diadem; etc., etc."]

One can readily understand why Voltaire would not expose himself, or France, to the reactions of Genevan sensibility to such allusions. Now, one day this second canto appears in print. Voltaire is beside himself with rage and anxiety, but he does not lose his head. Deliberately, thoroughly he conducts his inquiry, and it leads to the unquestionable conclusion that the culprit is La Harpe, that young man of letters whom he had entertained in his home for many months along with his wife, as if they were his children, and whose praises he had sung for two years in all his letters. It was he who had stolen the manuscript at Ferney, who had taken it to Paris in the same valise as the rouleaux of louis d'or which Voltaire was in the habit of slipping into his protégés' baggage when they left. Still worse, La Harpe had been encouraged, perhaps bribed, by Madame Denis. How? We shall never know for sure, although that woman's vulgar greed and her appetites even at the age of sixty allow us to guess the answer. As for La Harpe, Voltaire forgives him with a forbearance that continues to astonish us, as he always forgave those who offended him in a personal way. Not only does he forgive an especially disgraceful deed on the part of a guest, of a protégé; believing in La Harpe's talent, and in order not to harm him—the young man was very poor—Voltaire sends a denial to the newspapers, clearing La Harpe of all suspicion. And only a few months later (10 March 1769) he writes to him: "My dear panegyrist of Henri IV *et vitula tu dignus et hic*. You have a great deal of talent in verse and in prose. May it serve to make your fortune as it will surely serve to make your reputation!"

But as for Madame Denis, for whom this was not the first such offense, he quite simply throws her out. She feigns innocence. In an unpublished letter (19 May 1768) to neighbor Henri Rieu, the man who was to inherit the English books in Voltaire's library, she maintains that she does not know what caused the separation. "All I can tell you is that in spite of my uncle's bursts of temper I still love him. I do not impute his injustices to his heart, because he rectifies them as best he can." And she tries to blame it all on that "contemptible blockhead," the "Jesuit Adam."

This is just about all that was known of this incident, which was, in the final analysis, rather stupid and even sordid. But a lesson is in store for us, a lesson which will teach us once again, though never sufficiently, the urgent necessity of historical criticism, of documentary research.

Listen to an unpublished letter by Voltaire's secretary, Jean Louis Wagnière, addressed to Madame Denis "c/o Monsieur Tabareau, Postmaster General, etc. at Lyon"—already a precious detail, since it informs us as to the route taken by Madame Denis to return to Paris. I shall read you the letter in its entirety:

> Tuesday evening, 1 March 1768
>
> Madame,
>
> I thought I was going to be killed by Monsieur de Voltaire at a quarter past noon. After he had been alone for an hour with Father Adam, I was surprised to hear him say to me that you were sleeping very late. I exclaimed that you had left at ten o'clock, and that I thought Father Adam had told him so. He flew into a terrific rage against me, although I told him that you had all knocked for a long time at his doors, which were locked on both sides, and that Monsieur Dupuits had tried three times to get into his apartment. I was so stunned that I'm very sick over it. However, he did calm down a bit.
>
> He tore up his note for the twenty thousand francs he is to give you per year. I think he'll send you another one when you get to Paris. Monsieur Nicod has returned the power of attorney. My heart was pounding a bit when I handed it to him. He calmly read it through, and put it into his desk, saying that that was good.
>
> That, Madame, is how this sad day has passed by. My heart wishes you a happy trip, and I hope we shall have the good fortune to see you again at Ferney.
>
> You know the deep respect, the attachment, and the gratitude I feel toward you.
>
> Wagnière

Just a few words of comment on this letter. After her uncle's death Madame Denis behaved very badly, indeed very shabbily, toward the worthy Wagnière. It was, she said, because he had always been her enemy and had set her uncle against her. From everything that was known of Jean Louis's character, this accusation called for all possible reservations. We now have the proof of its falsity; in effect, all that was merely a fabricated and disgraceful pretext. Wagnière's letter reveals only a genuine friendliness, and even, if you will, some lack of discretion toward his master, in favor of the niece—a conclusion confirmed, moreover, by other unpublished letters which I shall soon present in my edition.

Next, and this is much more important, the words "He tore up his note for the twenty thousand francs" afford a glimpse, perhaps, of a Voltaire who, in his exceeding bitterness, decides to do nothing more for a woman to whom he has already given a large part of his fortune and who has lived at his expense—and very luxuriously—for thirty years. We may defend this gesture, we may deplore it or even condemn it, but we must above all tell ourselves that, although Wagnière certainly reported the truth, after all, neither he nor anyone can understand the real meaning of the gesture. And this attitude of caution is fully justified, for in reality Voltaire showered Madame Denis with gifts when she left, increased her pension, and that is not all. Here is the proof. Listen to a brief excerpt from another unpublished and very lengthy letter, the rest of which is too full of allusions that would be incomprehensible without long explanatory remarks. It dates from the same day, and is addressed to the future Presiding Judge D'Hornoy, born of the first marriage of Voltaire's younger niece, who was then the Marchioness de Florian. Even for this brief excerpt a few comments are indispensable: the "dear Judge" is, as I have said, the grand-nephew D'Hornoy; "Mamma" is Madame Denis; Madame Dupuits is Marie Corneille; the business arrangement with the Duke de Wurtemberg is the very irregular income from the life annuity which Voltaire had purchased from that prince; Abbé Blet was the Field Marshal Duke de Richelieu's business agent, entrusted with the inheritance of the De Guise family, which was heavily in debt to Voltaire, who had brought about the Princess's marriage with Richelieu by lending the money that made it possible.

1 March 1768

My dear Judge, Mamma and Madame Dupuits will soon do what I should like to do, they will embrace you. Mamma simply must spend some time in Paris on account of her gums, which are in dangerous condition, and I myself have to go and settle once for all my business arrangement with the Duke de Wurtemberg, who will never be twelve years in arrears like certain French field marshals.

I beg you to divide between her and me all that Field Marshal Richelieu owes me. It amounts, I believe, to 27,425 francs. The entire sum must be paid at once. Mamma, who lived with him a great deal, will get him to pay her more effectively than a tipstaff. It's true that she is past the age which unties the purse strings of dukes and peers; but an old liaison is always respected. Between the two of you, you will surely get the better of Abbé Blet.

Admire the discretion, the loyalty, the self-control of this old gentleman writing to his grand-nephew about the latter's aunt! Madame Denis's gums! What a marvelous man! What a splendid century! And do not forget that the Field Marshal's debt which Voltaire was so blithely offering to share with his niece would add up to fourteen million francs. It is true that if Richelieu, better known at the time by the elegant nickname of "old whoremonger," had had to pay for all his old liaisons at that rate, in order to meet his expenses he would have needed several campaigns as profitable for him in booty as the last one.

And now, the moment of truth. You are going to learn what Voltaire really felt that day in his heart of hearts. You will, in fact, learn it thanks to the discovery of one of his most remarkable letters, in a way perhaps the most remarkable. This letter was addressed to his niece. It has remained unknown up to now; I have the honor of presenting it first to you. Here is a large excerpt:

> At Ferney, Tuesday, 1 March [1768]
> at 2 P.M.
>
> Doubtless there is a destiny, and it is often very cruel. I came to your door three times, and you knocked on mine. I tried walking my grief about the garden. It was ten o'clock, I set the hand at ten on the sun globe, I was waiting for you to wake up. I came across Monsieur Mallet. He told me he was broken up about your leaving. I inferred he had just come from your apartment. I thought you were going to dine at the château, as you had said you would. No servant gave me any warning, they all thought I was fully informed. I sent for Christin and Father Adam. We talked until noon. Finally, I return to your apartment. I ask where you are. Wagnière says to me, "What, you don't know that she left at ten o'clock!" I go back to Father Adam more dead than alive. He replies just like Wagnière, "I thought you knew!" At once I send for a horse from the stable. There wasn't anybody there. So, in the same house with twenty servants, we looked for each other without meeting. I am in despair, and this persistent misfortune of mine presages a very sinister future. I know that the moment of separation would have been frightful; but it is even more frightful that you left without seeing me, while we were looking for one another. I quickly sent word to Madame Racle's, so that I might weep with her. She is dining with Christin, Adam, and her husband; but as for me, I am very far from being able to dine. I am consumed with sorrow and am writing to you. . . .
>
> You will see Monsieur de Choiseul, Richelieu, Argental. You will alleviate my misfortunes; that, too, is your destiny. You will succeed in Paris in your business and mine, you will see your brother and your nephew again. If I die, I shall die completely devoted to you; if I live, my life will be at your disposal. I tenderly embrace Monsieur and Madame Dupuits. I love them, I miss them, I am broken-hearted.

Such, in part, is the letter addressed by Voltaire to this niece who owed him everything, who had repeatedly betrayed him in his affections, who had perpetrated abominable injustices, and who had just left him without a word of farewell after forty years of friendship and love. Such is the letter of the man whose adversaries, professing a faith which should inspire, I do not even say more charity, but more justice, have tried to represent him as a rancorous and heartless monster. Let's not labor the point.

So it is two or two-thirty P.M. on 1 March 1768. Like the most ordinary mortal, Voltaire finds but one consolation for his distress: he immerses himself in work with a sad and noble serenity. The worthy Wagnière must have gone to bed that evening with a fine case of writer's cramp!

First of all, we find on that day a correspondence with the Resident of France at Geneva, Pierre Michel Hennin: I mean "correspondence," for on that Tuesday the post horse made the run between Ferney and the French ministry in Geneva four times, perhaps even six. In the morning Voltaire had already written a long letter to assure Hennin that a certain "Languedocian woman with her beautiful eyes"[5] could not have seen the second canto of *La Guerre civile,* and that it was La Harpe who was guilty of the betrayal; he also asks for the gazettes. Hennin sends them to him, adding: "Whenever you feel like not being alone, please let me know. You mustn't have any doubts about how pleased I shall be to prove my devotion to you at any time and in every way." The same evening Voltaire returns the gazettes to his "dear minister": "Mamma has left, I am now a hermit. You know that the devil became one when he grew old. But no matter what they say, I am not a devil."

Meanwhile there is a veritable avalanche of letters. Here is a note to his "divine angel" Count d'Argental, to send him a little publication which Voltaire disowns, to be sure, but which nevertheless appears among his works under the title of *Lettre de l'archevêque de Cantorbéri à l'archevêque de Paris*: it is a defense of Marmontel's *Bélisaire* against the thunderbolts of intolerance. That is what he is alluding to when he says to dear Argental that he is braving the thunderbolts of Rome to write to him. As for the trip of Madame Denis and the Dupuits, it is a necessary one. "Why can't I be with them?" But in this letter to his most intimate friend, Voltaire makes no reference to La Harpe. Why? It is precisely because loyal Argental would have had a lively and dangerous reaction.

[5] The French text here inserts the following parenthesis: "'Languedocian woman' is neither a pun nor a nasty allusion—the word was pronounced that way at the time." The modern spelling for "Languedocian woman" is "Languedocienne." Voltaire wrote "Languedochienne." "Chienne" means "bitch," and "Languedochienne" suggests "langue de chienne," i.e., "bitch's tongue."—Trans.

Voltaire explains himself a few weeks later (16 April 1768) in an unpublished letter: "You ask me, my dear angel, to open up my heart to you. . . . I haven't told you about the adventure involving La Harpe, who is, I believe, scarcely known to you, and whom, moreover, I don't want to hurt, and who never had any intention of harming me, however badly he may have behaved toward me. He is young, he is poor, he is married; he needs support, I have not wanted to deprive him of your esteem."

Here is a letter to young Chabanon de Maugris, whose *Eudoxie* had been written at Ferney, and had since been largely revised by our great man: "So Mamma will see *Eudoxie* before I do, my dear colleague. She is leaving for Paris, she will let Madame Dupuits judge whether plays are better performed in Paris than at Ferney. . . . She is going to take care of her health, her business affairs, and mine. All that went to rack and ruin during the twenty years that she lived far away from Paris. . . . So now Ferney has once again become the wilderness it was before I put my hand to it. I am abandoning Melpomene for Ceres and Pomona. Worthy young people, cultivate the fine arts and gorge yourselves on pleasure; I have had my day."

Here is a letter to charming Dorat. La Harpe had, in fact, already been guilty of a first indiscretion: he had sent a little epigrammatic shaft from Ferney to the graceful poet in Paris:

Bon Dieu, que cet auteur est triste en sa gaîté!
Bon Dieu, qu'il est pesant dans sa légèreté!
Que ses petits écrits ont de longues préfaces!
Ses fleurs sont des pavôts, ses ris sont des grimaces.
Que l'encens qu'il prodigue est plat et sans odeur!
Il est, si je l'en crois, un heureux petit-maître;
Mais, si j'en crois ses vers, qu'il est triste d'être
Ou sa maîtresse ou son lecteur!

["Good Lord, how sad this author is in his bursts of gaiety! Good Lord, how heavy he is in his light touches! What long prefaces his little pieces have! His flowers are poppies, his laughs are grimaces. How insipid and odorless is the flatterer's incense he lavishes! By his own testimony, he is a happy coxcomb; but by that of his poetry, how dull it is to be either his mistress or his reader!"]

Fine going! Not at all in the style of our great man, but inevitably attributed to him. Now, Voltaire preferred to fashion his own shafts, and above all to choose their targets, and he had no desire whatever to offend young Dorat. This is why he goes into lengthy explanations and protestations of innocence: "In a word, Monsieur,

I am too truthful and too frank not to be believed when I swore to Madame Necker on my honor that I had no hand in that troublesome business. It's up to you to know who your enemies are. As for me, I am not one of them. I have been deeply distressed by this imposture. I have proofs in my possession which would fully justify me [etc., etc.]." (This Madame Necker, to whom Voltaire swore his innocence, is the one who had just given birth to little Anne Louise Germaine, later Madame de Staël).

Here is a letter to François Louis Henri Leriche, Director General of Crown Lands at Besançon. He complains that his packets have been "brazenly seized at Saint-Claude"; he protests "that there is nothing which the insolent inquisition of certain people has not taken the liberty of perpetrating against the laws of the realm"; and he concludes: "A very great revolution is in the making in the minds of the Italians and the Spaniards. The entire world is shaking off the chains of fanaticism, but the shade of the Chevalier de la Barre cries out in vain for vengeance against his assassins."

Here is a letter to the Supreme Council of Montbéliard, fief of the Duke de Wurtemberg, who had sold him a life annuity. Now, the Duke and his business agents find it highly surprising and even shocking that a poet should expect to be paid regularly and punctually. Voltaire is obliged to ask over and over again for his money, to utter threats, and even to hale the Duke into court. This time he contents himself with moving the Supreme Council to pity: "I am under duress, and in a pit from which I could not possibly extricate myself, save for the arrangements you have been good enough to make. I await the transfers and the notes." And he adds: "If I were alone, believe me, gentlemen, I would not bother you; but I have a huge household which has only the income in question to live on."

Here is a letter to the Duke de Richelieu, one of his oldest friends, to announce the arrival of Madame Denis in Paris. "My adopted daughter née Corneille is accompanying her to Paris, where she will see her great-uncle's plays massacred. As for me, I am remaining in my wilderness. Someone has to stay and take care of the country household. This is my consolation." And he adds: "I already regard myself as a dead man, although I have made my death agony as cheerful as I could."

Here is a letter to the Chevalier Jean Amédée Honoré de Rochefort d'Ally to thank him for a gift. "You have sent me champagne, Monsieur, at a time when I am restricted to infusions; it's like sending a prostitute to a eunuch."

Here is a letter to the pastor Jacob Vernes. This one is exceptional for that particular date, since it is short, which permits me to quote the whole of it:

> Priest of a God who is father of all men, preacher of reason, tolerant priest, if you want to obtain *Le Militaire philosophe* by the late Saint-Hyacinthe, it's at the home of your illustrious and worthy friend, Monsieur de Moultou, who will lend it to you on presentation of this note.
>
> Have you seen the *Sermon prêché à Bâle*? I think it's by your little brother.
>
> Madame Denis is going to Paris on temporal business. When are you coming here to handle spiritual business?
>
> Liber libera liberrime.

There is no need to add that the little brother who was the author of the *Sermon prêché à Bâle le premier jour de l'an 1768, par Josias Rossette, ministre du saint évangile,* a sermon offering thanks to God "for the greatest event which has marked the century in which we live," i.e., the expulsion of the Jesuits, that this little brother was named Voltaire.

And now, with this thirteenth letter, let us grant Voltaire a rest from his emotions and his labors of that Tuesday, 1 March 1768.

It would have been only too easy to go into lengthy discussions of Voltaire the philosopher, Voltaire the poet, Voltaire the dramatist, and so on. In all these areas, and a score of others, there are new findings, often very important ones, among the thousands of unpublished letters which I have the honor of presenting in my edition, modifications to be made in the traditional image of the great man. But that was not the aim of my lectures. I have tried instead to let you see the real Voltaire by showing you the private side of his life, by taking you into his home as I might take you into an old friend's drawing room; rarely is one permitted to follow a single day in the life of a great man of the past in such detail and with so complete an outpouring of his thoughts and feelings. And if, in the words of Valéry, Voltaire "makes us admire, adore, abhor, hate and venerate, beat, and crown him with a sort of encyclopaedic mastery"—*I* think that, beyond this and above all, when thus directly observed in action, he inspires our affection.

Voltaire and Madame du Châtelet

by Ira O. Wade

It is clear that any final evaluation of the intellectual activity which took place at Cirey between 1733-49 will have to await further investigation. However, certain tentative remarks may be ventured. One result of this study is the conviction that the period's importance lies not in the romantic love affair of the poet and his Lady Newton, not in the social glamour which intrigued many of their contemporaries, but in an intense intellectual activity. An understanding of this intellectual activity is imperative, for as our knowledge of it increases, the years 1733-49 appear less and less an amorous interlude in the life of the poet, or a futile social venture into the life of the upper nobility and court, or a period of glorious inactivity. Desnoiresterre's two volumes, devoted to the Cirey Period, are primarily responsible for emphasizing its romantic and social aspects, and even Lanson has fallen into the error of stressing the futility of the years at court. In fact, all those who have become interested in this epoch have magnified the picturesque, the anecdotal, and the superficial at the expense of the intellectual.

For this state of affairs there is, as we have shown, considerable justification. All of the contemporary correspondence which referred to Voltaire and to Mme. du Châlelet stressed the picturesque, the anecdotal, and the superficial. Either, like Mme. de Graffigny, people were overawed by the feverish activity which they witnessed; or, like Mme. du Deffand or Mme. de Staal, they refused to take Mme. du Châtelet and Voltaire seriously; or, finally, like the Abbé Leblanc, they were incompetent to judge the intellectual progress of the two. Voltaire himself must be credited with some responsibility for these contemporary impressions, for in his correspondence as well as in his social conduct he veiled his intellectual activity behind a constant flow of witticisms and superficial clowning. Thus, the public was completely ignorant of certain key works of the period such as the *Traité de métaphysique,* or failed to understand others such as the *Mondain,* which to them was a "badinage," or knew nothing of Voltaire's excursions into new fields of thought such as critical deism. Later biographers have merely interpreted the reports left by contemporaries concerning his life at Cirey and ignored his intellectual preoccupations. Add to this the fact that the picturesque is always more attractive if less interesting than the intellectual, and one can readily understand how Voltaire's biographers would have preferred a superficial interpretation to a more intellectual one, even if they had been in a position to give it. Finally it appears evident that the very complexity of the years 1733-49 precluded any but a superficial interpretation. Properly speaking, there is no Cirey Period, unless one wishes to designate by that name the years 1736-40. Hence, for the years 1733-49, there can be no unity of locale, as at Ferney, and unity of activity is equally difficult to establish because of the diversity of interests involved. In reality, only Mme. du Châtelet gives unity to these years; in the final analysis it is not a Cirey, it is a Mme. du Châtelet Period. Voltaire's biographers, to be sure, have recognized this, but they have overstressed Mme. du Châtelet the mistress and forgotten the intellectual activity of the two.

None the less, it is more and more apparent that the picturesque interpretation is insufficient precisely because it explains nothing. Accepting it, one has difficulty in comprehending how a period so superficial in appearance can be so rich in literary and philosophical works. One understands less how there can be such diversity in Voltaire's intellectual activity. And one fails completely in an attempt to understand how this period unites with the preceding two and the two following to give coherence and unity to Voltaire's life. For until now, it has been somewhat generally accepted that the Cirey Period was an interlude which in no way explained the continuity of Voltaire's thought and interests from the English Period to the Berlin. Indeed, it has been assumed that the years 1733-49 were characterized by a break in the continuity of his development. Hence a whole series of assumptions to explain this discontinuity: the old assumption that Voltaire's life can be divided into a literary epoch (1719-50) and a philosophic epoch (1750-78); Lanson's assumption that it was only at Berlin in the "soirées de Potsdam" that Voltaire's religious impiety and philosophical daring developed; or finally, the assumption that he turned to a systematic consideration of critical deism only in 1762 after his establishment at Ferney.

The present study tends to prove the very opposite of this commonly accepted view. It has attempted to show that the Cirey Period grows logically out of Voltaire's youth and English sojourn and leads just as logically to the Berlin and Ferney years. It is evident from the meager details which we have been able to assemble that the Cirey Period is philosophical as well as literary, that it is replete with religious impiety and philosophical daring, and distinguished in part by biblical criticism. Moreover it is solidly grounded in the traditional French movement which had been evolving since 1710. It is enriched by English thought which Voltaire brought back from England, as well as by English thought which was already finding its way across the Channel. And it is broadened by the clandestine philosophical movement which was taking place in France. Out of these three movements, represented by numerous writers, philosophers, scientists, and literary works, Voltaire and Mme. du Châtelet created an atmosphere which is neither out of harmony with what had gone before nor with what followed. It is characterized by growth, evolution, expansion, but especially by broadened intellectual interests and feverish intellectual activity.

The main lines of this activity are now apparent and the contributions of its two important initiators made more distinct. Only in the drama which Voltaire produced between 1732-49 does the influence of Cirey seem negligible. He received his impetus in this field of activity from Corneille and Racine, from Shakespeare, and to a small extent from Destouches and Nivelle de la Chaussée. The critical assistance which he received came from D'Argental rather than from Mme. du Châtelet.

However, credit must be given the lady for turning Voltaire to a serious consideration of metaphysics. Not that he was unfamiliar with metaphysical problems before his liaison with Mme. du Châtelet began. But she, by making her own inventory in this realm of thought, encouraged him to make his, and in doing so, he began discussing problems which previously appeared to him of little consequence. Once he had received this impetus, there are reasons to believe that he strongly felt influences other than those of Mme. du Châtelet. His interest in Locke, Newton, and Clarke became intensified. And, by a reaction, he was attracted by the materialistic clandestine writers of the time. The central problem became for him, as it was apparently for Mme. du Châtelet, the doctrine of free-will. He chose to follow Locke and Clarke in preference to the clandestine materialists. But Frederick precisely at this time preferred the materialists, and a lengthy debate ensued. A field opened for Voltaire by Mme. du Châtelet became suddenly enriched by Locke and Clarke, and possibly by Malebranche, and the Cirey interests were broadened and considerably modified by Frederick.

In science, the story was somewhat different. Here Mme. du Châtelet's contribution was paramount. Not only did she turn Voltaire to the study of physics, but she guided him in his studies from Leibnitz to Newton. Never did she relinquish the lead in this field. Voltaire, however, though he could but follow, broadened it, and, to some extent, modernized it. To his study of Leibnitz whom he could not understand, and to Newton whom he only partially understood, he added his contemporaries Castel, Mairan, and Maupertuis.

In moral philosophy, on the other hand, Voltaire was the leader, Mme. du Châtelet, the pupil, though the fundamental equipment of both was the same, a knowledge of Cicero. But Voltaire had had the English experience and was acquainted with Pope, if not Mandeville. Moreover, his interest in moral philosophy was grounded in the experiences of his youth. Outside influences are also felt here. The central problem is "bonheur" ["happiness"], and Helvétius, La Mettrie, Mme. du Châtelet, and Voltaire, not to mention Pope and Mandeville, are all seeking "bonheur." Besides, it was the primary problem of moral philosophy in the first half of the eighteenth century, in England as well as in France.

In history, Voltaire had to find his way, encouraged but unaided by Mme. du Châtelet whose interest was purely incidental and whose critical historical sense was negative. Here the influences are all external to Cirey: Bayle, whose position was in the main that of Mme. du Châtelet, Lenglet, the Président Hénault, Montesquieu, and perhaps Middleton. And yet, it is unwise at this time to assume that Voltaire had to depend upon purely external influences for his inspiration in history, since our present information concerning his historical activity is very inadequate. If Hénault and others led him to write the history of Louis XIV and Louis XV, it was Mme. du Châtelet who reputedly turned him to the philosophic writing of history. And there is some ground for the belief that his philosophy of history was immeasurably influenced by his entrance into the field of critical deism.

In the field of critical deism, there is a strong presumption that Mme. du Châtelet is the leader. And yet, one cannot be too sure, for there are also reasons to believe that Voltaire is furnishing the criticism and Mme. du Châtelet is doing the transcription. At any rate, they are getting acquainted with Woolston, Calmet, Meslier, and the clandestine critics together, and while she is writing the *Examen de la Genèse,* he is composing portions of the *Bible enfin expliquée,* at least the first half of the *Examen important,* and the *Sermon des cinquante.* To be sure, there are external influences here: Calmet and Woolston and Meslier, and a fair number of clandestine manuscripts, among them the *Examen de la religion,* the *Religion chrétienne analysée,* the *Notes,* the *Preuves,* and portions of the *Examen critique des apologistes de la religion chrétienne,* and the *Examen critique du Nouveau Testament.* But the one fundamental influence is Mme. du Châtelet's *Examen de la Genèse.*

Thus the atmosphere of Cirey is a queer mixture of sudden enthusiasms, feverish activity, much confusion, and many external influences. The external influences can be easily detected. In metaphysics, they come from Locke, Newton, Clarke, Malebranche, and Frederick; in physics, from Newton, Leibnitz, Castel, Mairan, and Maupertuis; in moral philosophy, from Cicero, Pope, Mandeville, Helvétius, and La Mettrie; in history, from Bayle, Lenglet, and Hénault; in critical deism, from Calmet, Woolston, and the clandestine writers. The rôles of these individuals in the formation of the Cirey atmosphere are still not too clear, although their general contribution to it is readily apparent. On the other hand, we should now have a better acquaintance with the two powerful contributors of sudden enthusiasm, Voltaire and Mme. du Châtelet. Sometimes the honor for inaugurating an enthusiasm seems to rest with Voltaire, as in the case of drama, moral philosophy, and history; sometimes with Mme. du Châtelet, as in the case of metaphysics, physics, and biblical criticism. But it is, in the present state of literary history, difficult to apportion to each his exact share in this intellectual activity. Nor is it really desirable to do so. No one would care to prove today that Mme. du Châtelet was a great writer and a great thinker. It is more important to know in what ways she contributed to making Voltaire a greater writer and a greater thinker. It is significant that by 1749, at the age of fifty-five, Voltaire had completed his education. Never thereafter did he enter new intellectual fields. And when in later years his views on certain particular subjects shifted somewhat, he still based them on the same material which he and Mme. du Châtelet had assembled in the Cirey Period.

Voltaire and the English Deists

by Norman L. Torrey

Voltaire's early philosophical deism was strengthened and modified by the deistic disciples of Locke. And in his later attack against the Christian religion he adopted every method that was used by his English predecessors. He had his favorites, however, and borrowed chiefly from the English extremists who had brought the searchlight of common sense and common morality to bear upon the Scriptures. In this field his faults and failures were their faults and failures, and his successes their successes. It was only in ethically-minded England that this method of attack could readily increase and multiply, and it was naturally from England that Voltaire, with his command of the English language and his admiration for English thought, borrowed his material. The historical argument, on the other hand, was cosmopolitan; and though many noteworthy contributions of the English deists in this field affected Voltaire directly or indirectly, the English influence is here nearly lost among the wealth of scholarly sources.

The importance of Toland in England has been apparent throughout the whole study of the English deists. His catalogue of apocryphal works inaugurated a new era of documentary criticism. We have seen, however, that Voltaire borrowed very extensively from the apocryphal codes of the learned Fabricius, and thereby drew upon himself a greater reputation for learning than he might have secured in following Toland's more popular work. The apocryphal codices of Fabricius were probably Voltaire's most used single source. Yet without Fabricius, much of Toland's thought and spirit would have been passed on to Voltaire through Peter Annet, who saw most clearly and developed with the least hesitation the

"Voltaire and the English Deists." From *Voltaire and the English Deists*, Yale University Press, New Haven, by Norman L. Torrey. The pages reprinted here reproduce the chapter entitled "Conclusions," except for the omission of the opening sentence. Translations from the French have been supplied by the editor.

implications of Toland's researches. And it was in the spirit of Annet that Voltaire handled the material he found in Fabricius. Toland's other contributions to the historical argument were for the most part either lost upon Voltaire or derived from common sources, among whom Van Dale stands out as the most important. Greatly influenced by the labors of the Dutch scholars, Toland firmly laid the foundations of the English deistic controversy. The effect of his thought on Voltaire was therefore through the general movement more often than by direct contact.

The study of Collins has served to emphasize two distinct periods of pronounced English influence on Voltaire: first, the Mme. du Châtelet period of metaphysical research; and secondly, the late period of borrowings of method and material for the antibiblical attacks of the last fifteen years of his life. In the first period, Collins and Chubb were read in conjunction with Newton, Locke, and Clarke. On the important questions of determinism and of the nature of the soul, Collins' opinions finally emerged victorious. As early as 1734 he had entirely accepted Collins' proofs that not a single prophecy of the Old Testament could be honestly considered as referring to Jesus or as being fulfilled by him. In the second period he read with some care not only d'Holbach's adaptation, but the original English of Collins' *Grounds and Reasons of the Christian Religion* and *Scheme of Literal Prophecy Considered.* Voltaire's use of these works was fairly limited, for he wisely judged that he was writing to a different audience upon whom Tindal's remarks on the immorality of the prophets could be much more effectively stressed than the details of Collins' attack. Moreover, Collins' masterly defense of freethinking and his critical works on the prophecies again exerted a marked influence on Woolston and Annet, and hence indirectly on Voltaire.

Although Tindal was chiefly concerned in establishing the efficacy and sufficiency of the light of reason in matters of religion, his modest endeavors to show the inferiority of the revealed Scriptures by noting the barbarities and cruelties of the Jews, the questionable conduct of the prophets, and the contradictions and immoralities of Christ's teachings, were greedily received and magnified by Voltaire. Tindal's *Christianity as Old as Creation* was thus a very important source of Voltaire's deism. His adaptations of Tindal's material, however, depart from the usual moderation of the original to favor the more active animosity of Woolston and Annet.

Woolston's attack on the miracles was diabolical and purely destructive. To the opponents of the English deists he was a thorn in the flesh. Voltaire used his facile criticisms of the literal word in every critical work that came from his pen. Except in his major works on miracles, he reduced Woolston's ridicule of the letter to short and witty sarcasms, and abandoned those that could not be so reduced. His borrowings from Woolston thus modified, added a note of wit and levity to the fundamental seriousness of his attacks. He very wisely neglected Woolston's purposefully absurd typical interpretations, directed against the English clergy, but, in mocking this type of commentary, could be equally absurd himself when the occasion offered. He thought that Woolston, in his hatred for the clergy, had gone much too far in arousing the anger of bigots. But he adopted all that he dared of Woolston's intransigent spirit.

Chubb and Bolingbroke had relatively little effect on the critical deism of Voltaire. Chubb entered into the current of Voltaire's thought in the earlier metaphysical period, but the influence is negligible. Voltaire read Bolingbroke's philosophical works carefully during the later period, but chose for some reason not to use them. It is difficult, moreover, to see what material contributions Bolingbroke could have made to Voltaire's wealth of sources. Annet developed all there was in Bolingbroke that would have suited Voltaire's purposes, and in much more convenient form. In revenge, Voltaire used Bolingbroke's name to cover his most virulent criticisms, and on so many occasions that the Bolingbroke influence has become a legend, while of his many supposed quotations from Bolingbroke's posthumous works, probably not one is justifiable. Bolingbroke has been charged with being a god unto himself; and Voltaire took his name in vain.

On the other hand, Conyers Middleton looms up rather unexpectedly as an important source of Voltaire's attacks on the historical foundations of the Church. Middleton did for the latter-day miracles what Van Dale had done for the heathen oracles. His criticisms were mild and his attitude compromising. Voltaire carefully read and reviewed his works, admired them, and used extensively many passages marked for reference, especially in his *Dictionnaire philosophique,* which he was preparing when the Middleton volumes came into his hands.

Annet, the "last of the deists," took the most valid arguments of Toland, Collins, Tindal, and Bolingbroke, and transfused them with the spirit of Woolston for Voltaire's use. He was the most complete of critical deists, and at the same time the most intransigent. Voltaire appropriated and adapted his *Life of David* immediately after its publication, and was influenced by his *History of*

Saint Paul through d'Holbach, if not directly. Annet is responsible for much that is extreme in Voltaire's criticism, yet there is an underlying validity in his work that Woolston lacked. He realized fully that he was compromising in meeting his orthodox opponents on their own ground. Voltaire's use of Annet's *Life of David* shows with what rapidity he was receiving tracts from England in 1761, and how thorough was his reading knowledge of the English language. His drama *Saül,* based on this work, illustrates also the transforming power of his facile wit. His constant use of Annet for this subject on which Bayle could have been of great service to him, adds to the evidence of Bayle's relative unimportance in the inspiration of his antibiblical efforts, and at the same time illustrates the importance of Bayle's influence on the English deists.

There remains the danger that from the influence above indicated, there may still be some disagreement concerning the size of the debt that Voltaire owed the English deists. It is not enough to say that it was great or small; some distinctions must be made. In the development of his philosophical skepticism, Locke played a more fundamental rôle than any of the deists; yet Toland and especially Collins modified Locke's ideas to a considerable extent as they were gaining acceptance in Voltaire's mind. Again, the milder deism of Dryden, Pope, and the *Independent Whig* which interested him during his exile in England, was soon abandoned for the more pronounced deism of Tindal's *Christianity as Old as Creation.* In his later years, Voltaire plainly adopted the entire spirit and method of the extremists in the English controversy. He praised English philosophers, gave long lists of English deists as authorities, wrote very often under an assumed English name, and to give an English atmosphere to his works he adopted even their figures of speech and curt epigrams. "A Robinson Crusoe romance," "tales from Don Quixote," etc., were favorite expressions found in Annet's criticisms of the Scriptures, and many more were culled from Woolston's discourses on the miracles. In regard to the direct borrowing of material, it must be borne in mind that the great bulk of Voltaire's deistic criticism was historical, and that here the English movement, though it had much to offer, can account for only a small fraction of the total. Once imbued with the English critical spirit, Voltaire had only to draw his own conclusions from the learned works of Van Dale, Grabe, Fabricius, Fleury, and countless others, or from the commentaries of Dom Calmet. But next to the historical argument, it was the moral argument that Voltaire stressed the most, and here he was inspired by Woolston, Tindal, and Annet, and turned to their works again and again for his important material. Finally, considering this time the more general influences of the critical spirit, there seems to be no question but that the contributions of the French *précurseurs,* Bayle, Fontenelle, and Perrault, were not felt directly to any great extent by the later French school, but first crossed the Channel, only to return, greatly augmented by Toland, Collins, and their followers, to the welcoming arms of Voltaire and d'Holbach.

No generalizations can be formed concerning Voltaire's honesty in referring to the English deists as authorities. When he has grouped them in lists he is usually, to use the Abbé Guénée's expression, throwing dust in the eyes of his readers. Bolingbroke he mentions the most often, and with the least justification. Toland and Collins were accorded an almost even break between true and false attributions. Tindal is never mentioned in connection with the particular details which Voltaire borrowed from his work, even after Guénée had charged Voltaire with copying from him. On the other hand, Woolston is almost always correctly referred to, and although the name of Annet does not appear in all of Voltaire's work, the pseudonym "M. Hut" or "Huet" which Voltaire chose for him is properly used in almost every case. Yet the *Dialogues entre A, B, C; traduit de l'anglais de M. Huet* concern Annet not at all. The balance swings in favor of mystification rather than justification, and the crying example will always be the *Examen important de milord Bolingbroke.*

The English deistic attack was as complete and thorough as was possible without the advantages of modern researches in science, history, and archaeology, a field which Toland was approaching timidly and with some ideas far in advance of his age. His idea of evolution in the development of ideas and beliefs would have excused much in the conduct of the early patriarchs and prophets. But the later deists and Voltaire were too fond of their favorite argument that the "common ideas of morality" of the eighteenth century had been revealed by nature from the beginning, and were as old as creation. Their arguments were valid, therefore, only against their opponents who refused to consider the Scriptures as an historical document like any other, and are valid today only to that extent, considerable though it may be.

Voltaire had the methods and materials of this controversy well in hand from the very beginning of his openly critical attack. His later works are largely repetitions, enlargements, and modifications of his *Sermon des cinquante* and *Extrait des sentiments de Jean*

Meslier, both published in 1762. In the latter work appears the following significant paragraph:

> Quelles seront donc les vaines ressources des christocoles? Leur morale? elle est la même au fond que dans toutes les religions; mais des dogmes cruels en sont nés, et ont enseigné la persécution et le trouble. Leurs miracles? mais quel peuple n'a pas les siens, et quels sages ne méprisent pas ces fables? Leurs prophéties? n'en a-t-on pas démontré la fausseté? Leurs mœurs? ne sont-elles pas souvent infâmes? L'établissement de leur religion? mais le fanatisme n'a-t-il pas commencé, l'intrigue n'a-t-elle pas élevé, la force n'a-t-elle pas soutenu visiblement cet édifice? La doctrine? mais n'est-elle pas le comble de l'absurdité? (M. XXIV, 335-36)
>
> [What, then, will the Christ-worshipers' vain resources be? Their ethic? It is basically the same as in all religions; but cruel dogmas have been born of it, and have taught persecution and public disorder. Their miracles? But what nation does not have its own, and what sages do not despise those fables? Their prophecies? Has not their falsity been demonstrated? Their moral conduct? Is it not often infamous? The establishment of their religion? But is it not obvious that fanaticism began, intrigue raised, and force has supported that structure? Their doctrine? But is it not the height of absurdity?]

No more concise summary could be made of the main points of the English controversy. The foregoing study has revealed some of the sources of this *Extrait* of Jean Meslier. It would be interesting to know to what extent the deep note of sincerity and the passionate and uncompromising hatred for Christianity were due to the influence of this early French revolutionary. Even when this study is made, one must remember that Voltaire had at this time also read Tindal, Woolston, and Peter Annet.

In spite of the constant repetition of material, Voltaire avoids tediousness by the constant change of angle from which he directed his attacks. One of his most interesting adaptations is the famous *Traité sur la tolérance,* in which, in a mock effort to prove the tolerance of Moses and Jesus, he has nevertheless succeeded in heaping the customary ridicule upon them. It has been noted how, in that work, the ridicule of Woolston's treatment of the miracles of Cana and of the Samaritan woman was used to prove the innocence and tolerance of Christ's character. Here is indeed evident the diabolical spirit of Woolston. Tindal's criticisms of the prophets could only be used in one way, and on this subject, indeed, Voltaire is sometimes boresome through repetition. But no two works could be more opposite in nature than his *Saül* and his *Bible enfin expli-*

quée, in both of which Annet's *Life of David* figures prominently.

One final question arises: Did Voltaire anonymously publish his attacks against Christianity under the name or upon the authority of the English deists and at the same time withhold his personal sanction? The evidence is entirely in the negative. It has been argued that he had a sincere respect for the Pentateuch on the strength of his admission: "Le *Pentateuque* et l'Arioste font aujourd'hui le charme de ma vie" [1] ["Nowadays the Pentateuch and Ariosto are the charm of my life"]. This is merely an indication that Voltaire had a taste for extravaganza from no matter what source. It is as if Woolston had written that Swift and the Church Fathers were the charm of *his* life. One must look beneath the veil. In his volume upon volume of attacks upon the entire Old Testament, Voltaire is ready to admit in its favor only a lyric beauty, of a crude sort to be sure, in the Song of Solomon. Passages have been taken from the *Traité sur la tolérance* and the *Dictionnaire philosophique* either to show that Voltaire had an underlying respect for the person of Christ, or to prove him inconsistent. The study of Woolston again warns us to look with great suspicion upon either statement. There is likewise little evidence that in employing the phrase *Écrasez l'infâme,* Voltaire made any mental reservation in favor of Christianity as distinguished from superstition. One must turn way back to Toland for any sincere trust in this distinction. Voltaire's only reservations were due to his attitude of intellectual snobbery, a fear of the results of his efforts on the unthinking multitude. Following the extremists of the English school, he appears to have sincerely and consistently attempted, during the final fifteen years of his life, to demolish Christianity from top to bottom.

In conclusion, the English deistic controversy was a primary factor both in Voltaire's philosophical deism and in his attacks on the established religion. It renewed and fortified his convictions that the Christian religion, like other revealed religions, was founded on fraud and imposture and that the history of the Church was fundamentally unreliable. It convinced him that no comfort could be found for the orthodox in the arguments drawn from the miracles and the prophecies. It furnished him with many facts, but above all, it gave him the methods, the atmosphere, and the authorities for his own attack. The so-called moral argument of the English deists, represented by Woolston, Tindal, and Annet, had the most

[1] E. Champion, *Voltaire: études critiques* (Paris, 1893), p. 234; cf. M. XLI, 90, 153. Voltaire's letter contains an impertinence concerning Ezekiel which well illustrates his "respect" for the Pentateuch.

important direct influence upon Voltaire's work. While the more scholarly works of Middleton against the latter-day miracles, and of Collins against the prophecies, were by no means neglected, it was especially the tracts of their more facile and witty successors that found strength and increase in their continental transplantation.

Voltaire Historian

by J. H. Brumfitt

I. *Form and Style*

> On exige des historiens modernes plus de détails, des faits plus constatés, des dates précises, des autorités, plus d'attention aux usages, aux lois, aux mœurs, au commerce, à la finance, à l'agriculture, à la population: il en est de l'histoire comme des mathématiques et de la physique; la carrière s'est prodigieusement accrue (M. XIX, 365).
>
> ["One demands of modern historians more details, more solidly established facts, exact dates, authorities, more attention to customs, laws, manners, commerce, finance, agriculture, population. It is with history as with mathematics and physics: the field has expanded enormously."]

Voltaire is perhaps not fully aware of the extent to which these new demands necessarily imply a change in the form of historical writing. For he can still envisage history, as did the humanists, as being first and foremost a work of art. More than once, for example, he insists that history should be presented as drama. To D'Argental he writes in 1740:

> Il faut, dans une histoire, comme dans une pièce de théâtre, exposition, nœud, et dénouement (M. XXXV, 374).
>
> ["In a history, as in a play, there must be a beginning, a middle, and an end."]

And to Schouvalow, explaining the plan of the *Histoire de Russie,* he asserts:

> J'ai toujours pensé que l'histoire demande le même art que la tragédie, une exposition, un nœud, un dénouement, et qu'il est

nécessaire de présenter tellement toutes les figures du tableau, qu'elles fassent voir le principal personnage, sans affecter jamais l'envie de le faire valoir (M. XXXIX, 470).

["I have always thought that history requires the same sort of art as tragedy: a beginning, a middle, an end; and that it is necessary to present all the figures in the painting in such a way that they will draw attention to the main character without ever giving the appearance of wanting to set him off to advantage."]

As late as 1773 he writes to Marin in similar terms (M. XLVIII, 398). And one of his last words on history, appearing in a letter to Frederick the Great in 1778, is the apparently disillusioned conclusion that

Pour l'histoire, ce n'est, après tout, qu'une gazette; la plus vraie est remplie de faussetés et elle ne peut avoir de mérite que celui du style M. L, 338).

["As for history, it is, after all, only a gazette; the most truthful of histories is filled with falsehoods and can have no merit save that of style."]

It is hardly surprising, in view of the frequency with which this view is expressed, that some critics have tended to see in it the theory behind Voltaire's practice of history.[1] But to do so is to disregard entirely the whole tendency of development of his work. The early *Histoire de Charles XII* has some affinity with tragedy. Lanson has suggested that the narrative part of the *Siècle* has a similar form.[2] But even if this is true, Voltaire has destroyed the dramatic effect of the work as a whole by making the last part of it a series of purely descriptive chapters on arts, sciences, and religious affairs. And in the *Essai sur les mœurs,* the *Histoire du Parlement,* the *Annales de l'Empire,* and the *Précis du Siècle de Louis XV* there is no hint of such dramatic construction. Even in the *Histoire de Russie* the narrative of the life of the emperor is subordinated to the description of society.

Moreover, it is not only in his overall plan that Voltaire breaks with the humanists. He does so equally in matters of detail. In the first place, he makes repeated attacks on three features typical of the humanist historians—harangues, portraits, and anecdotes.

Harangues were regarded by the later humanists themselves with

[1] E.g., A. Bellessort, *Essai sur Voltaire* (Paris, 1925), p. 207; and J. W. Thompson, *A History of Historical Writing,* 2 vols. (New York, 1942), II, 66.

[2] G. Lanson, *Voltaire* (Paris, 1910), pp. 118-19.

some disfavour,[3] and even the *Histoire de Charles XII* is free from all but the shortest reported speeches. Voltaire's opposition, however, becomes more pronounced. In the *Supplément* to the *Siècle,* he insists that harangues should be totally omitted, asserting that there are only two examples of direct speech in the *Siècle* itself, and that both these speeches were actually made (M. XV, 124). Further criticism appears in the *Dictionnaire Philosophique* article, "Histoire," in the *Annales,* and elsewhere.[4] In all these works Voltaire rejects the fabrication of harangues as being contrary to the spirit of truth which should be that of history.

Portraits are similarly rejected. The article "Histoire" is willing to allow portraits of contemporaries, but it is ridiculous for the historian to produce those of people he has never seen (M. XIX, 362). This is emphasized in the preface to the *Histoire de Russie,* where Voltaire pours scorn on Sarrasin's portrait of Wallenstein. In the *Supplément* to the *Siècle* he indignantly takes La Beaumelle to task for having dared to suggest that the *Siècle* itself should have contained more portraits. And further criticism is to be found in the preface to the 1754 edition of the *Essai.*[5]

On the whole anecdotes are equally strongly condemned. We have seen that they played a considerable part in the *Histoire de Charles XII.* They are still prominent in the *Siècle,* but Voltaire feels it necessary to excuse their presence there with a special plea: "Louis XIV mit dans sa cour, comme dans son règne, tant d'éclat et de magnificence, que les moindres détails de sa vie semblent intéresser la postérité" (M. XIV, 422). ["Louis XIV infused into his Court, as he did into his reign, so much brilliance and splendor that the slightest details of his life seem to be of interest to posterity."] And usually he has no time for such trivial details, as can be seen from his ironical comments on the *Mémoires* of Dangeau which are full of them (M. XXVIII, 251ff.). Moreover, he is equally convinced that the majority of anecdotes are false. This is emphasized in the article "Anecdotes" in the *Dictionnaire philosophique,* in the letter *À M. * * * sur les anecdotes,* and in many other places.[6]

[3] F. de la M. Fénelon (*Lettre à l'Académie,* ed. A. Cahen: Paris, n.d.; p. 128) is sceptical, whilst G. Daniel (*Histoire de France:* 10 vols., Paris, 1729; Preface, p. lxxix) is openly hostile. But P. Rapin de Thoyras can still quote the harangue of a Breton ambassador to the invading Saxons, and excuse himself by saying that it does not appear to 'pécher contre la vraisemblance' [sin against verisimilitude] (*Histoire d'Angleterre*: 10 vols., The Hague, 1724-27; I, 92).

[4] M. XIX, 361-62; XIII, 503; and XXV, 185.

[5] M. XVI, 388; XV, 122; and XXIV, 47.

[6] M. XVIII, 193ff. and XXIX, 407. See also XVI, 385, and XXXIX, 70.

It is not surprising that the imaginative reconstructions of the historical novelist infuriate him even more. He finds them in the work of La Beaumelle, and in the *Lettre à l'auteur des Honnêtetés littéraires* he protests indignantly:

> On voit à chaque page un homme qui parle au hasard d'un pays qu'il n'a jamais connu, et qui ne songe qu'à faire un roman.
>
> "Mademoiselle de La Vallière, dans un déshabille léger, s'était jetée dans un fauteuil: là elle pensait à loisir à son amant; souvent le jour la retrouvait assise sur une chaise, accoudée sur une table, l'œil fixe dans l'extase de l'amour."
>
> Hé, mon ami, l'as-tu vue dans ce déshabille léger? l'as-tu vue accoudée sur cette table? est-il permis d'écrire ainsi l'histoire? (M. XXVI, 162).

> ["On every page we see a man who speaks at haphazard of a country he has never known, and whose aim is simply to compose a fiction.
>
> 'Mademoiselle de La Vallière, in a light dishabille, had thrown herself into an armchair. There she thought at leisure of her lover. The day's return often found her still seated on a chair, leaning on a table, staring fixedly in an ecstasy of love.'
>
> Come now, my friend, did you see her in that light dishabille? Did you see her leaning on that table? Is it legitimate to write history in this way?"]

All these criticisms are aimed at the various kinds of untruthfulness which characterize humanist historiography. But if Voltaire succeeds in defending and preserving factual truth, nevertheless, in rejecting the descriptive and anecdotal he is largely destroying the life and colour of history. The *Histoire de Charles XII* has been shown to be the least typical of his histories. The whole trend of his later development is away from the sort of approach it typifies. Yet the fact that some critics can think of it as his best work suggests that this later development was perhaps misdirected.

For it is not just the anecdote which is absent from Voltaire's later historical work: it is man himself, the living individual, facing the problems of his age and deciding his course of action. In the preface to the *Histoire de Russie* Voltaire asserts that it is no part of his task to pry into the inner secrets or motives of Peter the Great (M. XVI, 385). In this particular instance, this is a prudent way of avoiding saying anything which might embarrass his Russian patrons. But it is not only in the *Histoire de Russie* that he fails to bring his characters to life. Indeed, he hardly ever succeeds. The accumulation of anecdotes about Louis XIV helps to give some picture of the king, but this is because of their own intrinsic value, and is not the result of illuminating comment from Voltaire himself.

Even Charles XII and Peter the Great remain figures seen from outside; characters in a swift-moving adventure story rather than beings whose real personality is revealed. And other individuals in whom Voltaire is deeply interested, Cromwell, Richelieu, or Mahomet, for example, are never comprehended except in the most mechanistic terms.

This is not the fault of Voltaire's theory. It results from his general lack of psychological insight, visible in his *contes* and dramas, and in his tendency to assume that everyone who does not think as he does is either a fool or a hypocrite. But the weakness is a serious one in an historian. If Collingwood is right, and the historian's task is to rethink the thoughts of the past, then Voltaire is hardly an historian at all. And not only does he fail to penetrate the mind of the individual; he is no more successful in dealing with that of the group. S. G. Tallentyre's assertion, with reference to the *Essai sur les mœurs,* that "it was the first history which dealt not with kings, the units, but with the great, panting, seething masses they ruled"[7] is a masterpiece of misstatement. No one, least of all the masses, is allowed to pant or seethe in the *Essai.* The dress, habits, and customs of the people are portrayed, but they are portrayed from the outside, dispassionately, never, as with the romantic historians, with the aim of resurrecting a dead world. And when Voltaire does attempt something more vivid, he rarely succeeds. One cannot but applaud his decision to reject the majority of accounts of battles, when one reads a description such as this:

> Après la première charge, on vit encore un effet de ce que peut la fortune dans les combats. L'armée ennemie et la française, saisies d'une terreur panique, prirent la fuite toutes deux en même temps, et le maréchal de Villars se vit presque seul quelques minutes sur le champ de bataille: il rallia les troupes, les ramena au combat, et remporta la victoire (M. XIV, 359).
>
> ["After the first charge there was seen once again an effect of the power of chance in battles. The French army and that of the enemy, seized with panic, both took flight at the same time, and Marshal de Villars saw himself almost alone for a few minutes on the battlefield. He rallied his troops, led them back into the fray, and gained the victory."]

This impersonal, analytical style, which characterizes all Voltaire's historical works, but above all, the *Essai,* has an emotional aridity

[7] S. G. Tallentyre (pseud. of E. B. Hall), *The Life of Voltaire,* 3rd ed. (London, 1905), p. 273.

which is never really compensated for by the human feeling which obviously exists behind his outbursts of moral indignation at the events related, and the rarer expressions of approval when some brighter gleam is descried in the dark picture of human miseries. It is because of this that Voltaire, great as is his contribution to the science of history, cannot rank among the great historical artists. And yet this emotionally arid but intellectually sparkling style is obviously the one which most perfectly suits his peculiar gifts. It is an inimitable style, too, equally remote from the ornateness of the humanists, the lyricism of a Rousseau, and the picturesqueness of the romantics. It gives his work an unmistakable stamp of individuality.

II. *Conclusion*

It is in the work of Voltaire that the outline of universal history, as we know it today, is first clearly discernible. Earlier European historians describe a world some 6,000 years old, and their account of ancient history is dominated by a literal interpretation of the Bible and confined almost exclusively to the Middle East and Europe. Voltaire describes a world of great antiquity, in which societies have gradually come into being and decayed, and he emphasizes the importance of non-European civilizations such as those of India and China. It is he who, more than any other individual, brings about the Copernican revolution in historiography, displacing the Christian European from his comfortable seat at the center of the universe.

In so doing, however, he creates as many problems as he solves. He postulates the existence of thousands of years during which man is engaged in learning the rudiments of civilized life. But he has no knowledge of pre-history, no evidence of what actually happened during this long period. His attempts to fill the gap are almost pure speculation, and this speculation, inspired by the deist propagandist rather than by the historian, is as unsatisfactory in the way it deals with man's spiritual progress as it is in its failure to deal, except in the barest outline, with his material advancement.

These are important limitations; but they are largely imposed by the absence of knowledge of anthropology and pre-history which characterizes the eighteenth century. If it is legitimate to show the extent to which Voltaire clings to patterns of thought which have their origin in doctrines he sought to oppose, it is more important to stress the change which he does bring about and the extent to which his work stimulates his successors to further discoveries.

This is perhaps Voltaire's greatest achievement. Yet he has an important part to play in another transformation which may well be considered even more significant. In the nineteenth century history comes to be regarded as the equal of the natural sciences: the historian claims to show, in Ranke's words, "wie es eigentlich gewesen" [how it really was], and does not merely point a moral or adorn a tale. Modern historiography is not just concerned with the doings of the great or the adventures of the individual, but seeks to describe the totality of past human experience, the history of societies and civilizations in all their different aspects.

This transformation is not the work of any individual, but Voltaire's part in it is an important one. Not only is he one of the most outstanding advocates of "l'histoire de l'esprit humain" [the history of the human spirit], but in his own historical works he gives to social, economic, and cultural developments a far more important place than that allotted by most of his predecessors.

Once again, of course, there are obvious limits to his achievement. He is a popularizer rather than a scholar, and has to make what use he can of such information about social and economic history as others have provided for him. He is often narrow-minded and dogmatic—particularly in his views on art. Above all, though he is not a moralist in the seventeenth-century sense, he is a propagandist interested in changing society as much as in describing it. He shares the humanitarian ideals which characterize the Enlightenment, and if there is much in these ideals which is timeless, there is also much which is peculiar to the eighteenth-century *bourgeoisie* or to the struggle against Catholic authoritarianism.

Yet it is only rarely that these propagandist aims result in serious distortion. In the major works, like the *Siècle* and the *Essai,* they are balanced by a sincere desire for impartiality. If they flavor all Voltaire's work, they do not destroy its value as social history.

Voltaire attempts to recount the history of society. He also attempts to explain it; and here he must be considered less successful. If the puppets on the historical stage are not moved by the finger of God, there must be some other mechanism which is responsible for their antics. Yet Voltaire's thought lacks the profundity (or should one say, the rigidity?) to discover such a mechanism. Instead, he seizes upon the various explanations offered by others, and interprets history sometimes as the work of great men, sometimes as the result of the machinations of a capricious and ineluctable

ble fatality, and sometimes as the product of the deep-seated determining influence of climate, religion, and government. Anxious as he is to explain, he will rarely ponder over his explanation, and the result is often a disappointing superficiality.

It is to Montesquieu, Condorcet, or Lessing that one must turn if one wishes to discover an Enlightenment philosophy of history or a coherent explanation of causality, and not to Voltaire. Yet if his views are inconsistent, this does not mean that, individually, they are not important. In the emphasis he places, particularly in his later years, on economic causes, he appears to serve as a link between Machiavellian realism and nineteenth-century theories of economic determinism. His admiration for his heroes perhaps looks forward to Carlyle. And his ever-present scepticism tends to restrain the readers of Montesquieu, Turgot, or Mably from an uncritical acceptance of theories not always rooted in fact.

This same scepticism is most clearly visible in his critical method. It is he who, more than anyone else, inherits and, at the same time, fructifies the tradition of historical Pyrrhonism. Montesquieu does not appear to be affected by it, and the younger men, Rousseau, Mably, or Raynal, represent an age which is trying to construct a new faith rather than question an old one.

Voltaire's most positive achievement in this field is his application to history of principles drawn from the natural sciences in the belief that nature and human nature are unchanging. But these principles prove to be a mixed blessing. If they allow him to expunge the miraculous from the pages of history, they also tempt him to delete everything else which is not in accordance with his own nature or with the standards and values of eighteenth-century French society. As a result, and particularly because of his own lack of psychological profundity, his scepticism is often carried too far, and he is often led to denounce as fraudulent statements which can be shown to be in no way contrary to the "trempe du cœur humain" [temper of the human heart].

His scepticism is equally visible in what may be termed the field of lower criticism. Here it is particularly striking because the majority of the *philosophes* tend to be more credulous. It is because his historical method has been compared to theirs that its virtues have tended to be magnified. But when it is compared to that of the erudite historians, it is its inadequacy which is chiefly revealed. Voltaire's sources, except when he is dealing with the history of his own times, are almost exclusively second-hand. Moreover, he is entirely lacking in the technical skills necessary for a first-hand investigation of the distant past. In his treatment of evidence he shows an awareness of the importance of eyewitness accounts and the need for corroboration of testimonies, and he is adept at spotting anachronisms, contradictions, and improbabilities. Yet the rules he applies are those contained in every primer. If he applies them more boldly than many, his boldness is at times rashness. The extent to which he tends to leap to conclusions on the basis of insufficient evidence is exemplified by his criticisms of the *Testament Politique* of Richelieu. His controversy with Foncemange on this subject reveals the inferiority of his method to that of the more scholarly, if less imaginative, of his contemporaries.

Finally, the poet who hoped to create the French epic and to be the worthy successor of Racine reveals himself as an indifferent devotee of Clio the muse. His style has all the logical clarity and wit which everywhere characterize his prose. Yet though he has an intellectual understanding of things and ideas, he has no sympathetic understanding of men: and it is men, after all, who make history. Voltaire makes little attempt to explore the psychology of his characters; he lacks the deep interest in the past for its own sake which alone can lead to that "résurrection intégrale" [integral resurrection] of men and events of which Michelet speaks. In this context, at any rate, those who have accused him, and the Enlightenment in general, of being "anti-historical" have some justification. His effort to understand the past is an effort to review it in the light of the present, not to recreate it. He despises tradition, and is never willing to accept history as an authority; to argue from an historical fact to a right. Instead he uses history as a warning; as a constant reminder that men have long been stupid, cruel, and intolerant, and that the price of civilization is eternal vigilance. A society which cannot look back on the course of history with a certain contempt would, he seems to say, be a society in decay. If such an attitude can be the strength of a social reformer, it can be the weakness of an historian.

Can Voltaire, as some have suggested, be claimed as the father of modern historiography? It would clearly be absurd to answer such a question categorically. It is more valuable to observe how French Enlightenment historiography, as typified by its greatest and most universal figure, stands midway between that of the seventeenth century and that of modern times. The distance between Bossuet and Voltaire is great, but so, too, is the distance between Voltaire and Michelet or Taine. The gradual accumulation of knowledge and the impact of the Revolution and of romanticism brought about vast changes. So, too, did the development of the seed of a more imaginative understanding of the past which had lain dormant in the *Scienza Nuova* throughout the greater part of the eighteenth century. Yet Vico's seed would not have prospered had not the ground been prepared for it. Among those who accomplished this task, Voltaire's role is one of the greatest.

Candide's Garden

by William F. Bottiglia

Internal Analysis

A close analysis of the Conclusion of *Candide* will yield internal evidence which historians of ideas are prone to dismiss as beneath serious attention; but literary critics will accept it as objectively valid and will recognize in it the voice of Voltaire addressing his readers with authoritative immediacy. Once this analysis has been made, its results will be checked against, and correlated with, external considerations; and those results will be seen to shed light on the author's life and on his other writings. If the background of *Candide* helps illuminate its meaning, *Candide,* in turn, helps elucidate its historical context. This reciprocal relationship between art and history is a reality that needs to be constantly re-emphasized. *Candide* is not a mere passive product of "heredity, environment, and momentum." As a great literary statement, it has an agency of its own: it contributes to the making of history. More than this, as a work of art instinct with enduring values, it reflects and reveals the essential Voltaire in ways impossible to his humbler media of expression, such as his correspondence.

Since the Conclusion *is* a conclusion, and since the point at issue is one of meaning, it seems wise to begin by showing how the progression of ideas in the tale as a whole leads inevitably to the final climax. *Candide ou l'Optimisme* contains more—much more —than the promise of its subtitle.[1] Voltaire is not on exhibition

"Candide's Garden." From *Voltaire's "Candide": Analysis of a Classic,* 2nd ed. (Volume VIIA of *Studies on Voltaire and the Eighteenth Century,* ed. Theodore Besterman, Geneva, 1964), by William F. Bottiglia. The pages reprinted here are an abridged version of the chapter entitled "Theme: Candide's Garden." In this version all French quotations have been translated by the editor.

[1] Voltaire, *Candide ou l'Optimisme,* ed. André Morize (Paris, 1913), pp. vii, xlvii-xlviii.

here as a systematic philosopher. He does not dialectically anatomize a doctrine and throw it piecemeal to the dogs as lacking in logical coherence or in correspondence to reality. He displays himself as a theatrically self-aware artist, skillfully co-ordinating an atmosphere of clear ideas into a philosophic attitude charged with social dynamism. His central problem is that of human conduct in relation to the somber mystery of physical and social evil. His drive toward a solution of that problem develops as an assault on the vulnerable aspects of senescent classicism—its intellectual and its sentimental infirmities. But the assault alone, although it pervades the work from beginning to end, does not solve the problem. By routing the enemy and clearing the ground, it implies and prepares a positive solution. Meanwhile many hints are dropped along the way, prefiguring such a solution. Thus the great melioristic finale effectively concludes the tale by converging everything which has gone before into an epigrammatic statement of Voltaire's answer to the basic problem.

The intellectual presentation of physical evil in *Candide* includes natural disasters utterly beyond human control (e.g., tempest, earthquake), social calamities which outrun human responsibility (e.g., syphilis, plague), and misfortunes visited indiscriminately upon the good and the wicked (e.g., death of Jacques, naval battle)—all correlated with the view that the individual is helpless because completely predetermined by general laws. Throughout the tale there are repeated assertions that these workings of a "diabolical" principle mock the pursuit of happiness with miseries so numerous and so universal as to appear the normal lot of mankind, and so afflictive as to make one wonder at the tenacity of the will to live. Identical assertions are made with even greater frequency in the intellectual presentation of social evil, which occupies most of *Candide* with its grim catalogue of human ills rendered all the more execrable by their origin in human ignorance, weakness, and malice. A complete enumeration of these would rival the tale itself in length, and would show that Voltaire ranges with astonishing comprehensiveness through time and space as he satirizes man-made evils in their manifold appearances—metaphysical, theological, ecclesiastical, political, social, economic, and cultural.[2]

Brilliantly interwoven with the intellectual presentation of physical and social evil is the complementary assault on the sentimental foibles of the age—an aspect of *Candide* either ignored or under-

[2] Voltaire, *Candide, ou l'Optimisme,* ed. George R. Havens (New York, 1934), pp. xxix-xlix, lii-lv.

stressed by most critics. This takes the form of fictional parody, which saturates the work with ironic imitations of heroic, pastoral, picaresque, and utopian adventure-romances; also, by natural extension, of idealized travel-accounts. Numerous narrative devices, most of the character-types, many of the settings, and frequent turns of phrase are combined in this deliberate mimicry, which the author makes all the more amusing with occasional sly comments uttered through his personages.[3] In mocking the sentimental ideals of his period, Voltaire powerfully rounds out his treatment of physical and social evil, for he is thereby enabled not only to enlarge the area of his illustrations but also to re-emphasize ironically the helplessness of the individual, driven as if fortuitously by the necessary specific effects of the general, immutable, unhuman laws of nature.

The bulk of *Candide* is an attack, in accordance with Voltaire's conception of "true *philosophes*" as "decent persons who have no fixed principles on the nature of things, who do not know what is, but who know very well what isn't . . ." (Best. 12362). Yet the affirmation at the end is not thrust upon the reader suddenly, without preparation. To repeat, the attack itself is a preparation, in that it routs the enemy and clears the ground, thus implying a positive solution by elimination of its opposite. In addition, there are affirmative hints pointing in the same direction: two invincible biological drives, the will to live and the desire for food; the value of experience as a corrective for naïveté and as a means to practical wisdom; instinctive goodness, "conscience," and its normal civilized product, social goodness or "beneficence"; the benefits of culture, such as freedom of expression, good theater, good literature, good taste. And above and beyond all this, far-distant and half-lost in a luminous haze, the dream of Eldorado.

The final chapter of *Candide* funnels these many elements into an epigrammatic conclusion which summarizes and unifies the tale by answering the central problem. This answer, in keeping with the entire presentation, is not the scheme of a systematic philosopher, but the terse melioristic affirmation of a profound practical moralist doubled by a great literary artist.

Physical evil disturbs Voltaire for two reasons: (1) it calls into question the nature and purposes of a Creator whose general laws cause so much specific wretchedness for His predetermined creatures; (2) it gives rise to speculation which romances about the

[3] Morize, pp. l-lxi; Havens, pp. xlix-lii; Raymond Naves, *De Candide à Saint-Preux* (Paris, 1940), pp. 20-25.

unknown as though it were the known, with disastrous effects on the moral motivation of mankind. The answer given by Voltaire through the dervish is no attempt to solve the insoluble. It is the resort of a pragmatist concerned with preserving the moral initiative. Physical evil is declared to be ultimately unknowable, and men are exhorted to resign themselves to that which they can never know, hence never control.

Social evil, on the other hand, is knowable and to some extent controllable. Much of what men have constructed in ignorance, weakness, and malice can be torn down and replaced by those who are willing to work for the betterment of the human family. To the entrenched ruthlessness of man-made evil the champions of social goodness must oppose disingenuous tactics which spring from the will to live combined with a sense of practical necessities. Thus, like the old Turk and Candide, they will turn their backs on public abominations in a gesture of philosophic disdain. They will assemble in small, like-minded groups safely removed from the centers of corruption. As members of model societies, they will work concretely, each at his appointed task, and with a minimum of windy theorizing, toward the diminution of social evil and the spread of social virtue. Already, in this way, men can enjoy the pleasures of good dinners seasoned with good conversation, as well as the precious benefits of culture. They can also legitimately envision an ideal State which, though beyond complete realization, may at least be more or less approached through co-operative work, through practical action—through the weeding and the cultivation of the garden and the sale of its produce in the market of the world.

The progression of ideas just outlined is significantly punctuated by a series of symbolic gardens, or ways of life, culminating in the three which rapidly succeed one another at the very end:

1 the Westphalian "terrestrial Paradise,"
2 the kingdom of the Bulgares,
3 Protestant Holland,
4 Catholic Lisbon,
5 the Jesuit "vineyard" of Paraguay,
6 the primitive society of the Oreillons,
7 the model society of Eldorado,
8 Paris, the social and cultural hub of civilization,
9 Pococurante's ornamental garden,
10 Cacambo's accursed, backbreaking garden,
11 the modest garden of the old Turk,
12 Candide's garden, cultivated by a small model society.

Most of these are, of course, false Edens. Westphalia is the center of optimistic fatalism, sentimental quixotism, and petty aristocratic tyranny. The kingdom of the Bulgares is a naked military despotism, while Paraguay is a military despotism masquerading as a kingdom of God on earth. Holland is a mercantile utopia where "all are rich" and Christian charity is practised—with discrimination. Lisbon is the home of Inquisitorial fanaticism, with its attendant superstition and corruption. The country of the Oreillons is the habitat of state-of-nature savagery. The eighth garden symbolizes the tedium and the moral depravity of rootless and fruitless urban sophistication; the ninth, the sterile artificiality of blasé indolence; the tenth, the depression which accompanies work unillumined by a social purpose. Of the remaining three, Eldorado is negative in the sense that it is a myth, perfect and unreal; but it is also positive in the sense that it offers a philosophic ideal for human aspiration. Eldorado is the standard of perfection toward which the eleventh and twelfth gardens are dynamically directed. The old Turk's garden is a concrete example, however modest, of mankind advancing along the lines indicated above. Already less modest because involving a larger group than a family circle, and big with promise, is Candide's garden—a co-operative model society working ever so gradually, but with practical assurance, for the betterment of civilization.

The first and last gardens are specially related to each other by a common Biblical reference. The opening episode to some extent parodies the story of the Fall, with Candide, originally in a state of innocence, succumbing to temptation at the hands of a woman, and being expelled from the "terrestrial Paradise" by a very Teutonic Jehovah. In the final chapter the reader is reminded of the same story by Pangloss's quotation from the Vulgate. Before the Fall man was placed in the garden to dress it and to keep it. After the Fall he was condemned to work as a punishment. But the conclusion of *Candide* looks upon work as man's most wholesome activity (Havens, p. 145); hence the ironical aptness of Pangloss's quotation, which seems to ignore the malediction of God following "man's first disobedience."[4]

Before we look more closely at other key details of the finale, a few general observations are in order. In *Candide* the letter alone kills. Undeniably, the genre of the philosophic tale by its very nature invites interpretation that goes far beyond the naïve and unimagina-

[4] See also Voltaire, *Notebooks,* ed. Theodore Besterman (Geneva, 1952), II, 311, 383, 443.

tive oversimplifications of Fundamentalist criticism. It is not quite true, however, to say that the literal invariably serves as nothing more than a pretext for the symbolical. If the symbolical rightly understood is always true in *Candide,* the literal may also contain a measure of truth; but due allowance must be made for overstatement, duplicity, inversion, etc. Another, and related, point involves the negative emphasis which pervades the tale, and concerning which Havens correctly says: "Of course *Candide* is intentionally one-sided. No carefully balanced account of good and evil could shock mankind into revolt" (p. lv). In other words, the tale is a deliberately exaggerated polemic, which sets an example by protesting vigorously against current evils, so that its negations imply corresponding affirmations. A third point, related to the second, is that there are a number of direct affirmations strewn through *Candide,* and that these are not swept away by the Conclusion, but gathered up into it. The tale does not recklessly destroy the good along with the bad. It is an exemplary exercise in creative, or constructive, criticism. A final point, connected with the third, is that *Candide,* as Sareil rightly stresses, is a *comic* work with a *happy* ending.[5]

Now for those other key details of the finale. That the message conveyed by the dervish contains a certain degree of overstatement should be obvious. It is necessary to distinguish between what he literally says and what the author soberly means. Thus "be silent" appears to enjoin silence about ultimates, but actually would prohibit speculation on final problems only when it becomes a waste of time or is taken seriously enough to be exploited by power-hungry opportunists, to threaten moral initiative, to warp or obstruct social productivity. Earlier in the tale it was established that such discussion is permissible for purposes of intellectual stimulation and mutual consolation: "Candide continued his conversations with Martin. They argued unceasingly for two weeks, and at the end of two weeks they were as far advanced as on the first day. But after all they were expressing themselves, they were communicating ideas to one another, they were consoling one another" (Chapter XX). The dervish also prescribes resignation to physical evil on the ground that it can be neither known nor controlled. "His Highness" has instituted a certain general order and given men a certain basic equipment. The rest, it is implied, is strictly up to them. Let

[5] Jean Sareil, "De *Zadig* à *Candide,* ou Permanence de la pensée de Voltaire," *The Romanic Review,* LII (December 1961), 272.

them carve out for themselves whatever destiny remains possible within these limits. Those critics who insist that there is an effect of contraction or shrinkage at the end of *Candide* are obviously right, since Voltaire makes it clear through the dervish that all ultimates, including physical evil, are fated to remain forever beyond human reach. The author is so utterly convinced of this that he presents his dervish accordingly, self-assured to a point of being impatient and even curt with those who think otherwise.

The role of Martin has often been misconstrued because of a critical failure to catch some of Voltaire's finer distinctions. The Manichaean's arrival on the scene is strategically timed to symbolize Candide's drift toward pessimism in Chapter XIX. He serves as a devil's advocate, arguing consistently that all is for the worst and that man is powerless to change the situation. Now, the fact that Voltaire is attacking optimism does not mean that he is embracing its opposite. If he rejects optimism, he does so not only on the ground of its metaphysical bluff but also on account of its "devitalizing agency,"[6] its discouraging fatalism.[7] It is true that he treats Martin much more sympathetically than Pangloss, partly for polemical reasons, partly because the former's philosophy does less violence to the facts of life. But his handling of Martin in Chapter XXX shows plainly that pessimism does not triumph at the end. The author himself refers to Martin's principles as "detestable"—a valuation completely ignored by all critics who favor a pessimistic interpretation of the Conclusion. What is more, when Martin states that man was born to live "in the convulsions of anxiety, or in the lethargy of boredom," Candide *disagrees,* although he is not yet ready to voice a positive opinion of his own. Later, in the ripeness of time, it is Candide who makes the great affirmation, while Martin, like Pangloss, merely falls into line with an echoing judgment. Thus the pessimist and the optimist lose their respective identities to merge with their former disciple, now suddenly matured into the meliorist. In sum, Voltaire carefully shuns *both* extremes. Indeed, if, after his sustained assault on optimistic fatalism, he had concluded by adopting *pessimistic* fatalism, he would have perpetrated a glaring non sequitur, he would have killed the point of his tale, destroyed his case, lost the battle he had set out to win—the battle to preserve the moral initiative for his deistic humanism. In connection with Martin's echoing judgment, some scholars have under-

[6] Norman L. Torrey, *The Spirit of Voltaire* (New York, 1938), p. 49.

[7] Morize, p. xli; Arthur O. Lovejoy, *The Great Chain of Being* (Cambridge, 1953), pp. 210, 245.

stood the "let us work without arguing" to exclude from Candide's garden all forms of intellectual activity, philosophic or other. Actually, "without arguing" is the exact equivalent of the dervish's "be silent," which has already been explicated.

The first of the three gardens in Chapter XXX is Cacambo's. *Physically, it is the same garden as Candide's.* On this point Pomeau comments: "The survivors of the tale had been settled there for some time without knowing it. A profound lesson: all men are already in the only possible paradise. It is quite simply up to them to realize it."[8] Voltaire's full meaning is richer than Pomeau suggests. Cacambo's garden and Candide's are physically identical, but the one precedes and the other follows the dawning of wisdom through consultation of the dervish and the old Turk. Before that dawning Cacambo works alone and curses his fate; after it the entire group finds happiness in co-operative labor. The example had been set for both him and Candide by the Eldoradans. Neither, however, was then mature enough to appreciate the contentment that comes from socially purposeful collaboration. Torrey says of Candide's garden that it reveals a Voltaire at "the bottom of his emotional curve" (p. 51). More accurately, it is Cacambo's garden which represents such a depression of spirits, along with the attitudes of Martin, of Pococurante, and of Candide at Surinam.

The second of the three gardens in Chapter XXX is the old Turk's. Here the author has blended *overstatement* with *duplicity,* hammering home the former—"I know nothing about it," "I have never known," "I know absolutely nothing," "I never make inquiries"—in order to prepare the reader for the latter—"I content myself with sending the fruits of the garden I cultivate to market there." The old Turk is no rude, untutored peasant. He is head of a well-bred, hard-working family, and he is a master of literary utterance, climaxing his series of incisive, elegantly turned observations with the magnificent aphorism: "work keeps away from us three great evils: boredom, vice, and want." If such a person insists that it is best to remain rigidly indifferent, even ignorant, respecting the world, Voltaire is soberly implying: 1) that men of good will should turn their backs on public abominations in a gesture of philosophic disdain; 2) that they should seek positions wherein they can maximize their personal safety and provide the fullest possible scope for their self-determination; 3) that they should work to banish the basic evils of boredom, vice, and want by producing for the market of the world. Once again there is an effect of shrinkage. The *philosophe*

[8] René Pomeau, *La Religion de Voltaire* (Paris, 1956), p. 306.

must dissociate himself from all corrupt governments, since they would embrace him only to stifle him; and he must withdraw to where he is secure from their abuses of power. But there is also countermovement, with potentially explosive overtones. After so much ironic emphasis on the helplessness of the individual, Voltaire now seriously suggests that men have a certain freedom of action. He further suggests that they can exert an influence for the better on the world at large, not by overt participation in its political affairs, but by supplying it with nutriment, as well as by setting a good example. Considering the heavy exaggeration of the old Turk's opening remarks, his traits of character, the many values directly or indirectly affirmed throughout the tale as worth salvaging, and its calculated symbolism, what critic would be so rash as to propose that the nutriment being supplied is restricted to food? The fruits of the old Turk's garden include more than legumes; they include intellectual pabulum.

A comparison of Candide's garden with those of Cacambo and the old Turk reveals *a deliberate progression from lone individual to family circle to small model group;* also, in all three (explicitly in the first two, implicitly in the third), the practical enterprise of selling their produce in the metropolitan market. The progression is objectively there, and it has profound implications. It proves that the effect of shrinkage is accompanied and balanced by an effect of expansion. The former, however, fulfills its function within the limits of the tale. The latter projects beyond those limits. The Conclusion of *Candide* is an ending with a vista. The vista is neither infinite nor insipidly roseate, but it does hold promise of solid humanistic advancement, of augmentative and ameliorative evolution in the direction of Eldoradan values. The pattern of the final chapter, no less eloquent than its language, informs the alert and sensitive reader that Candide's garden is not a terminus, but a commencement. Animated by an inherent dynamism, it will outgrow itself—*provided* its inhabitants continue to work together and are spared a natural catastrophe. This vista suffices by itself to destroy the Fundamentalist interpretation, for the future of the garden must entail something more than the growing of bigger and better vegetables.

As for interpretations which dwell on "selfish indifference" and "the doctrine of minding one's own business," they are refuted by Voltaire's own words. Candide's garden is co-operatively cultivated by "the entire little community." Pomeau contends that Pangloss constitutes an exception: "He alone escapes the final reformation of the little community. Still addicted to metaphysico-nigology, still 'arguing without working,' he remains imperturbably Pangloss, the man who is nothing but talk."[9] The text of the tale, however, makes Pangloss a member of "the *entire* little community," and therefore one of its active workers. Moreover, it represents him as relapsing only "sometimes" into otiose speculation. Like his companions, then, he becomes socially useful in accordance with deistic doctrine. But social utility is not confined to the "little community." The garden is not "an Iland, intire of it selfe." The sale of produce establishes a connection with the big city—a connection wherein it is the small model group which influences the world, and not the other way around. But if the garden is to be understood symbolically as well as literally, then its yield must be such as to affect not only the bodies but also the minds of men.

In this regard it is a point of key importance that *Candide's garden involves more than gardening.* Each member of the group puts his particular talents to use. Cunégonde becomes a pastry cook, Paquette embroiders, the old woman takes care of the linen, Friar Giroflée does the carpentry. Cacambo presumably continues to grow vegetables and to market them in the metropolis. What of the remaining three members? Voltaire uses the others to illustrate very concretely the beginnings of specialized labor in a civilized society. Why does he say nothing specific about the work of Candide, Pangloss, and Martin? Several times in the course of the final chapter he focuses attention on them as *the intellectual subgroup* of the "little community." They undoubtedly help in the physical garden, but they, too, must have a specialty. Both Martin and Candide, applying the lesson taught by the dervish, discourage Pangloss from speculating about ultimates. That does not, however, preclude the composition and dissemination of socially useful literature. The activities of this civilization-in-miniature not only go beyond literal gardening to the extent of including carpentry, laundering, embroidery, and baking; they also include the life of the mind concentrated on the spreading of utilitarian knowledge. To argue the opposite would, of course, be absurd. Does Candide achieve mature wisdom by repudiating the life of the mind and degenerating into a brute fellah? Voltaire's silence respecting the intellectual activity of Candide's model group is not a denial of its existence. Once again, his patterns powerfully convey his full meaning. I have just mentioned the pattern of the intellectual subgroup. There is, in addition, the pattern of *the disingenuous stance.* The

[9] Voltaire, *Candide ou l'Optimisme,* ed. René Pomeau (Paris, 1959), p. 59.

duplicity of the old Turk's family circle prepares that of Candide's little band. Pomeau nonetheless flatly denies that there is any suggestion of "pamphletary activity" in the Conclusion of the tale.[10] He does find in the garden an "engineering philosophy" whose goal is to "develop natural resources." This is in itself a large admission. A society devoted to applied science is a society that believes in socially useful knowledge and in the indispensability of book-learning, hence fosters the life of the mind. Pomeau is certainly right to find this in the garden. In my judgment, if he had closely examined the *form* of Chapter XXX, as well as *the language in relation to the form,* he would have found more. In fact, he would have found enough to prove that the wisdom of the Conclusion is not narrow and disappointing (Pomeau, *Candide,* p. 72), but excitingly dynamic, expansive, and challenging at every level of the civilized adventure.

There is still another pattern which contributes in an important way to the elucidation of Voltaire's closing message. *Voltaire has Candide state his conclusion, not once, but twice, the second time with dilated meaning.* In good music the restatement of a theme after an intervening development constitutes something more than a mechanical repetition. It enables the listener to hear the theme with a new understanding of its meaning, to appreciate it in a richer perspective. And so with Candide's conclusion. The first time he makes his affirmation, it is already charged with considerable significance. It chokes off Pangloss's pedantic prolixity, opposing the Deed to the Word. It dramatically underlines the antithesis between those who bloody the earth and those who cultivate it. It proclaims the immeasurable superiority of productivity to power politics. It invites to reflection on the values preached and practised by the old Turk and his family. And it casts a fitful light over the long, fantastic road traveled by Candide and his companions. But all this is not yet fully clear. The author has said too much and moved too swiftly for the reader to be able to absorb the final wisdom in one abrupt, climactic judgment. With great tactical skill he goes on to the elaboration of his theme. First he varies it. The variation sounded by Pangloss harks back to the beginning of the tale and, with consummate irony, to the beginning of the Scriptural Revelation. That voiced by Martin picks up the dervish's message and beautifully fuses the effect of shrinkage with that of expansion.

[10] René Pomeau, Review of *Studies on Voltaire and the Eighteenth Century, VII, VIII, IX,* in *Revue d'histoire littéraire de la France,* LXI (January-March 1961), 86.

The effect of expansion, however, still remains to be clarified. Having stated and varied his theme, Voltaire now proceeds to develop it. He shows us the little band purposefully hustling and bustling about its business, achieving co-operative contentment, serving as a miniature model for the world, and seeking to help make the world's business more like its own. The picture is much clearer now, provided the reader has been alert to the stylistic and structural devices which the master-storyteller is dynamically interweaving as he approaches the end of his story. The end takes the form of a summation in two contrasting speeches. That of Pangloss, a parody of periodic eloquence and a caricature of optimistic dialectic, nevertheless manages to provide a rapid review of several major motifs and episodes: namely, both the intellectual and the sentimental aspects of optimism, the inhumanity of man to man, religious fanaticism, the aimlessness of the South-American adventure, the visit by special dispensation to Eldorado, and the worthlessness of unearned wealth. This review rings a number of changes on social unproductiveness, while reminding us of its ideal opposite. Candide's response, quietly tolerant of his comrade's occasional aberrations, pointed, terse, lapidary, reaffirms the theme of productivity, which this time, because of the intervening development, renews, enriches, deepens, and broadens the meaning of the garden. The restatement flashes both back and forward. It is a wondrous epitome of the tale's wisdom, coined neither for mere show nor for mere contemplation, but for *use*.

Among other things, after mercilessly caricaturing love and woman throughout his narrative, Voltaire redresses the balance at the very end, but with subtlety, so as to preserve congruity of tone. If Candide reluctantly agrees to marry an ugly and shrewish Cunégonde whom he no longer loves, but who later develops into an excellent pastry cook, the author is soberly suggesting: 1) that sentimental quixotism warps or obstructs social productivity; 2) that the dignity and the moral value of the individual's life depend strictly on such productivity; 3) that a sound marriage demands mutual respect, and mutual respect becomes possible only through such productivity; 4) that a sound marriage further involves the procreation and proper upbringing of children who may eventually, *like the sons and daughters of the old Turk,* themselves become useful citizens.

Thus one of the Conclusion's many functions is to blunt the cutting edge of the satirical sword wielded up to the final moments of the battle with a bravura relish which might otherwise be mistaken for sadistic abandon. But in addition, from the very beginning Voltaire has taken care to sow his recital with salutary affirmatives, with examples of moral sanity and true civilized refinement; and this seed will bear fruit in Candide's garden. One reason why the message of Chapter XXX has been so often misread is that readers fail to appreciate the constructive character of Voltaire's criticism. He razes in order to rebuild more solidly, but he does not raze indiscriminately. While demolishing he picks out what is worth saving and makes ready to re-use it. The cultivation of the garden must therefore be understood to include immediately a humanitarian feeling for the wretched and the oppressed,[11] and sooner or later the various cultural pursuits.[12] This salvaging operation effectively illustrates Voltaire's belief in *the conservation and exploitation of all truly human resources.*

Pomeau raises the interesting and very important question of how the garden is socially and administratively organized. "Good humor," he states, "prevents the problem of social relationships from being posed. No leadership, no subordination in 'the little community.' Voltaire, easy-to-get-along-with fellow that he is, assumes that work organizes itself . . ." (*Religion,* p. 306). Since it is Candide who makes the big decision while the others simply accept it, and since it is he who has the last word, I think it plain enough that he has now become the leader of the group. Moreover, Voltaire is under no obligation to do more than start the group on its way at the end. The rest is a matter of time, effort, intelligence, and good will. Nor must it be forgotten that the general direction of possible development may be inferred from the ideal society in the Eldorado episode. Voltaire definitely knows that it is men who organize work, and that in due course, if things go reasonably well, equality before the law will be preserved, but a social and economic hierarchy will take shape.

The nature of Candide's garden makes it dependent on those who work in it, to be sure, but also, as already noted, on the lucky avoidance of physical disasters, and, finally, on its security against destruction by hostile governments. There is nothing automatic or certain about it, then. Its existence is precarious. It is a beautiful but fragile thing. Yet it represents man's best hope—indeed, his

[11] E.g., Jacques offering a helping hand to Candide, Pangloss, and the sailor; Candide, Pangloss, and others succoring the survivors of the Lisbon disaster; Candide weeping over the Negro slave.

[12] E.g., the conversation with the Eldoradan sage; Candide's enjoyment of the theater in Paris; his discussion with Pococurante and Martin in Venice.

only hope *as* man; and it is therefore the only thing with which he has a human right to occupy himself.

One more point: Voltaire's conception of the garden is plural. Wherever a few persons gather in the name of social productivity, a garden comes into existence. Given enough of these developing, setting an example, and influencing the world, a global metagarden is conceivable. Conceivable, that is, as Eldorado is conceivable; but Voltaire is too much the realist to regard a global metagarden as fully realizable on this "globule." It is sufficient for him that men should move toward it, no matter how modestly, in attestation of their higher humanity.

The great mass of internal evidence proves that the meaning of the Conclusion is complex but not obscure, and that Voltaire does not end by abandoning the world to the wicked after flaying them with his verbal lash. He ends by affirming that social productivity of any kind at any level constitutes the good life, that there are limits within which man must be satisfied to lead the good life, but that within these he has a very real chance of achieving both private contentment and public progress.

External Considerations

Nothing outside *Candide* can be legitimately used to refute or to alter or to question what is actually expressed and communicated inside it by its author composing at a superconscious pitch of creative intensity. It is common sense to check the results of internal analysis against the available external evidence, to correlate the text of *Candide* with its historical context, to show how the work reflects the background and vice versa. But at no point should the work be treated as a mere result of mechanical forces functioning in time and space, hence susceptible of definitive measurement from without. The container theory of causation cannot be successfully applied to art, because the artist is a "sovereign Alchemist" who transmutes "Life's leaden metal into Gold," who creates new values. Investigations of origins and influences are therefore limited. Carefully conducted, they may prove highly suggestive. They should never be substituted for direct literary analysis of the work, and they should respect the great qualitative gap that separates the raw material from the finished product. This is why I have begun with a presentation of the internal evidence. What follows will serve to corroborate that evidence, both in general and in particular.

"Voltaire's tales," according to Torrey, "have a way . . . of summing up certain periods of his existence and certain problems with which he was then faced" (*Spirit,* p. 50). In the case of *Candide* the period was the decade of the fifties; the central problem, as already stated, that of human conduct in relation to the somber mystery of physical and social evil. And viewed as a whole, *Candide* pursues a course of argument which parallels the evolution of its author's philosophic attitude during that decade—a decade wherein he irrevocably abandoned the relative complacency of his earlier years, inclined toward pessimism, and finally won through to a melioristic affirmation.

The pessimistic trend of the fifties is clearly perceptible in several important branches of Voltaire's production: in the correspondence (Best. 3465ff.); in the tales, from *Zadig* (1747-48) to *Scarmentado* (1753); in poetry, from the *Poème sur la loi naturelle* (1752) to the *Poème sur le désastre de Lisbonne* (1756). Surveyed in broad perspective, this gradual, cumulative movement assumes dominant proportions between 1752 and 1756 (Morize, pp. xxxv-xlv). A mere enumeration of the major contributing factors will suffice to prove that this effect had its proper causes: the onset of old age coupled with poor health; the death of Mme. du Châtelet; the cynicism of Frederick's entourage; the rupture with His Majesty; the consequent sense of homelessness or exile; various literary and philosophic quarrels (Maupertuis, Rousseau, etc.); the Seven Years' War; the Lisbon disaster; the study of history, leading to disgust and skepticism; a painful awareness of the unresolvable conflict between the clocklike order of a rational, mechanical universe and the mad confusion of an illogical, capricious actuality. This last factor underlies the others. Metaphysics had become the unknowable. The purposes of God were inscrutable. Physical evil was a matter for stoical submission. Free will had been reluctantly abandoned in favor of determinism; yet optimistic fatalism was dispiriting and repugnant to one who could confront social evil only with programs of reform based on faith in man's progressive possibilities.

In the latter part of the decade, as the correspondence and the contributions to the *Encyclopédie* and *Candide* itself reveal, the pessimistic trend was checked and turned back upon itself by a melioristic countercurrent, which, gathering volume and momentum, swelled at last into an irresistible flood at Ferney (Morize, pp. xlvi-xlvii). Here again, sufficient reasons can be adduced to account for this fateful reversal of direction. The effect of Mme. du Châtelet's death wore off with time. Failing health and old age became conventional complaints, as Voltaire absorbed himself in active interests. He created for himself a secure haven, whence he was able to resume relations with Frederick at a safe distance. He attained genuine happiness through gardening and humanitarian projects. Confirmation of his genius all over the civilized world gave him renewed strength. Collaboration with the Encyclopaedists revived his confidence in at least a partial triumph of his ideas. And so his instinctive pugnacity spurred him on with increasing boldness against personal enemies, optimistic fatalism, "l'infâme," and social evil in general.

Thus the period of Voltaire's life which extends from the death of his mistress to the composition and publication of *Candide* can be summed up as a progression from relative complacency through pessimistic drift to meliorism. When due allowances have been made for literary license and accentuation, the movement of ideas in the tale is seen to follow pretty much the same line of development. Shortly after the beginning of the story Candide is ejected from his "terrestrial Paradise," the seat of optimism. The ensuing series of fantastically cumulated misadventures first disenchants, then disheartens him; until finally, in Chapter XIX, he renounces optimism as "the mania of maintaining that all is well when one is miserable," and is plunged into "a black melancholy," such that "the wickedness of men presented itself to his mind in all its ugliness, he harbored only gloomy thoughts." From this point on, symbolically accompanied by a devil's advocate in the person of Martin, he is drawn for a time toward pessimism; but concludes on a note which avoids both extremes by sounding the call to positive, practical action unobstructed by windy theorizing. This broad similarity between the evolution of Voltaire's philosophic attitude during the fifties and the movement of ideas in *Candide* lends no small degree of autobiographical distinctiveness and realism to its content.

There are certain principles of Voltaire's thought which, despite hesitations and vacillations, remain essentially consistent through the years. To see that this is so one need only look beneath the mercurial surface. As Berl expresses it, "one needs but a minimum of intellectual discrimination to distinguish his caprices from his serious ideas and his petulant outbursts from his permanent views. So it is pointless to say: 'He is a chaos of clear ideas'; the chaos is made up of ideas solid enough to have endured intact through a meditation carried on for seventy years with undiminished energy."[13] His attitude may evolve, as just shown, and it may even appear to shift from one pole to the other; yet invariably, in his serious moods, in his key works, it finds a way to avoid extremes. Thus he moves from free will to determinism, but interprets the latter as self-determination for purposes of human conduct, and so stays clear of fatalism. He attacks Jansenism from one direction and atheism from the opposite, again with the Golden Mean as his goal. What, then, of *Candide*? Is it a spectacular exception? "His entire intellect was an engine of war," says Flaubert (Morize, p. v) of the satirist who never wrote but to act (Best. 13221), who recognized that "he who takes pen in hand has a war on his hands" (Best. 4280), and who fought with a pen mightier than the sword for concrete social reforms. Did this same satirist, to indulge a fleeting mood of discouragement, compose his masterpiece on the problem of evil and pour into it all of his consummate artistry and ripened wisdom, only to arrive at a bucolic conclusion—the result of a paltry choice between cabbages and kings? Common sense tells us what the internal evidence and the evolution of Voltaire's attitude have already told us: that the Conclusion of *Candide* rejects pessimism no less than optimism, embracing instead a healthy, equilibrating meliorism.[14]

Another permanent principle of Voltaire's thought is his social conception of morality. In his seventh *Discours en vers sur lhomme* (1737) he had censured the piety of the hermit:

> Mais quel en est le fruit? quel bien fait-il au monde?
> Malgré la sainteté de son auguste emploi,
> C'est n'être bon à rien de n'être bon qu'à soi

["But what fruit does it yield? What good does he do the world?/ Despite the holiness of his august occupation,/To be good only to oneself is to be good for nothing."] (M. IX, 421)

In his *Traité de métaphysique (1734)* he had defined virtue as *"what is useful . . . to society."*[15] On this point he remains perfectly consistent from start to finish of his long career. Once more, what shall we say of *Candide*? Does his greatest work end in selfish withdrawal, indifference, escape, as some have maintained? The evidence

[13] Voltaire, *Traité sur la tolérance,* précédé d'un essai d'Emmanuel Berl et d'une préface d'Adrien Lachenal (Geneva, n.d.), pp. 37-8.

[14] Georges Pellissier, *Voltaire philosophe* (Paris, 1908), p. 51; Naves, pp. 17-18.

[15] Voltaire, *Traité de métaphysique (1734)*, ed. H. Temple Patterson (Manchester, 1937), p. 57.

inside the tale eloquently witnesses Voltaire's unbroken fidelity to his deistic ethic. Candide affirms that "we must cultivate *our* garden." Accordingly, the garden is co-operatively cultivated by the *entire* group. And what the group produces is fed to the *world.* Love of neighbor is thereby pursued in large as well as in small, and the meaning of "our garden" is expanded.

There are critics who defend a purely literal interpretation of that "garden" by reference to the author's gardening activities of 1758. Now, a Voltairean inclination toward allegorical and/or symbolical invention is clearly perceptible in as early a work as the *Henriade* (Best. 101), and has its roots deep in his psychology, his literary training, and his philosophic orientation. Long before 1758 this propensity had found apt raw materials for imaginative exploitation in the garden and the cultivation of the soil. In 1736 Voltaire had already utilized the Biblical garden of Eden in *Le Mondain,* contrasting its crudity with the "terrestrial paradise" of Cirey, and bantering Adam in these terms:

> Mon cher Adam, mon gourmand, mon bon père,
> Que faisais-tu dans les jardins d'Eden?
> Travaillais-tu pour ce sot genre humain?

["My dear Adam, my glutton, my good father,/What were you doing in the garden of Eden?/Were you working for our foolish human race?"]

The Leningrad notebooks include the following entry: "The soil of Florence seemed made to produce Petrarchs, Galileos. We must cultivate ours, fertilize it, etc. Geniuses, like fruit, have come to France from Greece" (*Notebooks,* II, 277-78). Part IV of the *Poème sur la loi naturelle* (1752) contains a prolonged metaphor representing France as a garden, the king as the gardener, and his subjects as plants of various kinds and sizes, which he "cares for and prunes in the interests of a better garden."[16] During the same year Voltaire writes to Argental, concerning his *Rome sauvée:* "It is by emendations that one must turn one's victory to account. This Roman soil was so unproductive that we must recultivate it after getting it, by dint of art, to bear fruit which was relished" (Best. 4244). A letter to Thieriot, dated 26 March 1757, affirms: "I have done everything I could throughout my life to help spread the spirit of philosophy and tolerance which seems today to characterize

[16] Voltaire, *Poème sur la loi naturelle,* ed. Francis J. Crowley (Berkeley, 1938), pp. 265-66, 192.

our century. That spirit, which inspires all decent Europeans, has successfully taken root in [this] country [Switzerland] . . ." (Best. 6517). In a letter of 3 March 1758 to Cideville, he says of his theater at Lausanne: "The actors trained themselves in one year. They are fruits which the Alps and Mount Jura had not previously borne" (Best. 6964). In another, also to Cideville, dated 1 September 1758, he writes: "You are content to pick the flowers of Anacreon in your gardens" (Best. 7131).

The remarkable early pamphlet, *Ce qu'on ne fait pas et ce qu'on pourrait faire* (1742), reproduces a Roman citizen's imaginary memorandum containing a program of reform which definitely prefigures the conclusion of *Candide,* and closes with the words: "The obscure citizen's memorial turned out to be a seed which gradually germinated in the minds of great men" (M. XXIII, 187). Also prefigurative is the following passage from the philosophic tale, *Lettre d'un Turc* (1750), with Omri saying to Bababec: "I value a man who sows vegetables or plants trees a hundred times more highly than all your comrades who stare at the tip of their nose or carry a pack out of excessive nobility of soul."[17]

But the most astonishing anticipation of all is Voltaire's ode on *La Félicité des temps, ou l'Eloge de la France,* read before the French Academy on 25 August 1746. Stanzas VII, VIII, IX, and XI of this poem develop the following line of thought: in olden times a wilderness infested with intestine wars, France is today a peaceful commonwealth overlaid with splendid cities and ennobled by cultural pursuits; this immense progress was made possible by industrious tillage of the soil; work increased fertility, fertility produced wealth, wealth gave rise to all the benefits of higher civilization; such is the history and the promise of our nation, as indeed of all mankind.

> Loin ce discours lâche et vulgaire,
> Que toujours l'homme dégénère,
> Que tout s'épuise et tout finit:
> La nature est inépuisable,
> Et le Travail infatigable
> Est un dieu qui la rajeunit.

["Away with the craven and vulgar opinion/That man is constantly degenerating,/That everything is giving out and coming to an end: /Nature is inexhaustible,/And tireless Work/Is a god who rejuvenates it."] (M. VIII, 456, n. 1; 458-59)

[17] Voltaire, *Contes & romans,* ed. Philippe Van Tieghem (Paris, 1930), IV, 12.

Here is one more fixed principle of Voltaire's thought, found from the *Lettres philosophiques* through the *Essai sur les mœurs* to the *Questions sur l'Encyclopédie*. Given time and good will, and unimpeded by earthquakes or invasions, human societies will advance by natural stages, beginning with agriculture and rising to culture in an ever more elaborate fusion of "pleasure" with "need." Agriculture is necessary for survival—which is why it has its indispensable place in the garden; but culture is necessary for higher civilization—which is why public works, the arts, and the general cultivation of the mind will sooner or later follow from the cultivation of the soil. In this connection I have already shown how the garden salvages the good seed from the experiences of the group in order to sow it for the future. Furthermore, in keeping with the values of the *Essai sur les mœurs,* the garden stands for every form of activity which helps produce civilization, as opposed to the criminally irresponsible and infertile practices of "the higher powers."

In addition to these inventions on the part of Voltaire, there is the striking passage from *Gulliver,* with which he had long been familiar, wherein the King of Brobdingnag expresses the opinion "that whoever could make two ears of corn or two blades of grass to grow upon a spot of ground where only one grew before, would deserve better of mankind, and do more essential service to his country than the whole race of politicians put together" (II, vii). There is the even more striking passage from a letter addressed to him by Bolingbroke as early as 27 June 1724.[18] Writing from his "hermitage" at La Source, Bolingbroke develops at some length a comparison between the cultivation of the literal garden and that of "the mind," "the heart," and "the talents." Shortly before the composition of *Candide,* Voltaire, writing to Alembert from *his* "hermitage" at Les Délices, preaches a crusade of ideas against "l'infâme" and in favor of tolerance, speaks of the advances already made, and states that the vineyard of truth is being admirably cultivated by such *philosophes* as his correspondent, Diderot, Bolingbroke, Hume, etc.[19] Bolingbroke had been dead for several years, yet Voltaire links him here with three other exemplary thinkers who are still alive and active. These associations, considered

[18] Best. 185; see Theodore Besterman, "Voltaire et le désastre de Lisbonne: ou, La Mort de l'optimisme," *Studies on Voltaire and the Eighteenth Century,* II (Geneva, 1956), 24.

[19] Best. 6800; see Besterman, "Voltaire et le désastre de Lisbonne," *Studies on Voltaire,* II, 24, n. 15.

in the light of Voltaire's remarkable memory, fully justify, it seems to me, Besterman's suggestion that the Bolingbroke letter should be regarded as "one of the sources of Candide's final conclusion" (Best. 185, n. 1).

Since a majority of these inventions and readings—the above list is by no means exhaustive—antedate Les Délices by a number of years, and since they prove that the metaphorical use of the garden is a literary habit with Voltaire, there is no compelling biographical reason for arguing a one-to-one relationship between the author's literal garden and Candide's.

There is a much closer relationship between the author's philosophic activities of 1758 and the old Turk's garden. The latter's attitude toward news of public affairs is an absolute contradiction of Voltaire's irrepressible curiosity. In fact, as already pointed out, the Turk professes ignorance and indifference with an overemphasis which broadly hints at, and prepares the reader for, an effect of duplicity. It happens that "a certain form of duplicity was the necessary condition of Voltaire's life and works" (Torrey, pp. viii, 120ff.). Now, the deceptions practised by Voltaire in his war against social evil, although they proved very effective in circumventing the established authorities, are never difficult to fathom. Like the author, the Turk and Candide do not withdraw completely from the world; they merely affect to do so. Actually, they turn their backs on public abominations in a gesture of philosophic disdain, and they retire to safe positions, where they will work concretely toward the spread of social virtue, and whence they will fight social evil with disingenuous tactics.

What was the justification for disingenuousness in 1758? Exile and homelessness were recent experiences and still-painful memories. The *Poème sur le désastre de Lisbonne,* issued in 1756, had had to be cautiously worded in order to avoid dangerous opposition.[20] A royal decree of 1757 had restored the death penalty for writers and publishers convicted of attacking religion.[21] In the very year 1758 the philosophic quarrel reached an acute stage, with the Encyclopaedic party deeply involved.[22] Shortly before the publi-

[20] George R. Havens, "Voltaire's Pessimistic Revision of the Conclusion of His *Poème sur le désastre de Lisbonne,*" *Modern Language Notes,* XLIV (December, 1929), 491; "The Conclusion of Voltaire's *Poème sur le désastre de Lisbonne,*" *Modern Language Notes,* LVI (June, 1941), 425.

[21] Daniel Mornet, *La Pensée française au XVIII*e *siècle* (Paris, 1926), p. 172; Pellissier, pp. 91-2.

[22] Best. 6848-7307, passim; Naves, p. 6.

cation of *Candide* a censorship of the mails was instituted (Best. 7327). Voltaire was an eminently practical fighter. He believed that false heroics leading to martyrdom would only play into the hands of the enemy; hence his elaboration of the adroit stratagems usually associated with his Ferney period, but already being practised in connection with the composition and the publication of *Candide*.

As a disciple of Bayle, a contributor to the *Encyclopédie*, and a master-tactician in his own right, he established his "four paws" (Best. 7283). He wrote *Candide* in great secrecy (Havens, *Candide*, p. xxviii). He published it anonymously and denied his authorship.[23] Shortly before its publication he feigned in his letters a loss of interest in the reading and the writing of books.[24] He included in the tale only a few anti-Biblical thrusts, and these mostly indirect. He scattered through his letters repeated affectations of complete withdrawal from the world,[25] and gave literary expression to this ruse in the final chapter of *Candide*. Finally, he may in part have chosen the metaphor of the garden because he could thereby screen an aggressive social intention behind a literal occupation. The old Turk's meaning, veiled yet strangely clear, shines through the following characteristic excerpts from the correspondence:

> (28 February [1757], to Diderot) "It is with pleasure that I forget in my retreat all those who are working to make men unhappy or to brutify them; and the more I forget those enemies of the human race, the more I remember you. I exhort you to diffuse as widely as possible through the *Encyclopédie* the noble freedom of your spirit" (Best. 6479);
>
> (26 March [1757], to Thieriot [the Damiens affair]) "We avert our eyes from those abominations in our little Romanic country. . . . We are doing here what one should be doing in Paris; we are living in tranquillity, we are cultivating literature without any cabals" (Best. 6517);
>
> (12 December [1757], to Alembert [the article *Genève*]) "There are some who accuse me of an impious conspiracy with you. You know I am innocent" (Best. 6813);
>
> (24 December [1757], to Vernes [same subject]) "I haven't yet received the new volume of the *Encyclopédie* and I know absolutely nothing of what it's about. . . . Let's be neither Calvinists nor

[23] Havens, *Candide*, p. xxviii; also Best. 7427, 7434, 7438, 7457, 7467, 7472, 7474, 7511.

[24] Best. 7273, 7289, 7291, 7322, 7364.

[25] Best. 6993, 6994, 7038, 7127, 7160, 7285, 7292.

papists, but brothers, adorers of a merciful and just God" (Best. 6835);

(15 May [1758], to Argental) "Do you have any news about the *Encyclopédie*? I prefer it to news of public affairs, which is almost always distressing" (Best. 7037);

(3 September 1758, to Mme. Du Bocage [the Encyclopaedic party]) "The few sages, Madame, must not expose themselves to the wickedness of those who are mad. They must live together and shun the general public" (Best. 7137).

As most of these excerpts plainly show, Voltaire was vitally interested in the victory of the Encyclopaedic party. He declared himself the "admirer and . . . partisan to his dying day" (Best. 6862) of those who were compiling "the greatest work in the world" (Best. 6363), and contributed not a few articles of his own to the great enterprise. In 1757, and especially in 1758, when the opposition was making progress on the work increasingly difficult, Voltaire repeatedly exhorted his colleagues to strengthen themselves by forming a closely-knit philosophic group: "Gather the little flock. Courage.—Unite all the *philosophes* as best you can against the fanatics.—Form a group, gentlemen; a group always commands respect. . . . Get together, and you will be masters of the situation. —This is the moment when all the *philosophes* should join together.—All the *kakouaks* should form a pack, but they separate and the wolf devours them."[26] Finally, recognizing the seriousness of their plight, he suggested that they flee from public life to where they could live together as free men, not in defeat, not in escapist retirement, but for the purpose of completing their task (Best. 6956). To that end he even invited them to share his own retreat, just as in 1766 he was to recommend withdrawal to one of Frederick's southern provinces (Best. 12557): (7 March [1758], to Alembert) "if we could reach an agreement, if we had courage, if we dared make a resolution, we could very well complete the *Encyclopédie* here. . . . If we were sufficiently detached from our age and our country to make this decision, I should contribute half of what I own to its execution. I should have the wherewithal to house you all, and very comfortably at that. I should like to see this project through and die happy" (Best. 6970).

The topical connection of the *Encyclopédie* with the conclusion of *Candide* is implicit in this epistolary evidence that Voltaire thought of the Encyclopaedists as a "little community," a model

[26] Best. 6426, 6443, 6894, 6937, 6998.

group of *philosophes,* who, like the old Turk and Candide—and Voltaire—should shelter themselves from exposure to public abominations, and work together toward the reduction of social evil and the spread of social virtue, by setting a concrete example and by enlightening the world. But the correspondence of the period immediately preceding *Candide* does more than imply such a connection; it explicitly links the Encyclopaedists with the metaphor of the garden:

> (30 January [1755], to Gauffecourt) "Speaking of philosophy, do you still get to see my lords of the *Encyclopédie*? They are the proprietors of the greatest domain in the world. I hope they will always cultivate it with complete freedom; they are made to enlighten the world boldly, and to crush their enemies" (Best. 5462);
>
> (6 December [1757], to Alembert) "I do as Cato did, I always end my harangue with the words: *Deleatur Carthago*. . . . It takes only five or six *philosophes* leagued together to overturn the colossus. It is not a question of preventing our lackeys from going to mass or attending Protestant services; it is a question of rescuing heads of families from the tyranny of impostors, and of inspiring a spirit of tolerance. This great mission is already enjoying success. The vineyard of truth is being well cultivated by Alemberts, Diderots, Bolingbrokes, Humes, etc." (Best. 6800);
>
> (7 March [1758], to Alembert) "If you again take up the ill-harnessed plow of the *Encyclopédie* and want some of those articles, I shall send them back proofread" (Best. 6970).

Torrey makes much of the fact that in his correspondence Voltaire differentiates the metaphor of the garden from that of the vineyard.[27] Actually, before the publication of *Candide* there is no such pattern, for the figure of the vineyard appears but once in the letters that have survived (Best. 6800). After the publication of *Candide* the "garden-vineyard" distinction does develop, and it is maintained with consistency, but it proves quite the opposite of what Torrey would have it prove. The "vineyard" metaphor becomes the ironic battle-cry of the philosophic party in its attack on "l'infâme": e.g., (13 February 1764, to Alembert) "so labor in the vineyard, crush 'l'infâme' " (Best. 10858). The "garden" figure, which tends to recur especially at times when "l'infâme" seems to be gaining the advantage over the philosophic party, becomes the

[27] Torrey, Review of William F. Bottiglia, *Voltaire's "Candide": Analysis of a Classic* (Vol. VII of *Studies on Voltaire*), in *The Romanic Review,* L (October 1959), 220; "Candide's Garden and the Lord's Vineyard," *Studies on Voltaire,* XXVII (Geneva, 1963), 1657-66.

symbol for an affectation of retreat accompanied by vigorous clandestine activity, so that, in the correspondence as in the Conclusion of *Candide, the garden includes the vineyard.* An excellent example of this fusion by absorption is found in Voltaire's letter of 2 April 1764 to Damilaville: "So we shall have to end like Candide by cultivating our garden. Good-bye, dear brother. Crush 'l'infâme' " (Best. 10969); another, in his letter of 14 July 1773 to Alembert: "We must cultivate literature or our garden. . . . Please do not fail to remember me to Monsieur de Condorcet and your other friends who are very quietly supporting the good cause" (Best. 17382).

In fine, the correspondence posterior to *Candide* corroborates the message of its Conclusion as expressed and communicated in the text itself. The note of duplicity which is sounded in the letters echoes that of the old Turk's garden and Candide's, and so is necessarily present to Voltaire's mind. After the tale even more than before he is aware that the inherent dynamism of the garden inescapably compels its figurative extension. I have taken pains to describe the limitations which circumscribe and the dangers which attend that extension; but limitations and dangers notwithstanding, the basic, concrete example of gardening and/or farming has in it the stuff of expansion, so that it cannot be confined within a purely literal conception.

Concluding Remarks

It is difficult for historians of ideas to accept the principle that in a genuine work of art material and efficient causes are transcended by formal and final causes; but art critics know that to enter a work of art is to enter a sanctuary where the raw material of experience becomes aesthetically significant form-fused-with-content, and where quantitative measurement must accordingly be replaced by qualitative insight. I have been careful here to consider every kind of external evidence which has relevance either as raw material for *Candide* or as a subsequent reflection of *Candide,* and to consider it with a proper respect for its real importance—and a sensible appreciation of its limitations. My approach, in sum, has steered clear of both the Scylla of *in-vacuo* analysis and the Charybdis of unimaginative historicism in order to do full justice to a literary masterpiece risen out of time to timelessness.

Voltaire's Politics: France and Constitutional Absolutism

by Peter Gay

These then are the politics of Voltaire: realistic and serious but rarely solemn, reformist and hopeful but rarely abstract. His assertion that he took no interest in political questions is as untrue as his critics' assertion that his radical program was merely the random energy of a creature of air and flame, the playfulness of an old child who quickly kindles and as quickly tires. Like Shaw's Don Juan he rebelled against a philosophy that looked at the world and found it good, and he cultivated the instinct that looked at the world and found that it could be improved. But unlike Shaw's Don Juan, he believed that it could be improved by political means.

Voltaire's practical political style vividly emerges for the last time in his polemics against the French *parlements,* the culmination of his life-long fight for the *thèse royale.* His admiration for English institutions, his royalism, his hostility to censors, his hatred of fanaticism, his passion for a humane and rational jurisprudence—all his political convictions, all his rancors and enthusiasms, were enlisted in his last great battle for French absolutism.

Voltaire had left France in 1750 defending the royal cause against the clergy; at Ferney in the late 1760's and early 1770's he defended the royal cause against the *parlements,* a far more energetic adversary to the crown than the church. The French clergy had forced the king to abandon his tax program, but the church's influence was waning. The *philosophes* were occupying stronghold after stronghold; by 1770 they had infiltrated the censorship, conquered the *Académie française,* and invaded the administration. Most Frenchmen did not accept the bold materialism of the Holbachian clique and hesitated to accept the more sedate deism of the Voltairians, but they were strongly anticlerical. Unsavory controversies within the church, slyly publicized by philosophic propaganda, had done the faithful much damage.

The expulsion of the Jesuits in the 1760's suggests how little control the crown had over these controversies. Ultramontane, royalist, urbane and sophisticated, the Society of Jesus had long excited the resentment of the Jansenist magistrates. Since Pascal's brilliant and cruelly unfair *Lettres provinciales,* the Jesuits had been a safe target for jokes, rumors, and slander. Even a good Christian could allow himself the pleasure of painting them as servants of a foreign power, sinister intriguers, and probably all pederasts. These dark accusations, some well-founded but mostly imaginary, came to be generally accepted in 1761, after the bankruptcy of a Jesuit house on Martinique. A Marseilles court made the Society financially responsible for the commercial losses of a single mission, and the Jesuits appealed the verdict to the hostile *parlement* of Paris, which was perhaps as good a sign as any that their celebrated shrewdness was in decline. The Jansenist judges gleefully confirmed the verdict, and initiated a comprehensive investigation into the statutes and political ideas of the Jesuit order. To no one's surprise, the investigators found what they were looking for: the Jesuits preached tyrannicide. Men who followed their maxims, Voltaire wrote drily, "could gain paradise and the rope" (M. XV, 398). In August 1761 the *parlement* ordered the burning of twenty-four Jesuit works as irreligious and seditious, and moved to close the Jesuit *collèges,* while the *philosophes,* many of them products of these schools, fervently applauded. The king and the bishops tried to save the Jesuits, but they succeeded only in postponing their inevitable suppression until the following year.[1]

While Jansenist Christians persecuted Jesuit Christians, unbelievers rejoiced. D'Alembert wrote excitedly to Ferney that the *parlements* were executioners serving the *philosophes* without know-

[1] The "destruction" of the Jesuits, as it was called, took several years. In 1762, the various *parlements* suppressed the Society, the Jesuit *collèges* were closed; in 1764, a royal edict expelled the Society from France, but permitted Jesuits to remain in the country as secular priests; in 1767, finally, they too were ordered expelled.

ing it.[2] Voltaire, far more politically acute than his brethren, was afraid that the *parlements* were executioners serving no one but themselves, and that the magistrates were right to celebrate the suppression of the Jesuits as a great victory. He had savagely and ungratefully lampooned his old teachers in their prosperity, assiduously spread stories about their politics and their morals. Even the cannibals in *Candide* were Voltairians: they threaten to eat Candide only while they mistake him for a Jesuit.

But now that the French cannibals had eaten the Jesuits, the delicate natural balance that kept the enemies of philosophy and of the state at each other's throats had been disturbed:

> Les renards et les loups furent longtemps en guerre:
> Les moutons respiraient; des bergers diligents
> Ont chassé par arrêt les renards de nos champs:
> Les loups vont désoler la terre.
> Nos bergers semblent, entre nous,
> Un peu d'accord avec les loups.

["The foxes and the wolves were long at war with one another:/The sheep were breathing easily; diligent shepherds/Drove the foxes from our fields by decree:/The wolves are now going to ravage the land./Between you and me, our shepherds seem to be/Somewhat in league with the wolves."] (M. XLII, 505)

Voltaire had no reason to like these wolves. They had burned his books, and after they had chased the foxes, they began to burn people.

Voltaire had observed the growing political influence of the magistrates with dismay. After the regent restored the *parlements'* right to remonstrate in 1715, they emerged as the supreme enemy of reform. On more than one occasion an angry Louis XV exiled them to their country houses, but his attacks of courage failed to reduce the magistrates' power and only increased their popularity.[3] After the suppression of the Jesuits gave them a monopoly of resistance to the crown, the *parlements'* conduct fully justified Voltaire's fears:

[2] Henri Carré, *Louis XV*, p. 327 (Vol. VIII, Part 2 [ed. 1911] of Ernest Lavisse's *Histoire de France*).

[3] In 1753, the *parlements* took an aggressive part in the debate over the refusal of sacraments to Jansenists; against the king's explicit orders, they debated and remonstrated. The robe nobles, Louis XV told his intimates, are an assembly of republicans: "The regent made a great mistake to restore their right to remonstrate. They will end up by ruining the state!" To stave off that ruin, he dispersed the *parlement* of Paris in May 1753, but meekly recalled it in October. Carré, *Louis XV*, p. 239.

they strengthened their united front and launched demagogic appeals to a public already suspicious of "despotism" and "centralization."[4]

The crown could either surrender or fight. It chose to fight. The political crisis erupted in Brittany in 1764, when the estates refused to levy the royal *corvée* on the ground that the tax illegally infringed time-honored rights; the Breton *parlement* at Rennes, led by its Attorney General La Chalotais, sustained the estates and went on strike. A violent war of words broke out between La Chalotais and the duc d'Aiguillon, the military governor of Brittany; the central government, determined to enforce obedience, arrested La Chalotais and five other Breton officials. True to their policy of vocal cooperation, the other *parlements* energetically remonstrated with the king.

It was against this subversion of royal authority that Louis XV launched his celebrated lecture at the *séance de flagellation.* On 3 March 1766, he sternly told the *parlement* of Paris that provincial affairs were none of its business, that he would not tolerate a "confederation of resistance," that sovereignty and hence the law-making power were his alone, that the authority—indeed, the very existence—of the courts depended on the royal will, and that the *parlements* had the duty to register decrees if the king insisted on them.

These were powerful words, and they delighted Voltaire who was following matters closely from Ferney. "You have sent me a truly beautiful present in sending me the king's reply to the *parlement,*" he wrote to Damilaville. "It's been a long time since I have read anything so wise, so noble, and so well written" (M. XLIV, 243). But the king's forceful tone ill concealed his defensive mood. The *parlements* were no longer afraid of royal bluster. Following their brief exile of 1753, they had perfected a bold aristocratic interpretation of the French constitution which pushed the *thèse nobiliaire* to unprecedented, dizzying heights. They adopted Montesquieu's notion that they were "intermediate powers" indispensable to civic

[4] There were perhaps no more than 2,000 robe nobles in the country, but they became more and more exclusive in the eighteenth century. It was precisely the relative recency of their noble status that made them so punctilious and so eager to limit their caste to a few families. *Parlement* after *parlement* decreed that new posts carrying nobility be restricted to individuals who belonged to families that were already noble. By the end of Louis XV's reign, the stream of social ascent had become a narrow and obstructed trickle. "The road is blocked in every direction," wrote the young Barnave. The frustrations of a whole generation of ambitious bourgeois are in that sentence. Georges Lefebvre, *The Coming of the French Revolution* (English tr., 1947), p. 41.

freedom; in the words of one of their ideologists, the lawyer Le Paige, they claimed that "sovereign courts" were as essential to the French constitution as the monarchy itself. They revived the fanciful history of Boulainvilliers; they asked the crown to acknowledge that the registration of decrees was a legislative rather than an administrative act—a sign of the people's consent, a guarantee that the king's edict did not violate the fundamental laws of France. The French constitution, said the magistrates, adopting the language of natural rights and even of popular sovereignty, was a contract between king and people.[5] Since the people could not speak for itself, the *parlements* spoke for the people in a single voice: "All the companies of magistrates, known under the name of *parlements,* compose the court of the king, and are the diverse classes of a single and unique corps, animated by the same spirit, nourished by the same principles, occupied with the same object."[6] To remove magistrates from their posts, to treat the dozen *parlements* as separate bodies, to compel registration of edicts—all this was to overstep the boundaries of legitimate kingship and to move in the direction of despotism. Such claims sounded old, but in their sheer boldness, they were new; Louis XV significantly denounced them in the *séance de flagellation* as "pernicious novelties" which disregarded "the true fundamental laws of the state."[7] For even the most royalist of lawyers and the most vigorous of kings carefully distinguished between absolutism and despotism. They maintained that the crown had a monopoly of the legislative and executive power, but it did not follow that the king could do as he pleased. Advocates of the *thèse royale* from Bodin to d'Argenson subjected the crown to the unwritten fundamental laws of France and assumed, further, that the king would obey the decrees he had made.[8]

[5] It should be remembered that during and after the French Revolution the *thèse nobiliaire* was transformed into a weapon of French liberalism, while the *thèse royale* became a weapon of conservatives and authoritarians. But this subsequent history, which makes such present-day royalists as Pierre Gaxotte strong advocates of the *thèse royale,* does not affect my argument in the text.

[6] This is from a declaration of the *parlement* of Paris. Jules Flammermont, *Le Chancelier Maupeou et les parlements* (1895), pp. 126-27.

[7] *Remontrances du parlement de Paris au XVIIIe siècle,* eds. Jules Flammermont and Maurice Tourneux (1895), II, 557.

[8] Since the fundamental laws were unwritten, the precise nature of the French constitution was legitimately a matter of debate. There was general agreement that the fundamental law consisted (1) of the inalienability of the king's domain (usually interpreted to mean French territory), (2) of the Salic Law, which excluded women from succeeding to the throne, (3) and of the hereditary

This legal tradition was perhaps illogical in that it mixes elements from two positions usually treated as incompatible, constitutionalism and absolutism. But logical or not, it was this "constitutional absolutism" rather than naked despotism on which eighteenth-century royalists, including Voltaire, rested their case against the *parlements.*

This fine distinction between a legitimate and an illegitimate absolutism did not find a wide response. The magistrates' exiles were triumphant processions, their remonstrances were popular manifestos: it was the *parlements'* position that impressed the general public, and alternately intimidated and infuriated the king. It neither impressed nor intimidated Voltaire—it only infuriated him. He said again and again that he hated the "assassins of Calas," but his enmity to the *parlements* antedated the execution of Jean Calas and was political opposition more than abhorrence (M. XLVII, 421). He condemned the magistrates' interpretation of the French constitution as a defense of archaic institutions and privileges, a verbal counterrevolution. The *parlement* of Paris, he wrote, "seemed to take the side of the people, but it obstructed the government and seemed to wish to establish its authority on the ruins of the supreme power" (M. XVI, 106).

In the late 1760's, the *parlements* appeared close to success in this enterprise. They persistently refused to register royal edicts, ordered the arrest and trial of royal officials, inundated the country with remonstrances ever more seditious in tone. "This astonishing anarchy could not subsist," wrote Voltaire. "Either the crown must recover its authority, or the *parlements* must prevail. In such a critical moment, an enterprising and audacious chancellor was needed. He was found" (M. XVI, 107).

That chancellor was René-Nicolas de Maupeou, member of an old robe family and former *président à mortier* at the *parlement* of Paris. He had exercised considerable influence in the government even before Louis XV appointed him chancellor in September 1768 —it is probable that he inspired the king's harangue at the *séance de flagellation*—and there was nothing he liked better than to exer-

---

character of the crown, which kept it Catholic and confined it to legitimate sons of the king. Louis XIV, who knew these obligations well enough when he needed to cite them to escape an onerous duty, violated the last of these when he legitimized his bastards in 1714. Voltaire knew of these violations and admitted that the status of the fundamental laws was far from clear. See *l'A,B,C,* M. XXVII, 379-82.

cise influence. Serious, active, unscrupulous, indifferent to literature and hostile to men of letters, he was a man to fear. Diderot derisively called him "a nobody, without great fortune, without good family, without great talents, who made up for these deficiencies with servility, duplicity, a vengeful spirit, ambition and audacity."[9]

The *parlements* had good reason to fear their former colleague. So did his present colleagues: the duc de Choiseul, minister of foreign affairs and secretary of war, a powerful court favorite and the king's chief adviser, became the victim of Maupeou's machinations. As soon as he held the chancellor's seals, Maupeou plunged into the congenial tasks of trying to tame the *parlements,* undermine the position of Choiseul, and muzzle the *philosophes.*[10] Here was indeed a strange ally for Voltaire, and the *philosophes,* who disliked and dreaded Maupeou, were appalled to find Voltaire ready to overlook the chancellor's vices for the sake of his program. But then Voltaire was never particular about his tactical affiliations.[11]

In the spring of 1769, Voltaire supported Maupeou's program, probably upon the chancellor's instigation, with a tendentious *Histoire du parlement de Paris.* It is a relatively minor achievement, but it is a full-scale history, remarkably informative and objective. Voltaire disavowed it immediately and pointed out that a "M. l'abbé Bigore" had written it, but he let it be known that he found this work, which pernicious gossips had falsely attributed to him, a sound and reasonable history.

In the preface, Voltaire-Bigore hinted suavely that earlier historians, including Hénault, had been hampered by their obligations or their prejudices. "Freedom alone knows and tells the truth."[12] It was regrettable (Voltaire wrote without regret) that the truth was not wholly pleasant. In France's perennial conflicts with papal ar-

[9] "Essai historique sur la police," *Diderot et Catherine II,* ed. Maurice Tourneux (1899), p. 127.

[10] In an autobiographical memorandum that Maupeou submitted to Louis XVI, he acknowledged without apology that he had "severe views" about literature, and had intended to strengthen the censorship to "purify" the profession of letters. Flammermont, *Maupeou,* p. 606.

[11] In *Le neveu de Rameau,* "He," who occasionally speaks for Diderot, says: "You would never have been able to write *Mahomet,* but then you wouldn't have praised Maupeou either."

[12] M. XV, 445. Despite these bold words, it is evident that once the history was published, Voltaire had one of his attacks of panic. Even to his best friends—d'Argental and d'Alembert—he disclaimed authorship, and contended that only an author who had access to archives could have written this history. This disclaimer only suggests that Maupeou in fact supplied Voltaire with documents. See Gustave Desnoiresterres, *Voltaire et Genève,* p. 382.

rogance, the *parlement* of Paris had served its country well. In the fifteenth century, it had sensibly opposed the payment of annates to the Papacy; in the sixteenth century, after much vacillation, it had accepted Henri IV and "returned to its earlier sentiments of patriotism which have been France's firmest ramparts against the enterprises of the court of Rome" (M. XV, 558); in the seventeenth century, it had vigorously supported Bossuet's Gallican declaration; in the eighteenth century, it had risen in justified wrath against the Bull *Unigenitus,* against the refusal of sacraments to Jansenists, and against the Jesuit order. This was an enviable record of service.

Further, Voltaire impartially acknowledged, in many a civil conflict the *parlement* of Paris had been no more at fault than its opponents. The Frondes had been produced as much by the cruelty of Richelieu, the rapacity of Mazarin, the ambition of Condé, as by the irresponsibility of the magistrates; in the ridiculous squabbles between Jansenists and Jesuits, the fanaticism of the Jansenist *parlements* had been hardly more reprehensible than the obstinacy of the Jesuit bishops.

A prejudiced, unrelieved attack on the *parlement* would have been much less damaging than this judicious praise: it was the magistrates' occasional service that threw their frequent disservice into pitiless prominence. Voltaire approvingly quoted the self-denying ordinance of a fifteenth-century magistrate—the proper business of a *parlement* is to administer justice rather than to meddle with political, financial, and military questions (M. XV, 481)—and reminded his readers that unfortunately such rational modesty was rare. Over and over, the *parlements* had proved themselves reactionary, selfish, divisive, irresponsible, superstitious, and intolerant. They were reactionary, for they had persistently opposed salutary innovations in French life, from the establishment of the *Académie française* to the *Encyclopédie,* from inoculation against smallpox to the gratuitous administration of justice. They were selfish, for they claimed to safeguard the traditional rights of Frenchmen, while they defended the interests of only a small privileged caste. They were divisive, for they had instigated religious wars in the sixteenth, civil war in the seventeenth, class war in the eighteenth century. They were irresponsible, for without a shred of legal jurisdiction, they had tried the dauphin Charles in 1420. They were superstitious, for they had condemned the first printers in France, applauded Saint Bartholomew, and condemned the maréchale d'Ancre to be burned as a witch. They were intolerant, for they harassed men of letters, persecuted Protestants, and tortured the innocent.

This parade of facts, offered soberly, with few tricks of rhetoric and few appeals to emotion, adds up to an unsparing condemnation of the aristocratic position. For the most part the *Histoire* is history; it makes few contemporary allusions, but it makes its contemporary point forcefully: from its medieval beginnings, the *parlement* of Paris has acquired no legislative or administrative rights. Since it did not have the right to try a peer in 1420, it has no right to try the duc d'Aiguillon in the 1760's; since the *parlements* were created one by one during the Middle Ages, they have no right to associate themselves into a single corps in the eighteenth century (M. XV, 455); since the first deposit of laws under Philip the Fair was no more than an administrative convenience, eighteenth-century *parlements* have no constitutional right to veto legislation. This is the burden of Voltaire's *Histoire du parlement de Paris.* It restates the king's speech at the *séance de flagellation,* at greater length and with more impressive documentation.

The magistrates, persuaded that royal actions would never match royal words, did not choose to take seriously the warning implicit in Voltaire's book. In the summer of 1766 Louis XV had recalled the duc d'Aiguillon and restored the old *parlement* of Brittany except for its attorney general and his five associates. The Bretons were not satisfied with this partial victory; stirred by La Chalotais' account of his sufferings, they demanded the restoration of all their members, and initiated a prosecution of d'Aiguillon for a series of sensational and improbable crimes. D'Aiguillon, eager to be cleared, requested a trial by his peers, and such a trial actually began in April 1770 before the *parlement* of Paris, but the king quashed all proceedings at the end of June and ordered all to observe silence on the case.

But silence was not to be had, for Maupeou was trying to precipitate a crisis. His program of reform and his dependence on Madame Du Barry, d'Aiguillon's intimate and Choiseul's enemy, made him decide to move quickly and decisively. He persuaded Louis XV that the crown must finally crush parlementary pretensions, and that Choiseul, the ally of the magistrates, must go. In September, he delivered an offensive harangue to the *parlement* of Paris, haughtily demanding its dutiful obedience. Two months later, he sent it an edict which stigmatized the magistrates as "victims of the *esprit de système*"[13] and as disseminators of "new ideas" dan-

[13] Voltaire, himself a lifelong opponent of the *esprit de système,* was much amused to see Maupeou denouncing the nobility of the robe for being infected

gerous to the public order, and forbade them to use the terms "unity, indivisibility, classes," to send proceedings concerning one *parlement* to others, to go on strike by resigning or refusing to sit on cases, to reopen discussion or obstruct administration of edicts that had been registered: "We permit them once again to make such remonstrances or representations as they deem fit for the good of Our people and the good of Our service before Our edicts, declarations, or letters patent have been registered. . . . *Car tel est notre plaisir.*"[14]

The king's pleasure was not the magistrates' pleasure. Protesting that it had always labored to enhance royal authority, the *parlement* of Paris defied the king, and refused to register Maupeou's edict. But Louis XV could be firm when he had someone to lean on—on 7 December 1770 he presided over a *lit de justice* in which Maupeou delivered an able address restating and clarifying the crown's constitutional position.[15]

Half persuaded that its legal position was untenable, and wholly unwilling to make this fact official by accepting the edict, the *parlement* continued its resistance, closed its doors to legal business and sent its *premier président* to the king. He was not admitted. Louis XV was now determined to prevail: on 20 December he signed Maupeou's draft of *lettres de juission,* ordering the magistrates to abandon their disobedience. Four days later, Choiseul was dismissed and d'Aiguillon was brought into the cabinet.

Thus the fortunes of politics placed Voltaire in a cruel dilemma which he resolved in characteristic fashion. Cultivated and witty, Choiseul had been an adherent of Madame de Pompadour and an enemy to the Jesuits; he, his wife, and his wife's intimate, Madame du Deffand, had long been Voltaire's correspondents. During his rivalry with Maupeou, he strongly supported Voltaire's plan to build the free port of Versoix near Geneva. Voltaire had much rea-

---

with it. M. XLVII, 290. It is probable that some of the correspondence between Voltaire and Maupeou has been lost, but we have a flattering letter from Voltaire to Maupeou of 22 August (1770), which proves that they were in direct touch. M. XLVII, 182.

[14] Flammermont, *Maupeou,* pp. 116-20.

[15] There is nothing new in this address: the *parlements'* pretension to "free verification" of edicts, he said, has no place in the French constitution: "When the legislator wants to manifest his desires, you are his organ, and his goodness permits you to be his counsel; he invites you to enlighten him by your intellect, and orders you to show him the truth. Your office ends there." Flammermont, *ibid.,* p. 141.

son to regret his dismissal, and regret it he did, loudly and unconvincingly (M. XLVII, 317). Maupeou, on the other hand, was everything that a man of letters must distrust. But Choiseul had made himself into an instrument of the magistrates, and Maupeou, whatever his character, was the most inventive and the most energetic advocate of the *thèse royale* since Machault. So like Byron's Julia, who "whispering she'd ne'er consent, consented," Voltaire, proclaiming that he'd ne'er desert his friend, deserted him.[16]

Politically, at least, Voltaire's choice was wise. Maupeou needed and deserved support. The magistrates continued to refuse to register the edict, and the public, inflamed against the chancellor by libelous brochures, angered by the dismissal of the popular Choiseul, vocally abetted this disobedience. On 3 January 1771, and again a week later, the king repeated his orders; the magistrates agreed to go back to work, but submissively informed their sovereign that they could not register an act that violated the fundamental laws of France. On 20 January, between one and four in the morning, every Parisian magistrate was awakened by two royal musqueteers bearing a *lettre de cachet,* which ordered him to signify his obedience or disobedience in writing, "without evasions or dodges."

The proud nobles of the robe were not to be intimidated. An overwhelming majority, protesting its love for Louis XV, replied in the negative. Within the next two days, 165 members of the Paris *parlement* were deprived of their posts and exiled to the country. Voltaire was pleased but not wholly satisfied: "It is a pretty feeble consolation," he wrote to d'Alembert on 2 February 1771, "that the assassins of the chevalier de La Barre are in their country houses; but we can no longer hope for justice in this world."[17]

This callous and vindictive observation placed Voltaire in the vanguard of a small minority who applauded Maupeou's *coup d'état.* Condorcet, d'Alembert, and to some extent even Diderot, sometimes echoed Voltaire's tone, but none of them had Voltaire's political sagacity, none of them saw as clearly as Voltaire that Maupeou's program was the best, perhaps the only, hope for saving the country from revolution.[18]

[16] Naturally enough, both the duc and the duchesse de Choiseul regarded Voltaire's act as a betrayal.

[17] M. XLVII, 340. The remark is inaccurate; fewer than half of the magistrates were exiled to their properties, and some of the elderly judges suffered real hardships on the icy roads to their places of exile.

[18] Kingsley Martin writes: "The *philosophes,* indeed, had supported the King against the *Parlements.* They favoured 'enlightened despotism' and criticized

The immense and unshakeable popularity of the *parlements* suggests how little rational political discussion there was in eighteenth-century France. Every single charge of Voltaire's against the *parlements* could be documented over and over again; the counterrevolution of the robe nobility was what German sociologists have called a "reinfeudation" of society in an age when feudal institutions, feudal exemptions and privileges were becoming more and more damaging to stable government. It should have been obvious that in the midst of prosperity France was nearing bankruptcy, that taxation weighed most heavily on those least able to bear the burden, that trade and industry were crippled by archaic restrictions and absurd customs barriers, and that fiscal and administrative reforms were overdue.

But it was not obvious, and the central government, which might have explained its policies to gain public support, never explained them. Under Louis XV, the target of flattery and contradictory advice, minister succeeded minister and cabal succeeded cabal. Many of the king's ministers were incompetent, and when they were competent administrators, they were all too often inept politicians, like Turgot,[19] or unpopular, like Machault, or indifferent to public opinion, like Maupeou. The government operated privately, and seldom asked men of letters to come to its aid. The case for its policies was often excellent, but it was rarely made. Catherine II, looking back upon the royal fiasco at the beginning of the Revolution, rightly observed that the king and his ministers had failed to make themselves masters of public opinion.[20]

The magistrates, on the other hand, were united by ties of profession, family, and interest; they knew what they wanted and they were highly sensitive to the public mood. They exploited each bread riot, each grain shortage, each rise in prices, to pose as the defenders of the public interest. They staged spectacular investigations, spread stories about the speculations of royal officials, and resorted to demagogy the crown was too proud or too foolish to

---

Louis, not for his despotism, but for his lack of enlightenment." *French Liberal Thought in the Eighteenth Century* (2nd ed., 1954), p. 86. This greatly underrates Voltaire's isolation; it suggests that all the *philosophes* had the good political sense that, in fact, Voltaire displayed almost alone.

[19] An exception must be made for Turgot's work as intendant of Limoges: there he adroitly explained his tax and road building program to the public and as a result had wide public support—an instructive experience.

[20] 10 August 1789, quoted in Albert Lortholary, *Les "philosophes" et le mirage russe,* p. 308.

refute. To the public, politically uninformed, superstitious, and conservative, the magistrates were the guardians of the general interest, the enemies of the Jesuits, the representatives of the people. It saw the central government at its worst—the dragoon and the tax farmer; it overlooked the government at its best—the intendant. Most Frenchmen lived near the starvation level; their favorite topics of conversation were the price of bread and rumors about government officials making fortunes in the grain market. Magistrates were popular heroes, but representatives of the king all too often appeared as speculators in starvation. The tenacity of this parlementary mystique can be surmised from Tocqueville's comment, made eighty-five years after the event: "When in 1770 the *parlement* of Paris was dissolved and the magistrates belonging to it were deprived of their authority and status, not one of them truckled to the royal will. . . . In the history of free nations I know of no nobler gesture than this."[21]

It was this attitude that drove Turgot and Voltaire to despair. Turgot tried more than once to rouse the government from its lethargy. "The magistrates have always sought to display themselves as the protectors of the people against the crown," he wrote, "but the crown would do well to unmask these magistrates and to show them as they really are—as corporations little interested in the well-being of the masses."[22] Maupeou worked against, rather than with, public opinion. For a month after the exile of the Paris *parlement* he tried in vain to carry on with a makeshift court composed of cabinet ministers and administrative officials, but lawyers refused to serve before this "interim *parlement*" and even the princes of the blood, usually so docile, protested that an "arbitrary absolutism" was being introduced into the French government. On 23 February 1771, Maupeou therefore proceeded to the second, constructive stage of his *coup d'état:* he published several edicts over the king's signature introducing drastic reforms into the magistrature. They abolished the venality of office and of justice, and greatly reduced the territory and jurisdiction of the *parlement* of Paris, creating in its place six "superior councils" to administer justice. Voltaire was delighted with this reform. "Nothing is nobler and more useful," he wrote on 27 March 1771, "than the establishment of six

[21] *The Old Regime and the French Revolution* (English tr., 1955 by Stuart Gilbert), pp. 116-17.

[22] Quoted in Douglas Dakin, *Turgot and the ancien régime in France* (1939), p. 71.

sovereign councils. This alone should make the reign of Louis XV precious to the nation. Those who rise up against this benefit are sick people who complain of the doctor who restores their health" (M. XLVII, 402).

Most Frenchmen were complaining heartily about their doctor: Louis XV was compelled to enforce registration of the February edicts in a *lit de justice* of 13 April. In words that Voltaire might have written, the king praised the Maupeou reorganization for reducing the expense and increasing the certainty of justice. "You have heard my wishes . . ." he concluded dramatically. "I shall never change."[23]

For once in his long reign the king meant what he said. By 1772, more and more lawyers and magistrates consented to serve in the new courts, fewer and fewer libels circulated against the chancellor. Some minor scandals, greatly exaggerated by a hostile public opinion, marred the work of the new courts, but in general the reform appeared successful and promising. At last it seemed possible that the counterrevolution of the robe nobility might be stopped, and that a bureaucratic absolutism, rational and modern, might be imposed on the country.

This was Maupeou's aim, and Voltaire's as well. To achieve it, he followed up his *Histoire du parlement de Paris* with a series of short pamphlets, containing nothing new, and important only as propaganda efforts designed to undermine the popularity of the magistrates. This popularity, Voltaire argued, rested on ignorance of their history, misunderstanding of their function, and susceptibility to their rhetoric. "You seem to be afraid that tyranny might someday take the place of reasonable power," he told the magistrates' partisans, "but let us be even more afraid of anarchy, which is only a tumultuous tyranny" (M. XXVIII, 424). The English estates general, which represent the people of England, are called a "parliament," but the French bodies with a similar name are neither estates nor representatives of the people. French magistrates are exploiting a purely verbal resemblance and are turning the facts inside out: "How do you begin? By declaring that the benefits of the king are oppressions; by forbidding obedience to the most salutary orders" (M. XXVIII, 423). They are equally untrustworthy in their interpretation of the French constitution: it is the king and his ministers who know the common good, not the *parlements*, with their narrow *esprit de corps;* the king is sole legislator and has

[23] J. de Maupeou, *Le chancelier Maupeou* (1942), p. 121.

full authority to call the nobles together to advise the crown; the *parlements'* duty to register decrees is no more than a convenience; the courts are "respectable organs of the laws, created to follow and not to make them."[24]

Voltaire found it incomprehensible that the people should so stubbornly resist the very reforms it needed so desperately, but he expressed confidence that good sense would conquer prejudice. "It is raining remonstrances," he wrote hopefully, but, as it turned out, inaccurately. "People read the first, skim through the second, yawn at the third, and ignore the last" (M. XXVIII, 383). He predicted that Maupeou would win enduring popularity: "I watch the battle with tranquillity . . ." he wrote on 24 June 1771. "I am absolutely sure that the chancellor will carry off a complete victory and that people will love the victor" (M. XLVII, 460).

But Louis XV died on 10 May 1774, and his successor, who had enthusiastically applauded Maupeou's program when it was first proposed, promptly destroyed it with no less enthusiasm. Before the year was out, Maupeou had been dismissed, the old *parlements* had been recalled, and the robe nobility was again entrenched in its strategic position.

It has often been suggested that with Maupeou's great *coup d'état*, "the whole of the ancient Constitution of France had been wiped out."[25] This is to exaggerate Maupeou's break with the past and to accept the magistrates' version of the fundamental laws of France. Supplanting the *parlement* of Paris with six councils was indeed a frontal attack on an ancient institution, but it was largely a defensive measure, a revolution designed to stave off a revolution. In his letters patent of 1673, Louis XIV had almost completely silenced the *parlements;* in his reforms of 1771, his successor had gone further only because the magistrates had driven him further. "The *parlement* lost its liberty by its license," wrote Voltaire in his note-

[24] M. XXVIII, 413. Since Voltaire's pamphlets are nothing more than restatements of what he and others had been saying for years, I have summarized them in this brief paragraph. His contributions to the Maupeou debate are: *Lettre d'un jeune abbé, Réponse aux remontrances de la cour des aides, Fragment d'une lettre écrite de Genève, Avis important d'un gentilhomme à toute la noblesse du royaume, Sentiments des six conseils établis par le roi et de tous les bons citoyens, Les peuples aux parlements, L'Equivoque,* M. XXVIII, 383ff.

[25] Kingsley Martin, *French Liberal Thought,* p. 82.

book about the events of 1673.[26] He could have written the same words about the events of 1771.

As a proponent of constitutional absolutism for France, Voltaire rejected the widespread assertion that Maupeou's *coup d'état* established despotism in France. It led toward absolutism, but absolutism need not, indeed must not, be arbitrary. It is not only in his play *Les lois de Minos,* which the angry duchesse de Choiseul thought had been written to glorify Maupeou, that Voltaire distinguished between the legitimate and the illegitimate exercise of royal authority.[27] The distinction appears as early as 1731 in the *Histoire de Charles XII* and 1734 in the *Lettres philosophiques,* and as late as 1777, in his drama *Agathocle.* The tyrant of Syracuse, Agathocles, hands his throne to his son, who in turn renounces power and gives it to the people to whom it rightfully belongs. In a dramatic speech in the last scene, the new, just tyrant descends from the throne:

> Peuples, j'use un moment de mon autorité:
> Je règne . . . votre roi vous rend la liberté.
> (*Il descend du trone.*) (M. VII, 430)

> ["People, for one instant I shall wield my authority:
> I reign . . . your king gives you back your liberty.
> (*He descends from the throne.*)"]

We should not dismiss this drama of self-abnegation as the Utopian dream of a senile poet: Voltaire had never been an indiscriminate royalist. In his major histories, he had supported the king's cause in France, but he never hesitated to criticize those—like Louis XI, Richelieu, and even Louis XIV—who advanced that cause at the expense of the rule of law. Long before the abbé Sieyès became famous for asserting the claims of the third estate, Voltaire wrote that the third estate was the nation itself (M. XV, 5; XVI, 12), and praised Louis XII for the edict of 1499—"forever memorable"—which ordered people "always to follow the law, despite the orders contrary to law which importunity could wring from the monarch" (M. XV, 484-85).

Voltaire's constitutional absolutism is patently open to a serious objection: it fails to provide institutions to determine whether the king is observing the rule of law, and to resist him if he should dis-

[26] *Voltaire's Notebooks,* ed. Theodore Besterman (1952), I, 97.

[27] For Madame de Choiseul's remark on this play, see Desnoiresterres, *Voltaire et Genève,* pp. 401-02.

obey it. "Enlightened despotism," as I have repeatedly said, is not an apt phrase to characterize Voltaire's political program, even for France. But his royalism seems to leave him almost defenseless against despotism, enlightened or unenlightened.

It is improbable that Voltaire would have admitted the force of this objection. He was willing to use Maupeou, but his version of good government was not the same as the chancellor's.[28] Maupeou sought absolute centralized power for the sake of reform, unhampered by competing institutions or by criticism. Voltaire too wanted to employ royal power as the engine of reform in France, but as a radical man of letters, with a firm faith in education, he wanted to check and guide that power by the force of public opinion. That opinion was not embodied in formal institutions as it was in England, a country lucky enough to have a real parliament and rudimentary political parties. But public opinion could exercise influence, and as the enlightenment of the middle classes grew, that influence too would grow. Voltaire's persistent demand for free speech in all matters, including religion and politics, envisaged a rational administration, governing through fixed rules and cooperating with a free and informed public.

Moreover, France was faced with a condition, not a theory. The only available institutions to check the crown in 1771 were the *parlements* and the provincial estates, but Voltaire had no faith in either of them, and modern historians have come to accept his judgment. Not long after Maupeou was dismissed, the *parlements'* treatment of Turgot gave another, conclusive demonstration that they were bodies dedicated to the preservation of privilege rather than to the securing of the general good.

Anne-Robert-Jacques Turgot was a public servant of exceptional intelligence and independence. He was identified with the physiocrats, but he rejected their tenet that land was the only source of wealth; he was counted among the *philosophes,* but he did not share their hostility to organized religion; he was a Catholic, but he advocated toleration of Protestants. As a young intellectual he had

[28] I cannot emphasize enough that Voltaire's tactical alliances do not necessarily give reliable testimony concerning his permanent preferences. He was even willing on occasion to support the *parlements.* On 13 November (1765), in the midst of his mediating efforts in Geneva, he reread the Bull *Unigenitus* and wrote to d'Argental: "If I hold an even balance between the Citizens and the Council of Geneva, it is not thus with the quarrels between your *parlement* and your clergy. I declare myself flatly in favor of the *parlement,* but I make no promises for the future" (M. XLIV, 109).

delivered an epoch-making discourse on the theory of progress; as a mature administrator he had served brilliantly as intendant of Limoges. Voltaire was greatly taken with Turgot; he was delighted when Louis XVI took him into his cabinet, first as secretary of the navy, and then in August 1774, in the strategic post of controller general.

It was inevitable that a man as able and as disinterested as Turgot must make powerful enemies. "Woe to France," Voltaire wrote prophetically in December 1774, "if he were to leave his post!" (M. XLIX, 171).

Energetically, Turgot attacked the problems facing the grain trade and initiated some modest reforms of the tax system. Opposition soon arose; it was not only his ability, it was also his policies that endangered his future in the cabinet. His advocacy of toleration aroused the clerical party; his opinionated honesty annoyed the remaining supporters of Choiseul; and his economic and fiscal program offended the vested interests of the privileged classes. Turgot, wrote Voltaire to Condorcet on 26 April 1775, was the greatest man in France, whose policies were being obstructed by "abominable popular and parlementary superstitions" (M. XLIX, 286).

Superstitions were Voltaire's specialty, and he tried to dispel them in Turgot's behalf, not always adroitly. His *Diatribe à l'auteur des Ephémérides,* circulated in Paris in August 1775, was a vigorous defense of free trade. But it was also, to Turgot's intense embarrassment, a vehement attack on the French clergy (M. XXIX, 359-70). Far from disarming opposition to Turgot, Voltaire's pamphlet stimulated and united it.

Turgot was neither a politician nor a courtier. He was an administrator who knew that he was right and his opponents wrong. Early in 1776 he persuaded Louis XVI to support an expansion of his reform program. The celebrated Six Edicts brought free trade to Paris; suppressed archaic duties on food and unnecessary offices connected with the food trade; destroyed the systems of guilds that hampered the movement of skilled labor, investment, and the growth of technology; and abolished the road tax, the *corvée.*

Naturally, the *parlements* refused to register such revolutionary measures, and in March 1776 the king ordered them registered in a *lit de justice.* But the staying power of Louis XVI was even less impressive than that of his predecessor. Other ministers were indifferent or hostile; the *dévots* were outraged; the *parlements* were roused to resistance. Against all this opposition Turgot could do nothing without the king, but the king dismissed him in May and his successor rapidly reversed his policies. "Ah! *mon Dieu,* monsieur, what disastrous news!" Voltaire exclaimed on 15 May. "What will become of us?" (M. L, 17-18).

Voltaire's hopes for France had been aroused by Maupeou's ministry, but dashed by Maupeou's dismissal. Turgot had revived them, but French kings seemed unable to learn from experience. "The dismissal of this great man crushes me," Voltaire wrote to Du Pont in June (M. L, 43). "I have been in a perpetual depression since we were deprived of the protector of the people and my province," he complained to Condorcet as late as September 1776. "Since that fatal day, I have not followed anything, I have not requested anything of anybody, and I am waiting patiently for someone to cut our throats" (M. L, 81).

Voltaire was lamenting more than the fall of a man, he was lamenting the fall of the *thèse royale.* In the eighteenth century, Frenchmen could take one of three major political positions: the *thèse nobiliaire,* the *thèse royale,* or Rousseau's democratic theory. But Rousseau's position was Utopian and, in any event, had never been intended for France, and the *thèse nobiliaire* was no more than an ideology for special interests. What remained was the *thèse royale,* and all his life Voltaire had placed his trust in it. "Neither Louis XV nor Louis XVI," Franz Neumann wrote in his brilliant essay on Montesquieu, "could possibly arouse the hope that a monarch could and would have the courage to cut himself loose from all ties with the aristocracy, to wipe out all privileges, to create economic freedom, to put the finances on a sound basis, to establish a reorganization of the administration, clean out the drones, and throw himself into the arms of the masses of the people. . . . Turgot's short-lived administration proved the Utopian character of the *thèse royale.*"[29]

The beginning of this statement seems too harsh: for years the only realistic political position in France was Voltaire's. But its conclusion is just: with the dismissal of Turgot the *thèse royale* collapsed, and all positions became equally unrealistic. When Voltaire returned to Paris early in 1778, there was much prosperity and much gaiety, but some kind of revolution was now inevitable.

[29] "Montesquieu," *The Democratic and the Authoritarian State* (1957), p. 112.

The Voltairian Reformation of France[1]

by Gustave Lanson

If virtue resides only in social action, then the moral life is inconceivable without an involvement in politics, and the good man will be he who does good for everyone by working to improve society. And that is what Voltaire did, with unremitting fervor, during his last years at Ferney. Anxious for results, distrusting philosophical and theological systems, he did not apply himself, as Montesquieu and Rousseau had done, to the formulation of a political theory or to drawing up a plan for an ideal society. He did not refine on abstract principles. He was a realist to the highest degree, accepting France as she was with her social classes and her conditions so ripe for reform. He tried to discover what could be done immediately, what was within the realm of possibility, and limited his efforts to that end. He reviewed all phases of government and administration, criticizing them in the light of two or three moral principles of his own. He drew up a list of abuses and reforms, avoiding when possible any head-on collision with reality, the better to change it more effectively.

He regarded society as an established fact, a fact of life, and governments as the powers deriving from this fact. Governmental powers had, in the course of time, succeeded in disguising their rule by force as rule by law. But there is no law, save in the free consent of men (M. XXVII, 197), for men are by nature free and equal.

[1] *Dictionnaire philosophique Mélanges,* M. XXII-XXXII. Ed. Hertz, *Voltaire und die französische Strafrechtspflege,* 1887. Masmonteil, *La Législation criminelle dans l'œuvre de Voltaire.* E. Faguet, *Politique comparée de Montesquieu, de Voltaire et de Rousseau.* L. Robert, *Voltaire et l'intolérance religieuse.*

The following pages are the résumé of a more comprehensive study in which all the references will be given.

There is no divine right. Democracy is the most rational kind of government. But because it can survive only in small countries, and also because monarchy is the most ancient form of government in France, a concern for peace and order requires the Frenchman to be a royalist. A constitutional, representative régime is good in itself, but, for France, feudal anarchy had made a régime of absolute monarchy both useful and necessary. The force of royal power saved the people from petty tyrants. Yet one must require a respect for laws on the part of absolute royalty itself, and these laws must have as their object the preservation of freedom, the only "fundamental law of all nations" (M. XXVII, 388). But general freedom, in practice, consists of a number of individual freedoms which must be guaranteed to each citizen through laws.

Here is Voltaire's list of required freedoms: (1) *Freedom of person:* slavery is against nature. (2) *Freedom of speech and the press,* even in matters of politics and religion. This freedom is the safeguard and basis of all others. Character assassination, outrages against authority and laws, even seditious libel, must be punished. (3) *Civil liberty: habeas corpus* should be introduced. (4) *Freedom of conscience.* (5) *Security of private property:* if required for reasons of public utility, private property may be expropriated with compensation for the loss sustained. All citizens must have the right to possess private property, but there shall be no law enforcing an equal distribution of goods. (6) *Right to work* and to sell one's work or product to the highest bidder. Work is the property of those who lack property.

Property ownership confers an obligation to hold public office and the right to participate in public affairs. In the present state of France an enlightened bourgeoisie governs both the weak and powerful and controls public opinion. Finally, there is no other guarantee for liberty and freedom than the will of the governed. One is free when one so wills it, and only to the extent that one desires freedom. There is little need to recall that Voltaire hated war, but he doubted that it would soon disappear from the earth. Armies were therefore a necessity. The best sort would be a militia. A professional and permanent army is constantly tempted to embark on external conquests, or else it poses a threat to the people's freedom. Since it is impossible at the present time to do without a military establishment, we must limit its size and strength in accordance with the needs of self-defense. It is folly for a nation to ruin itself under the pretext of self-preservation. With fifty thousand married soldiers, well paid, to be retired at half pay at age

50, France would have all the army she needed and have it with a minimum of social disruption or inconvenience.

Patriotism in the eighteenth century had nothing to do with war and the military. Voltaire was patriotic because, like Montesquieu and Rousseau, he was interested in the public weal. In the English manner, he linked his country, his *patrie,* to the concepts of liberty and property, and it seemed to him that only those who possessed private property could really claim a native country. He felt that such people were bound by common interests and would intervene in one way or another in the preservation and development of those common interests. He believed that in large nations millions of people still had no *patrie,* no country they could call their own.

In theory he would make education a function of the state, but in practice he accepted freedom, that is, the University and the religious schools and congregations brought under state control. He did not think it either possible or desirable that the masses, the common people, should be educated.[2] Otherwise, who would perform the disagreeable and difficult chores that must be done? But his concept of the masses, *le peuple,* was restricted to the lowest class of manual laborers. He desired through education to enlarge the middle class. He wanted manufacturers, artisans, masons, carpenters, blacksmiths, and farmers to become educated and enlightened. He wanted them to look beyond their trade or profession and acquire a knowledge of public interests. Voltaire's school would thus be essentially a citizens' school.

Voltaire did not seek separation of Church and State. His ideal was the English system. In France *Catholicism* would be *the state religion,* but the Church would be subordinate to civil authority and respectful of civil law. There would be an end to Roman jurisdiction and the abolition of all taxes paid to the Roman chancellery. Church property would be subject to taxation just like the property of every other citizen. The state would supervise these funds and intervene in their distribution to ensure all priests an adequate income. In this sense Voltaire was moving toward the idea of a clergy paid by the state, thereby permitting the state to limit the number of priests and to dispose, as it saw fit, of excess ecclesiastical profits.

Voltaire advocated civil marriages; state control over all rites, catechisms, and educational and devotional books; and state super-

[2] He meant by education what we would call the secondary level, the one enabling a pupil to read "the best chapters of *The Spirit of Laws.*" He opened an elementary school at Ferney.

vision of the pulpit. Civil authority would not intervene in matters of dogma, but it must ensure respect for public order, laws, and morality. Priests would retain the right to teach faith and morals and the practice of charity. Voltaire would discontinue burial within a church edifice, and he would reduce the number of religious feasts observed as public holidays. He would have religious communities supervised and permit the renunciation of monastic vows at the age of twenty-five. He favored a progressive reduction in numbers leading to the eventual abolition of monasteries, convents, and religious communities. He would transfer their wealth to charitable institutions.

He wanted freedom of conscience but not an equality of religions. Voltaire said nothing about freethinkers and atheists. Their beliefs he regarded as individual matters of no concern to the state. But churches, other than the Roman Catholic, would not be officially recognized. *Tolerance and test;* it was the English example Voltaire wanted France to follow. For Protestants, Voltaire demanded freedom for private worship, recognition of the validity of their marriages, the right of Protestant children to inherit family property, freedom from any sort of physical harassment, and the right to engage in business or to practice any profession. To the Jews, whom he despised, he offered personal safety and a status as resident foreigners, and he invited them to rid themselves of their uncouth manners and become a cultivated people.

Instead of an ambitious policy of conquest and military glory, Voltaire preferred a peaceful, economy-minded government. He wanted, not great cabinet ministers, but good administrators. The government should devote itself, above all, to promoting conditions favorable for work and population growth. He found that, unfortunately, most governmental regulations impeded work and caused a decline in population. The financial system of France was detestable. Taxation should be proportional without restriction or regard for social privilege. The exclusive system of the physiocrats was as absurd as tax exemption for the clergy and nobility. Taxes should bear most heavily on the wealthy. It is despicable to take from a wage earner part of the bread he earns.

The farm system of taxation was a bad one. Direct taxes would be less burdensome on the treasury and less vexatious and ruinous for the people. Changing the values of money, abolishing *rentes* [interest from stocks and bonds], creating offices, lotteries, and salt taxes, and collecting internal customs—all these were just so many abusive or detestable means of taking money from the citizenry.

Free trade for wheat, at least within the country, was essential. Taxes must be levied where the money is. Tax receipts must be increased by lowering the tax rate. Taxes must be collected with the least possible expense. The tax structure must be organized in such a way as to promote, rather than paralyze, the nation's economic activity. Feudal taxes, forced labor, and tithes must also be abolished.

As for agriculture, commerce, and industry, everything could be summed up in one word: freedom—that is, freedom from hindrances of all sorts, from onerous or tyrannical regulations, from the *jurandes* and *maîtrises* [the corporation of craftsmen, which restricted the liberty of industry], from the requirement to sell only at the market, and from the prohibitive taxes on wine, etc. Voltaire's liberal policies nevertheless allowed for protection against foreign competition, but in such a way that wheat, that is, bread, should remain inexpensive. He recommended the establishment of standard weights and measures.

Voltaire was thinking primarily of commerce and agriculture as practiced by the large property owner and the wealthy businessman. He was hardly aware of industrial problems although he had created factories himself and was acquainted with the unhappy plight of the Lyonnese weavers. So far as the worker's interests were concerned, Voltaire limited his demands to advocating the worker's right to sell his service or his product to the highest bidder and to earn a salary permitting him to live and to bring up his family. To enable the worker to earn more, he proposed merely an increase in the number of work days. And yet he believed that factory work was stultifying and degrading. His whole economy was basically tied to a theory of affluence, *la théorie du luxe*. To spend one's income was a social obligation. The wealthy man, both in his needs and in his pleasures, provides a livelihood for the poor man. His expenditures stimulate business, industry, and agriculture. All his delights and pleasures trickle down into the populace in the form of wages and salaries and thereby promote general prosperity.

Prosperous and well-run nations can afford to pay heavy taxes, but taxes are not meant to be squandered by the court and used to nourish parasites. Taxation is first of all a guarantee, serving to establish order and security. It must also be a cooperative venture intended to subsidize enterprises of public utility. Money would be better employed for water and markets in the cities, for canals and highways across the country, than for waging wars. Productive expenditures are those that protect public health and facilitate business and agricultural activity.

Of the postal system Voltaire asked only for freedom from censorship, a respect for the secrecy of private correspondence. In this matter there was no requirement more urgent. In welfare matters, Voltaire regarded public assistance as a duty of the state. He wanted to end public begging. He urged hospital reforms, the creation of new hospitals, particularly maternity hospitals, foundling homes, and homes for the aged and infirm workers. To provide for these necessary establishments, one must use "the poor tax" levied on theatrical entertainment, and available funds of the clergy and monasteries.

Lastly, the administration of justice needed a thorough reorganization. The worst abuses of all were in the judiciary. Voltaire was to applaud the abolition of the *Parlements,* for he hoped this would result in two capital reforms he had long advocated: the termination of the right to acquire judicial office by purchasing it, and the separation of judicial powers from political powers. He also desired a reduction in legal costs for litigants and fewer delays in the administration of justice. He wanted a single body of laws, a civil code and a penal code, that would put an end to contradictory and arbitrary judgments in legal decisions.

Into civil law he would introduce divorce. But for criminal law Voltaire demanded sweeping reforms. Criminal justice was atrocious, absurd, blind, and ridden with theological ideas. It struck hit or miss. While severe on little people and lesser crimes, it was lenient with those committing great crimes, with persons who happened to be powerful and influential. One should punish only those felonies that directly affect men and harm the social order. Offenses against God, sacrilege, sorcery, suicide, heresy, and sodomy are not within the province of the judiciary. One must carefully define cases of legal repression, distinguish misdemeanors from more serious offenses, make the punishment fit the crime, and not abuse the use of sentences to the galleys or, above all, the death sentence. One must remove from the death sentence the refinements of cruelty which men have added to it. Punishment must be a purely personal matter, not be extended to an innocent family by the confiscation of its property, or otherwise.

Legal procedures continued to disregard the rights of the individual. An accused man must not be treated as guilty. Innocent people must not be thrown in jail frivolously only to be released after many long months, ruined, demoralized, and with no indemnity whatsoever. Voltaire wanted the abolition of *monitoires* [secret ecclesiastical informers]. Such testimony appealed only to witnesses for the prosecution and encouraged secret denunciations. He advocated the abolition of torture and secret trials. Witnesses must not be intimidated or disregarded. The accused must be allowed to confront his accusers. He is entitled to legal assistance in both criminal and civil cases. One must abandon the barbarous and puerile system of partial proofs—half-truths and quarter-truths. There must be an end to this accumulation of uncertainties twisted into a legal certitude. Motives for arrest must be clearly established, whether in criminal or civil cases.

And so we have given a very matter-of-fact summary of the reforms Voltaire sought over a twenty-year period. He did so with an indefatigable zeal, alternately sarcastic and indignant, trying to win over to his views human reason and public conscience. Their collective effect is not that of a fine philosophical treatise developed in the abstract to the glory of the human intellect. It was a series of corrections, of repairs to the old social structure, not to be judged apart from the realities on which they had an immediate bearing. Voltaire asked himself what modifications and retouches were demanded in every phase of government and administration in the name of liberty, equality, and humanity, those principles which, in his eyes, expressed the social conscience and rational views of his age.

We are tempted today to underestimate and to belittle the importance of this criticism because it was not organized into a system, and because the majority of the reforms called for have either now long since been realized or else have become outdated and irrelevant through the evolution of our institutions and our society. But his contemporaries were grateful to Voltaire for his realistic and precise analyses indicating what improvements were possible of attainment in all parts of the body politic.

And if we will just think of it for a while, if we pause to visualize the France of Louis XV with all its many abuses and shortcomings: the capricious despotism of its government, the self-centered and extravagant court, the powerful clergy and judiciary, more concerned with their own special privileges than with the welfare of all, the financial disorder and its oppressive fiscal system, the poverty of the parish priest, the chaotic conditions of the laws, the conflict and confusion between various authorities and their jurisdictions, the intolerance that condemned Protestants to concubinage or hypocrisy and consigned their pastors to the galleys, the multitude of rules and privileges that were just so many sources of vexation and misery for the masses—if we apply to those conditions the reforms

Voltaire advocated, and if, into this France of the Old Régime, a France Catholic and monarchical, if we introduce tolerance, freedom of the press, proportional taxation, a uniform code of laws, reforms in criminal procedure, a submissive and salaried clergy, a program of public assistance, liberal and peaceful principles of government and of honest, conscientious administration, one truly concerned with the public interest—then, and only then, can we realize the extent of the transformation that Voltaire's criticism was bringing about. Only then do we realize how wide of the mark it is to regard Voltaire's work as negative and timid. His criticism was in process of producing a new and different France, a France disengaging herself from an old feudal and monarchical chaos that was Roman and ecclesiastical, anarchical and tyrannical. It was a new France that was becoming, under the very Christian Bourbon king, somewhat like the France that emerged during the peaceful moments of the Consulate or the Second Empire. More precisely, the Voltairian reform, in its main outline—except for the two Chambers [the Chamber of Deputies and the Senate] was the design for the bourgeois government of Louis-Philippe [1830-1848]. It is the France that would have come into being had Turgot been able to stay in power for twenty years and been permitted to do what he wanted. Broadly speaking, Voltaire was the journalist and propagandist for the work of which Turgot was the statesman.

We would also be wrong about Voltaire's spirit or intentions if we believed that they did not go beyond the reforms he championed. He was not a revolutionary or a visionary. He was an opportunist and a realist. He indicated what could be accomplished immediately, under the pressure of public opinion. Having achieved a certain limited objective, he did not give up asking for something else. He did not claim to be a republican. He did not call for a constitution on the English model. He did not expressly ask for the direct participation of property owners and industrialists in the management of public affairs. He did not ask for the right for Protestants to hold public office or be given the freedom of public worship. He did not demand that all professors be nominated by the state. But these were matters he regarded as altogether reasonable. He contented himself with declaring the right of the state to supervise religious communities. He did not demand their immediate dissolution, though he desired and hoped for it.

Voltaire was, beyond any doubt, a conservative. But he was conservative in the manner of any true liberal. He did not want a violent upheaval. He did not try to abolish social classes or the unequal distribution of wealth. He put France into the hands of the enlightened bourgeoisie, whose limits he would expand to include greater numbers of common people through the process of education. But his program, precisely because it was a practical one, contained nothing absolute or definitive. He maintained the constant attitude of seeking certain limited and realizable reforms, toward which he bent every effort, and then anticipating additional improvements made possible by having accomplished his first objectives. And thus it would continue to be so long as we find evil in the world and, with the aid of human reason, can conceive of something better. Thus it would always be so long as humanity and justice are, in one place or another, wounded and suffering, and so long as society remains imperfect and men unhappy.

Voltaire's Religion

by René Pomeau

Voltaire's religion reflects the concurrence of a character and an age. It is impossible to impute his deism or theism to frivolity. It was not a huckster's doctrine, borrowed from Chaulieu and the English, and propagated out of mischievousness to flout the priesthood. In such a view Voltaire's passion—that relentless thrust of a lifetime which turns into a mania—becomes incomprehensible. In so immense a production, almost every page of which is occasional, one can ignore what is said once, in passing. What counts is what Voltaire repeated throughout his entire life. What counts is the ideas to which he clung tenaciously, his obsessions. Now, from one end of his long life to the other, Voltaire was ardently and aggressively a deist. For some sixty years he kept seeking historical and philosophical justifications. A Fontenelle, an Anatole France were perhaps characterized by frivolity—surface and, as it were, inadvertent rationalists. As for him, he never stopped fighting for and against, for so-called natural religion and against Christianity.

We must search for Voltaire's secret in depth, in that soul of his which was so out of the ordinary and difficult to plumb. Few writers have expressed themselves so copiously. There is perhaps no other figure whose biography is so richly detailed. Yet, for all that, Voltaire eludes us. We have at our disposal vast inventories on the man, but we do not know him. Extroverted, obstreperous, blabbermouthed though he was, his unceasing agitation conceals his true self. His notebooks contain not a single word about his intimate feelings. He who wrote about everything wrote almost nothing about himself. Can it be that he is invincibly averse to looking into the depths of his soul? He did, nevertheless, give himself away somewhat on the day when he let slip the words: "Où fuir loin de moi-

"Voltaire's Religion." From *La Religion de Voltaire,* by René Pomeau (Paris, Librairie A.-G. Nizet). Translated from the French and reprinted by permission of Librairie A.-G. Nizet. The pages reproduced constitute the chapter originally entitled "Conclusions."

même?" ["Where can I flee far away from myself?"] But what does this brilliant, light veneer cover over? Some secret inhibition? We have seen him experience and express mystical emotions, not just once or during a temporary crisis. But when he is seventeen, the rumor spreads, among those who know him, that he is going to become a Jesuit. Ten years later he cries out to God: "Je ne suis pas chrétien, mais c'est pour t'aimer mieux!" ["I am not a Christian, but it is so that I may love Thee better!"] In the *Henriade* of 1730 he adds a hymn to the glory of the Eternal Geometer. On a bitter-cold night he is enraptured by the divine spectacle of the starry universe. At Ferney he worships the sun, image of the Supreme Being; he repeatedly hymns the cosmos; he dies "adoring God." These facts and these texts testify to Voltaire's religious propensity; but they add up to very little in so long and so busy a life and in an immense output, compared with countless negations. Did he deliberately stifle mystical tendencies which he feared beneath fiercely negative sarcasms? This hypothesis would make it possible to explain Voltaire's irreligious religion: very critical, yet still retaining a few positive elements, his deism may have rendered innocuous an inhibited mysticism, barely allowing it an occasional vent. In such a light the development of his life takes on a meaning.

In his youth Voltaire begins by combatting the double obsession of the terror-inspiring God and the cruel priest. As far back as one can go, the Voltairean complex is already fully developed: a rather morbid picture of men's sufferings would have it that those responsible for them are the priests serving a blood-thirsty God. What traumatic experience had torn little Arouet apart, for him to employ his talents at the very outset in composing an *Œdipe,* an *Henriade*? All we know is that he did not find in the Jesuits' engaging religion a refuge against the cruel God, perhaps because, under Father Le Tellier's administration, the champions of Molinism had abandoned their erstwhile insinuative approach and become persecutors. The godson of Abbé de Châteauneuf preferred to give himself over to free-thinking frivolity; he exorcised the tyrant God by means of Chaulieu's facile deism. But Voltaire remained aggressive in his writings and in his speech. He was already an anti-Christian soldier; already he saw in the Christian religion only his two enemies, a sanguinary God and priest. It is true to say that, from the very beginning, Voltaire "grounds his peace of mind (or that which he would like to have) in his denial of the faith,"[1] provided we specify

[1] André Rousseaux, "Un philosophe impertinent," in *Les Lettres françaises* (2 December 1944).

that the object of this denial is the terror-inspiring God he identifies with the God of the Christians.

Suddenly the revelation of English philosophy lends substance to the Divinity who represents the antithesis of the Christian God, that clement and until then rather vague God of the merry abbés of the Temple. Henceforth Voltaire knows that his God is the God of Locke, of Clarke, and of Newton, the God attested and demonstrated by the order of the cosmos, who partakes of the cold majesty of outer space. The metaphysical, scientific, and historical labors of Cirey consolidate this acquired knowledge. The obsession of a pettily vindictive God is shunted aside; God is rendered remote by his very sublimity, and life is gay, whatever Pascal may say about it. All that remains is to concentrate on the fraudulent and persecuting priests: they are told off in *Mahomet*. But the end of the Cirey period reveals the permanence of Voltaire's obsessions. He doubts free will; he feels dominated by a superior power; he feels futile and frail; his imagination sees crawling on the surface of our little pile of mud a denigrated humanity composed of insect men. He discovers the style of the philosophic tale at the same time that he is arguing the problem of evil, and again the image of the terror-inspiring God appears in clear outline.

The pessimistic crisis, aggravated by the death of Madame du Châtelet, prolonged by the Prussian tribulations, quickened anew by the Lisbon disaster, divides Voltaire's life into two parts. But he reacts against pessimism, as he had fought the tyrant God, without being able completely to liquidate this haunting idea either. Up to the moment of his death Voltaire is tormented by the insoluble problem of evil. His recourse is to escape pessimism through action. It is at the height of the crisis that he attempts to launch the campaign against *l'infâme*. He expects Frederick II to destroy Christianity and to impose on Europe a "pure" religion, that deism which Voltaire has framed for his personal use. The King of Prussia has not the slightest interest in these fine schemes. So Voltaire turns to the "enlightened" pastors of Geneva, but these "faint-hearted Socinians" slip away. A moderate and reasonable temperament would have given up. Prudence dictated that the old man enjoy his glory in peace and quiet, *by cultivating his garden*. But once again the obscure forces which possess him plunge him into battle. The wear and tear of age have weakened the other inclinations of his soul, but the irreligious passion has gathered strength with the passing of the years. Since the King of Prussia and the Genevan clergy have failed him, the Patriarch will himself be the apostle of modern times, the successor of Luther and Calvin. Solidly entrenched in his ambush at Ferney, he leads the attack, armed with his pen. He pounces upon the enemy with all his might: he is going to *crush* it beneath arguments, sarcasms, insults, lies. This paradoxical champion of tolerance abandons himself to the fanaticism of a savage hatred. Passionate but practical, he foresees the replacement of the old-time religion. He has railed so profusely against the imposture of the founders of religions that he imitates it. We must, he says, preach to the masses that the Eternal Geometer "rewards and punishes." Voltaire is not at all certain that the Being of beings concerns Himself with punishing and rewarding creatures as insignificant as man. No matter, the interests of society and morality demand this pretense: *"fingo, fingo."* But Voltaire is at least sure that the Supreme Being exists. He adores Him in His handiwork, the world: "I believe, I believe in Thee"; and when the free-thinkers of the younger generation seek to bring him into their atheistic fold, he balks. Fully half of his last quiverful of arrows is aimed at the "fourth impostor." The mystical need which remains buried in the inmost recesses of his being holds fast to the naked affirmation that God exists.

It is therefore unfair to accuse Voltaire of substituting mind for soul.[2] The arguments and behavior of this vehement polemicist are motivated by deep-lying forces which he embellishes with his consummate intellectual charm. He made it his calling to crush the Christian religion; he found, not his peace of mind, but his well-being in the religious struggle; he rode to his salvation on the back of *l'infâme.*

This negation, required by his most intimate being, was in harmony with the option of a society which actively preferred earth to heaven. All those who, in Paris, London, Amsterdam, even Geneva, want to live for enjoyment, pursue wealth. In all those localities business prosperity is bound up with the appetites of flesh and spirit. Voltaire's irreligious propaganda is not the only one which provides assurance of a good conscience for those who neglect to merit heaven by denying themselves earthly pleasures. But by reason of its bulk and its expressive force it is the most persuasive. To be sure, its brutalities are not always approved. Madame du Deffand and the Choiseul coterie censure excesses that are shocking to good form. But all these well-bred persons live, and when the opportunity offers, the Duke governs, as if

[2] André Rousseaux, *loc. cit.*

Voltaire were right. Voltaire is the natural ally of enlightened despotism practised by princes and ministers who have chosen, or at least maintain they have chosen, to ensure the temporal happiness of their people, and no longer their eternal felicity. The attempts at an "enlightened" policy sketchily initiated in France by Madame de Pompadour and Choiseul, the philosophical and military régime of Frederick II, the enlightenment propaganda disseminated by Catherine of Russia, find in Voltaire a guarantee and a support.

On the level of ideas, those which the *philosophe*'s temperament appropriated were the key ideas of the century. His first negations took the form of the free thought in vogue under the Regency. Then he came up against the philosophies of Leibniz, Locke, and Clarke, which issued from a classical rationalism that was Christian only by compromise. Even Malebranche and Fénelon yield to the trend which is drawing the thought of the great century toward deism: by a dialectical necessity the mechanistic representation of the cosmos eliminates the supernatural, and the existing religion therefore seems encumbered with superstitions. When Voltaire appears on the scene, the war against the supernatural has already been declared. Before him the century has begun to lose the feeling of God's immediate presence. Voltaire, who means to substitute for the Christian Divinity a God too pure to have anything human about Him, moves to the forefront of this current of thought. He has sworn to destroy faith in the God of the Incarnation. So it is not accurate to assert that he attacks only the vulnerable positions on the periphery of Christianity after isolating them from the whole.[3] He doubtless does practise this tactic when he dins into our ears the harlotries of Oholah and Oholibah, and the incestuous affairs of Alexander VI. But when he denies that the Supreme Being kept providential watch over the destinies of the Jews and the Church, when he would have it that Jesus was a man and only a man, he attacks the very citadel of Christianity. Details aside, it is his denial of the Incarnation which sets him against the Christian religion. All his hatred of Christianity is centered upon this negation, in which he persists on his death-bed, when to the question posed by the curate of Saint-Sulpice on the divinity of Christ he replies: "Let me die in peace." But all around him the religious crisis of the eighteenth century was a crisis focused on

[3] Léonce de Grandmaison, "La religion et l'irréligion de Voltaire, en marge d'ouvrages récents," *Etudes,* CLXXXVI (5 January 1926), 25.

the Incarnation. In Protestant Europe the Socinians and Neo-Arians, in France the clerics who had more or less secretly shifted to deism, denied with all possible respect that Jesus had possessed a divine nature. The former welcomed Voltaire; and do what he might, there are some, as we know, whom he never succeeded in scandalizing.

However, despite his general agreement with his time, and despite the insinuative pliancy with which he accommodates himself to ideas very different from his own, certain trends of the century proved alien or repugnant to him. He paid the penalty of great men who outlive their generation. Those who resisted his influence became more and more numerous after 1770. His coquettish stratagems failed to relieve the conflict which opposed him to the atheistic group. As is well known, the *Système de la nature* created a following; that following has still not forgiven the Patriarch his deism.[4] Whether one deplores it or not, Voltaire originated no form of modern atheism, neither the indifferent nor the vehement variety. Voltaire felt an even greater aversion to Rousseau's sentimentalism. When, after 1730, he realized that the public was asking for sentiment, he had perfected in *Zaïre* the formula for tearful tragedy. But when he saw that that Rousseau fellow, after riddling Christianity with Voltairean gibes, confessed his love for this religion of his childhood, Voltaire lost patience: Jean-Jacques must be a "malicious madman." Voltaire is alien to the sentimental logic of all those who will say, after Rousseau, that one must be a Christian because Christianity stirs the emotions.

When he dies, his gospel, which he called "today's Gospel," has become yesterday's, while Diderot and Rousseau are preparing the future. Vistas are opening up in the direction of atheism or of a religion of the heart, not of Voltairean deism. Is Voltaire, then, as a man of his century, for that very reason a prisoner of the past? It is a fact that the deistic attempt of the theophilanthropists failed, for reasons that are obvious enough. Not only was Voltaire, the apostle of the new faith, too fond of buffoonery for his most determined admirers to take him quite seriously, but his inhibitions had reduced this "pure" religion to less than a bare sufficiency. Granted that God exists and that one must practise virtue; what then? The ceremonies of the artless theophilanthropists are a crashing bore, or a farce. Being purely allegorical, this cult cannot be

[4] The book *Paul Thiry d'Holbach et la philosophie scientifique au XVIII*[e] *siècle* (Paris, 1943) by Pierre Naville, who makes the Baron a precursor of historical materialism, is frankly hostile to Voltaire.

saved even by the mystical efficacy of its rites. Finally, Voltaire, like the audacious reformers of the Revolution, did not know how durable religions are. The god outlives the city. After the furious assaults of an entire century, after the tidal wave which swept away a throne and a social order, the Church is still standing at the dawn of the new century. The failure of Voltairean deism is a definitively established fact of history, confirmed by the later failures of an Isambart who, in 1829, invited the theists to reorganize themselves into a Church (a police investigation put an end to that undertaking); of an Henri Carle, who during the Second Empire founded the periodical *Alliance religieuse universelle* and polemicized for a few years against Dupanloup and the materialists; of a Décembre, whose "Philanthropic Commission" and journal managed a meager existence from 1882 to 1888; of a Camerlynck, who contented himself with publishing a bulky theistic treatise in 1900.[5] The lay spiritualism of Jules Simon, author of a noble and frigid work on *La Religion naturelle,* likewise failed of its effect. It is not in these otiose repetitions that the spirit of Voltaire lives on.

It does, nonetheless, live on. The wounds inflicted by Voltaire are still bleeding. He continues to be detested by some to an extent that is rare for so old a writer.[6] The smile of the dilettante Renan allows for compromises, but not Voltaire's grin. His enemies will not forgive him for having known God and for having so fiercely vilified the Christian religion. Poor Father Adam, Reverend Gal-Pomaret, estimable Abbé Gaultier, and bizarre Abbé Marthe had judged correctly. There is something about Voltaire that tempts proselyters. It is not surprising that even today there are critics who try their luck at it. But the old man resists; his case is hopeless. So others prefer to get rid of him by disqualifying him: he has no sense of mystery, they say, he does not understand religion at all. But this is not true either. The old fox had made arrangements to have his tomb at Ferney half inside and half outside the church. It is no longer possible either to admit him completely into the sanctuary or to eject him from it altogether. This Voltaire fellow remains a very awkward corpse for the guardians of the temple.

An anti-Christian, but not without a sense of the divine, Voltaire ushered in a form of religiousness which does not adhere to

[5] Albert Mathiez, *La Théophilanthropie et le culte décadaire (1796-1801): essai sur l'histoire religieuse de la Révolution* (Paris, 1903), pp. 710ff.

[6] See, for example, the pamphlet by Father Albert Condamin, *Le "grand homme" de M. Albert Bayet, Voltaire* (Paris, 1936).

established faiths, even when it does not combat them. After him the religion of some persons became a marginal one, an individual state of mind, manifested, not by the practice of a cult, but through literary expression. That is how it was with Rousseau, and Lamartine, and Vigny, and Hugo, and Lamennais, who sought his way outside the communion of the faithful, and even Péguy, who died before he could put himself right with those whom his popular anticlericalism continued to call "the curates."

No indeed, all is not dead in what Voltaire wrote. Over the ashes of yesterday's gospel plays the flame of the eternal gospel. Voltaire has not finished inciting readers to thought and action. The life which sparkles in the slightest phrase of his production is infectious. He has no equal in bestirring the sluggish. He is the best tonic one can find in our tradition to remedy a decline of French vitality. He is as eternal as his enemies, the fools and the tyrants.

> "Nous savons qu'il naîtra, dans le lointain des âges,
> Des dominateurs durs, escortés de faux sages . . ." [7]
>
> ["We know that in the far-off future harsh rulers will arise, escorted by false sages . . ."]

announced Vigny, that reader of Voltaire. The rulers, who have come with their escort of theologians and inquisitors, continue to find in Voltaire a formidable adversary. It was not the fashion of a day that he was initiating when he said that "freedom [i.e., free will—Transl.] in man is spiritual health" (M. IX, 391) and that freedom of thought and expression is the law of civilized societies. Has the lesson lost its vital pertinence in the twentieth century?

Even in the churches Voltaire has not ceased to exert an influence. Father Lacordaire has been credited with the following astonishing statement: "God, by a diabolical (sic!) ruse, sent Voltaire to combat His Church for the purpose of regenerating it." [8] This spokesman for liberal Catholicism doubtless meant that the Church, once it had abandoned its untenable outposts, had established itself solidly in its main positions. Without attempting here to weigh precisely the importance of this influence by reaction, one may admit, with Albert Monod, that the crisis of the eighteenth

[7] Alfred de Vigny, *Les Destinées,* ed. Edmond Estève (Paris, 1942), p. 119.

[8] Quoted without a source reference by Félix-Titus Courtat in *Défense de Voltaire contre ses amis et contre ses ennemis* (Paris, 1872), p. vi.

century profoundly transformed religious life. In order to reply to the attacks of Voltaire and the *philosophes,* it would seem that the defenders of the Church sought their inspiration chiefly in the Christian humanistic tradition. This accounts for the strengthening of the old party of those who refuse to oppose heaven to earth; and it may be that there are not many individuals left today who would support that conception of religion which led Bossuet to affirm: "A Christian is never alive on earth, because he is always practising mortification here, and mortification is a trial, an apprenticeship, a beginning of death."[9] In the disputes over China, did not the Society of Jesus win on appeal the trial which opposed it to Monsieur de Meaux? But it won with the support of Voltaire. It is the *philosophe*'s propaganda which spread abroad the idea that every religion contains something valid. To cite but one or two instances, Durkheim was in the tradition of the *Philosophie de l'histoire* when he revealed that there was a sort of eternal truth running through the various faiths; the noblest elements of the spirit of Voltaire also permeate certain of Alain's *Propos sur la religion.*[10] It is Voltaire who dissuaded men from believing that any one sect had a monopoly on truth. Today the sense of the universal and the mockery of all that is petty and limited remain living values in his works: "All of you who are listening to me, remember that you are men before being citizens of a certain city, members of a certain society, believers in a certain religion. The time has come to enlarge the sphere of our ideas, and to be citizens of the world. . . . We are all of the same religion without realizing it" (*Sermon de J. Rossette,* M. XXVI, 583). That Voltaire still has something to say to us Jean Guéhenno, who knew it, was able to confirm when he dropped in on a class of young Africans engaged in reading the *Prière à Dieu:* "May all men remember that they are brothers . . ."[11]

Voltaire, old friend, if we may address you after writing so many pages about you, we must begin by apologizing: how can one be laconic in speaking of you who were so interminably brief? What was it that you had to say at such great length? You were malicious, jealous, mendacious; but when you had before you a man, your fellow-human, you felt him to be your brother. "Quiconque avec

[9] Jacques Bénigne Bossuet, "Oraison funèbre de Marie-Thérèse d'Autriche," in *Œuvres complètes,* ed. Abbé Guillaume (Bar-le-Duc, 1877), VII, 295.

[10] Paris, 1951, pp. 171-72, 191.

[11] Jean Guéhenno, "Tournée africaine: Les noirs à l'école," *Le Figaro littéraire* (10 May 1952).

[toi s'entretenait semblait] disposer de [ton] âme" (M. II, 538). ["Whoever conversed with you seemed to have your soul at his disposal."] You dreamed of a fraternal humanity, and you were right to do so. For after all . . . But Pangloss has held forth long enough. If the Being of beings has somewhere preserved the flame of your spirit, you are murmuring: "That is well said, but may all men who crawl about on this globe or globule where I once stirred things up a bit remember that they are brothers."

Voltaire's Wisdom

by Raymond Naves

The Unity of His Thought

Fréron initiated a critical method of attacking Voltaire which has enjoyed great success among his adversaries up to our own time: it involves making him contradict himself by means of carefully chosen passages taken out of context. This is an easy thing to do with a production which, as we have seen, is strictly dependent on circumstances. Serious intellectuals have often repeated this reproach of inconsistency, being persuaded of its merit by a sort of tradition, and trusting to a superficial reading. Chateaubriand said: "Voltaire eternally upheld the pros and the cons." Nisard thought he was separating the wheat from the tares by distinguishing in the *philosophe* a praiseworthy thought and evil, indeed almost diabolical, intentions. Faguet made famous his "chaos of clear ideas," excelling in presenting Voltaire's politics and morality as "disjointed" congeries.

This impression, which can be justified if one piles up references without checking them historically, disappears as soon as one restores the man behind the work. First of all, there is in Voltaire's thought a psychological unity: everywhere we see the same spirit, impatient, prying, hostile to posturing and mystery, taking hold of all subjects with an equal craving for clarity; and this kind of ardor already forms a philosophy: it gives priority to and puts its trust in freedom of the mind.

But, as we have just come to understand, his thought also possesses a critical unity: the attack on absolutes and certainties, the condemnation of all extremes and all forms of fanaticism, in the name of humanity, but also in the name of logic and science, in the name of nature, since it does not become a limited, ignorant, and mortal creature to want to impose his conclusions by conferring upon them a value that brooks no question. In every sphere Voltaire pursues this educative mission with an impressive constancy. The *Questions sur l'Encyclopédie,* forty-five years after the *Lettres anglaises,* resound with the same blows aimed at the same adversaries. Besides, those who reproach him with retractions generally do not fail to hurl another, rather contradictory reproach at him: "Never has anyone repeated himself so frequently"—which would at least be proof of continuity.

Was there, however, an evolution on certain points of detail? To tell the truth, the real changes (i.e., those that cannot be eliminated by shifts in viewpoint) are few in number. In literature Voltaire moved slowly toward a broader, more relaxed taste, admitting of more fantasy and attempting innovations in the use of spectacle; but this result is potentially present and, as it were, under consideration in his earliest works. Philosophically, he slides toward determinism, above all he redoubles his attacks on Providence, which he had at first treated with an indulgent smile; but this intensification of his pessimism merely expresses his repeated disillusionments, it is a fleeting reflection of life rather than a transformation of his thought which, as early as 1730, in the *Remarques sur Pascal,* conceived the equilibrium to which it will return after each oscillation of his mood. The only important evolution is that which concerns his historical works. Here the writer explicitly spoke of repentance, and acknowledged that he was late in achieving awareness of his object, the study of civilization, and not of a few great men; but here, too, it is a matter of his blossoming forth rather than of his contradicting himself, and in any case the lucidity of this evolution can only accentuate the spiritual unity of his effort in the direction of greater human richness.

The psychological and critical unity of Voltaire's thought is therefore an indubitable fact; all our preceding pages are an ample demonstration of this. It remains for us to present its practical or constructive unity, that which has most often been called into question, and which we shall call his *wisdom.*

Man and His Destiny

It is a commonplace to repeat, after Bernardin de Saint-Pierre: "Voltaire is concerned with little else than to destroy," or to say, with André Bellessort: "He founded nothing." It is another to spread abroad Cousin's remark: "Voltaire is nothing but superficial common sense," embroidered by Faguet: "He failed to scale the summit of any art, just as he failed to plumb the depths of anything," or by Schlegel's disdain: "It was impossible for that mordant wit to treat any subject whatever with the proper attention and with sustained seriousness," or Jules Lemaître's aversion: "He has a certain dryness, a certain brevity of spirit which no longer satisfy." It is, moreover, the Patriarch himself who helped to circulate this fiction, comparing himself to limpid but shallow streams, and meaning to imply thereby the unpretentiousness and the perfect propriety of his discourse, like the first-rate classicist that he was.

Certain critics have gone farther and have taxed him with unworthiness and immorality. "It became necessary to acknowledge," declares Léon Crouslé, "that Voltaire's doctrines lacked solidity in history, were extremely weak in philosophy, and in morality constituted an attack on true virtue and on the dignity of the human soul." On this ground, which is the most important of all, it seems to me that the most serious charges against Voltaire have been brought by Vinet, and I think it useful to transcribe the essential part of his judgment:

> To substitute nature for convention, common sense for authority, to prefer things to words, facts to persons, the whole to details, to unite what the average man separates, to distinguish what the average man confuses—all that is philosophy. But this is all that Voltaire's philosophy amounts to. He rises no higher. He does not allow for the noblest elements of human nature, faith, the infinite, Providence; he is acquainted only with the lower and middle regions of the soul. He came to know only the social side of man; he does not know what man is face to face with himself, and all the less face to face with the infinite. He lacked a true sense of moral values; in morality he has instincts, prejudices, habits, but no principles.

This passage, nuanced and restrained in its severity, is by reason of its arguments the best summary of the basic criticisms which it has been possible to make of Voltaire's thought.

Destruction without a constructive counterpart, superficial levity, moral baseness and blindness, these are the usual themes. Such accusations have a polemical flavor, even in the most serious critics, and the origin of this hostility lies invariably in the resistance of that same mystical romanticism which Voltaire had dealt unforgivable blows. We shall see, as we take up anew the great ideas of his positive philosophy, whether in actual fact he founded nothing and whether his morality has no principles. Let us note for the moment that if his thought has been caricatured above all by literary critics or dilettantes, philosophers properly so called have not always held it in contempt. Bersot took a great deal of interest in it; he assigns Voltaire a "distinguished place in the history of modern philosophy," and is grateful to him for having been "zealously insistent on evidence" to a point of never being satisfied with any hypothesis. "He blasted," says Bersot, "more than one belief, but for the benefit of natural truths."

J.-R. Carré has very felicitously stressed the dissatisfied character of Voltaire's thought, the demands of a mind that is not content with approximations and does not confuse possibilities with certainty, the profound homage which a strictness of this kind pays to truth. "This taste of his slowly, gradually led Voltaire to be, in part, the Pascalian man satisfied by nothing, and even to be such, in one sense, perhaps more completely than Pascal himself, that is, refusing to stop being such and to take refuge, in order to forget, in the obscurities of faith." And J.-R. Carré does Voltaire the honor of considering him, in this respect, the typical philosopher: "The distinguishing characteristic of philosophers is perhaps to know how to live quite alone under an iron sky; and not to betray reason in order to seek euthanasia, or beatitude, at any price, not even by throwing oneself into the arms of the unknowable."

Such is what one might call the austerity of Voltaire's wisdom, and we are a long way from that alleged levity, which is only its elegant embellishment, or more exactly its protective cover of modesty. Sincerely, or somewhat complacently, many readers have been taken in by this mocking appearance, this cursory unconstraint. The feigned epicureanism, the cynical statements mask a permanent uneasiness, and there is no question which interested Voltaire so passionately as that of man and his destiny.

Metaphysics fails us, or rather leads us to the proof of our insignificance and our incapacity. So it is not in the metaphysical mode that Voltaire will speak of destiny, and that is doubtless one of his original slants:[1] he will speak of destiny as a moralist. The

[1] One may believe that it is also one of his weaknesses. Voltaire takes no interest in metaphysical systems, which strike him as being otiose and which he does not try to understand, both out of levity and out of contempt. Here, as with religious matters, there is clearly a sense that is lacking in Voltaire. This contempt, it should be added, is based on the very sincere conviction that such quests will never lead to anything, and so, methodically, it represents for him the beginning of wisdom. This means denying oneself profundity, but it also means avoiding empty profundity and contenting oneself with primordial common sense.

question he asks himself is not: where are we going? It is: how shall we live? what is the best use to which we can put the life our nature permits us? And this nature, this life he does not define hypothetically: he analyzes them in accordance with the very experience which is offered us.

He pondered life at length, and his ponderings, taking into account circumstantial variations, brought out a predominance of evil, although, all things considered and carefully judged in conformity with the modesty which is imperative for man, a certain equilibrium is established or rather can be assumed, if only to make the whole endurable. There is always a touch of pragmatism in Voltaire's relative optimism; pessimism is more natural to him. Babouc comes to judge Persepolis as inspector general of manners and morals. His impressions are very mixed; the acts of violence, the duplicity, the corruption incline him toward the destruction of the city, but he spares it for the sake of its civilization and its civility. This mingling of crude vices and refined qualities seems indissoluble to him, like the symbolic statue he presents to Ituriel, "composed of every metal, of the most precious and the basest clays and stones. . . . 'Will you,' he said, 'break this pretty statue because it is not completely made of gold and diamonds?' Ituriel caught the hint. He made up his mind not even to think of chastising Persepolis, and *to let the world go as it goes;* for, he said, *'if all is not well, all is tolerable.'*"

Voltaire often took up this formula again, and he adopts it even when, in order to refute one extreme, he seems to plunge into its opposite. The *Désastre de Lisbonne* stresses evil because it is a matter of discrediting the axiom: all is well; it ends, however, with the word: Hope. *Candide* piles up misadventures and disasters; yet, when all is said and done, the garden to be cultivated is a sufficient tonic for human activity. To the morose Jansenists and the myopic pleasure-seekers the *philosophe* replies simultaneously: "To regard the universe as a prison, and all men as criminals who are going to be executed, is the notion of a fanatic. To believe that the world is a place for enjoyment where one should have pleasure and nothing but, is the dream of a sybarite. To think that the earth, men, and animals are what they should be within the order of Providence, is, I believe, proof of wisdom" (*Remarques sur Pascal*). And the reference to Providence is not a mere ruse here: Voltaire does not recognize a Providence which intervenes by means of special acts for our personal benefit and above all in accordance with our conceptual categories; but he does recognize it as the irrational and incomprehensible origin of the world. The "order of Providence" is also the "world as it goes"; it is at any rate what we cannot change and must accept as an incontestable fact of our destiny.

So human life is livable, provided we willingly submit to the "order" within which it must be lived. At the basis of Voltaire's wisdom there is a profound resignation, and this resignation is justified in his eyes by our powerlessness to modify the laws of nature in any way. What good is it to wear ourselves out with ineffectual protests or never-ending quests, when other tasks await us, in the properly human sphere where our actions are creative? *What lies within our control,* that is the only reasonable arena of our activity, and that is why Candide becomes a gardener. So this wisdom, which, as it turns out, smacks somewhat of Antiquity, is composed both of a thoroughly pondered renunciation and of a lucid call to action: this is what distinguishes Voltaire from Montaigne, for whom all hustle-and-bustle was futile. Thus, whatever Vinet may have said about it, Voltaire came to know what man was before the infinite, to know it so well that the modesty of his metaphysical thought is the very result of that contemplation.

After pondering life, he pondered the nature of man; and here, too, he reacted against extreme interpretations. He views man as neither basically good, like Jean-Jacques, nor basically bad, even if only through the theory of original sin, like certain "fanatics." Man is simply a being adapted to a tolerable world; he himself is tolerable. He is not inclined toward evil, "he is inclined toward his own well-being, which is an evil only when he oppresses his fellow men" (*A, B, C,* 3rd conversation). And herein is already a basis for morality: freedom through respect for others.

But there is more than immediate self-interest in man; there is also an instinct of elevation and transcendence which drives him to imagine himself beyond his natural possibilities. Voltaire was anything but unaware of this instinct, and on this theme he even composed a supremely expressive philosophical verse, which Lamartine had only to elaborate: "Tes destins sont d'un homme, et tes vœux sont d'un Dieu." ["Your destiny is that of a man, but your aspirations are those of a God."] (2nd *Discours*)

But instead of seeing man's greatness in these unbounded aspirations, like the romantics, he sees in them precisely man's weakness, his lack of proportion, and the source of his worst defects: false judgment, presumption, intolerance.

That is why he returns to material self-interest as a principle that is less dangerous, easier to control and to direct toward goodness. His moral realism here comes to the aid of his philosophical criticism in order to condemn and destroy the craving for the absolute; but he allows the "passions," which are an integral part of the human condition, and which it is a question of putting to proper use.

These passions themselves are very mixed, as is the case with every reality: "God has given man legitimate pride, which is useful to him, benevolence, which is useful to his neighbor, anger, which is dangerous, compassion, which disarms it, sympathy with a number of his companions, antipathy toward others. Many needs and much activity, instinct, reason, and the passions, that is man" (*A, B, C*). There is a great deal to be drawn from this composite whole, and the art of the moralist consists in drawing from it as much goodness as possible. Now, "it is love of ourselves which promotes love of others; it is through our mutual needs that we are useful to the human race. This is the foundation of all social intercourse; it is the tie which eternally binds men. . . . It is very true that God could have made creatures solely concerned with the good of others. . . . But God has set things up otherwise. Let us not criticize the instinct He gives us, and let us make use of it as He enjoins" (*Remarques sur Pascal*).

Thus Voltaire accepts the world as it goes, and man as he is: that is the basis of his wisdom. Let us note how far this removes him from the utopianism for which his century has been so heavily condemned, and often very thoughtlessly at that. Let us also note that if he gives prominence to "social man" in his morality, as Vinet observes, it is not because he was unacquainted with the problem of destiny: on the contrary, it is after posing this problem and ascertaining that it was insoluble. Such being the case, the only problem within our range remains, in all modesty, that of happiness, and resignation before destiny has as its logical counterpart the struggle for human betterment.

Man and Happiness

"Le paradis terrestre est où je suis." ["The terrestrial paradise is where I am."] Such is the conclusion of *Le Mondain*. A provocative conclusion addressed to gloomy temperaments, a youthful optimism, but also a very firm decision to make use of life such as it is; and here there is no difference between the conqueror of

1730 and the hermit of 1770. This man who entertained so many hopes and encountered so many setbacks, never despaired of life; his moments of lassitude are very brief, and always resolve themselves into recoveries.

So the first condition of happiness is to make the best of one's era; and carefully considered, this "iron age" offers many opportunities for pleasure and for interesting activity: at the same time by its resources, its refined modernism, and its deficiencies, which call for effort on the part of pioneers and reformers. Doubtless at the beginning of his life Voltaire was tempted by a desire to enjoy more than by a desire to crusade; but the worldling in him quickly gave way before the *philosophe,* and it is above all a *philosophe* we have to examine, without overlooking that worldly coquetry whose traces preserved a grace and a swiftness of thrust that are rather rare in a thinker.

Since our nature debars us from lofty speculation, our destiny, and our duty, is to *act.* No one displayed this principle better than Voltaire; and this rehabilitation of useful work is at first a novelty for the age, but is soon introduced into the vast Encyclopaedic movement. Confronting Pascal, who despises the diversion of action, Voltaire shows that it is an illusion to want to escape this law of our being: "Man is born for action as fire tends upward and a stone downward. Not to be busy and not to exist are the same thing for man." Indeed, thought itself is a mode of action according to him; pure contemplation is a chimera. So it is futile to oppose the physical act to the intellectual: both represent an "occupation," a diversion, to use the Pascalian term. Pascal diverted himself, like anyone else, by thinking of God and by pleading the Jansenist cause. Activity is the very fabric of human life: "the entire difference lies in gentle or tumultuous, dangerous or useful activities."

Happiness will entail choosing one's activities in accordance with this scale of values; social duty, providing this happiness for all men—which is doubtless in itself the best of activities. As a matter of fact, there is in Voltaire a parallel need to make a success of his life and to improve the lives of others. He very quickly recognized the right way to make a success of his own life, despite all the temptations of false glory: the *summum bonum* is freedom. He finally gains it at Ferney, and writes to Madame du Deffand (17 September 1759): "I have carved out for myself a modest destiny apart. . . . I have made up my mind to become a completely free individual. . . . I have become aware that the greatest pleasure consists in being personally and usefully occupied." However, to be free one must shake off bondage to material needs, in a word one must have wealth; and Voltaire realized that, too, very early. Already when young he learned how to make sound investments and, after thirty years or so, he had at his disposal what was doubtless the largest fortune ever managed by a man of letters. Ferney, his territorial setup, his practical immunity, his workshop for concocting subversive writings, became possible only because of this foresight. "I can no longer write anything but what I think," he then said with an air of naïveté; such a result presupposes a splendid perseverance.

But it is easier to attain this freedom and this happiness for oneself, when one firmly resolves to do so, than to bestow it on other men. Voltaire always saw two great categories among them: those who deceive and those who let themselves be deceived; and then, outside these two massive groups, the small company of enlightened men. He never had great hope of liberating the "rabble"; and if, in his confident moments, he dimly envisages a certain emancipation and esteems the common people enough to think that one must not "make use of pious frauds" in dealing with them, on the whole this possibility seems very remote to him, and for the time being wisdom demands many precautions, and, when it is a question of primitive minds, a clever conformity: "If Bayle's maid dies in your arms, do not speak to her as you would to Bayle, nor to Bayle as you would to his maid" (*Dictionnaire,* article *Blé*).

But this ordinary concession to prejudices must not make one lose sight of the basic struggle which will progressively eliminate them: "Gradually weaken all the old superstitions, and introduce no new ones." Actually, the cruelties of the domineering not only result in the exploitation of the weak: they ceaselessly threaten the honorable, and the very credulity of the weak is a source of fanaticism whose eruption places the wisest in danger. It is therefore as much out of a concern for self-protection as out of a desire to better the lot of others that the *philosophe* will intervene in civil affairs.

His first task will be to denounce men's responsibility in misfortunes not visited upon them by nature. And there are two of these above all whose idiotic horror he will demonstrate: persecutions and wars. Persecutions are the consequence of fanaticism, on the one side as on the other; Voltaire is no more indulgent toward the Calvinists than he is toward the leaders of the dragonnades. The real cure for this evil lies in the extinction of the "enthusiasm" which creates factitious parties and passions. As for wars, he details their useless barbarity and illogical confusion, which almost always dupe the very persons who expected to reap advantage from them: "Luck, a mixture of successes and failures, intrigues, lassitude extinguished a conflagration which had been kindled by other strokes of luck, other intrigues, greed, jealousy, hope" (*A, B, C,* 11th conversation). Pending progress, the more peaceable nations must "defend themselves against the robbers called conquerors," but the true solution here, too, lies in the spread of enlightenment. This spread of enlightenment, whatever difficulties it may pose, is not in Voltaire's view utopian: it is actually based on self-interest properly understood, and it is not possible that men should not finally arrive at a better understanding of their self-interest. Up to now they have been duped by their short-sightedness, and also by the big empty words with which they artificially oppose one another. First it was for food that they killed each other, then for the glory of their village or the triumph of their opinions. So peace and happiness can be instituted only following two decisive forward steps: the economic organization of the world, the rational education of the mind.

Voltaire brought to the attention of his contemporaries a plan for a society in which maximum security and well-being might reign. Struck by the destitution and disorder which had long plagued the countries reputed to be the richest, he encourages agricultural and industrial production both by word and by deed, without, be it added, lapsing into the physiocrats' biased approach, in which he still sees the systematizing fallacy. His Ferney undertakings are well timed to transform his predilection into active proficiency (see *Dictionnaire,* article *Agriculture*) and to enable him to discover, within the framework of a seignorial estate, the principles of intensive management which at the same time are already inspiring Frederick II's domestic policies.

However, commerce remains for Voltaire the vehicle of true well-being and of civilization. The attainment of self-sufficiency is the indispensable precaution against scarcities; but this is only a first-stage ideal. Transcending it are the expansion of free trade, general prosperity achieved through judicious distribution of local products, and, finally, luxury, which is the natural perfection of great nations. And at this point economic preoccupations merge with artistic concerns. Voltaire emphatically advocated great, publicly useful works and, generally speaking, all city-planning projects. Paris, with its winding, dirty streets, its irrational accumulations of leprous houses, seemed to him unworthy of a people in other respects enamored of so many refinements.

How finance such works and find the necessary manpower? Governments do finance wars! And there are so many unproductive citizens: soldiers, monks; and there is so much misdirected leisure: a hundred twenty holidays per year, which workers spend in the tavern! And all the hoarded money profitlessly dormant, and the embezzlement of public funds! "Well, if one contributes to the misfortune of the human race, will one give nothing for its happiness and for its glory? What, since your establishment as an organized nation, you still have not found the secret of compelling all the rich to provide work for all the poor! Then you still have not arrived at the rudiments of civilization!" (*Embellissements de la ville de Cachemire*). All these demands are very modern in tone and are valuable less, perhaps, for their substance than for the new conception of life which they presuppose. Man is no longer provisionally encamped on earth, on the look-out for dangers under the oppressive burden of the original malediction. Henceforth he will settle down here, and if the life of the individual is too brief to carry through the task of civilization, other men will come, of whom he must think, and who will carry on. The main thing is to have initiated the right approach, which is a sort of economic and administrative rationalization.

For administration, whose sound functioning prevents as many evils as that of production and exchange, is in a lamentable state in France: "It is said that there are a hundred forty-four customs in France which have the force of law; these laws are almost all different. A man who travels in this country changes laws almost as often as he changes post horses" (*Dictionnaire,* article *Coutumes*). The new administration must have two qualities: it must be effective, produce more efficient results; it must offer the citizens guarantees of personal security. More than anyone else during the century, Voltaire demanded a respect for the individual, and his most authentic imprint on the Declaration of the Rights of Man is in the condemnation of arbitrariness, the proportioning of punishments to crimes, the protection of the accused prior to judgment (articles VII, VIII, IX): in sum, the *habeas corpus* principle acclimated and articulated into maxims.

As for government proper, this is doubtless the subject which has most confused his commentators. Louis Blanc declared: "Although he was a revolutionary in religion, he did not want any part of revolution in politics," and this summary view has prevailed to the point where Voltaire still passes today for a conservative as against Rousseau and even Montesquieu. This is the wrong way to put the question. Actually, Voltaire's politics is less interested in theoretical and general problems than in immediately applicable reforms. When he happened, very rarely, to discuss some theoretical problem, his views proved to be as "advanced" as those of Jean-Jacques; like the latter, Voltaire believes that democracy is applicable only to small States, but he is not far from seeing in it the least pernicious form of government, and he praises it highly: "Usually there is no comparison between the crimes of the high-and-mighty who are always ambitious and the crimes of the masses who never want and cannot want anything but liberty and equality. These two intuitive notions, *liberty* and *equality,* do not lead straight to calumny, rapine, assassination, poisoning, the devastation of one's neighbor's lands; but ambition in high places and lust for power plunge men into all these crimes in all times and in all places" (*Dictionnaire,* article *Démocratie*). Thus Voltaire, despite all his distrust of mass passions, regards the common people as less likely to provoke the great catastrophes than the irresponsible despot; and his hatred of arbitrariness is sufficiently well known for us to conclude that, theoretically, he condemns despotism on the same ground as Montesquieu.

But for him the main thing is not this intellectual game: as a realist, he studies the practical conditions of specific reforms. He had a great deal of good to say about the English government, and no doubt his dearest wish was for the constitutional representation of the most enlightened classes of the nation. But in France the moment does not seem to him to have arrived: the *Parlement,* which in one sense claims to express public opinion, is attached to privileges and routines; moreover, it is intolerant, and Voltaire condemns its meddling in political matters just as he does that of the clergy. In short, what he wants is a central power freed from the partisan influences which lead it astray, and impregnated with the social and economic role it is more and more called upon to play. The liberal nobility and bourgeoisie seem to him to be the groups best prepared for this task. It is up to the king to choose his ministers from these groups, then to grant them all the necessary power to do good; and this wise policy is linked with a wise administration and a wise economy: to make men happy, protect them, make daily life easier for them, maintain order with a maximum of freedom. This is the government of a Providential Aristocracy; it is the one whose birth Voltaire hailed when Turgot appeared, the man who could doubtless have prevented the Revolution.

The economic organization of society already implies *per se* the education of the mind: a certain level of culture is necessary if one is to understand the utility of a common order. But in the opposite direction, material harmony must favor the flowering of an intellectual and moral élite. Society must create happiness for all, but it must also create beauty, and in creating the latter it need never halt its forward movement. The servants of beauty are those same aristocrats to whom the management of the State naturally falls; in them can finally be fulfilled that destiny of man on earth, that supreme civilization whose watchwords remain: Peace, Prosperity, Lucidity. The pursuit of the fine arts, the pleasures of good company, conversations on philosophy, enlightened contributions to public utility are so many occupations capable of captivating the members of the élite and of making them forget, through the attractions of beneficence or through artistic creation, the eternal mystery on whose threshold their intelligence makes its renunciation, when their imaginations resist temptation.

Humanism and Morality

Humanism can be a pious inventory of the spiritual treasures bequeathed by the past; on this ground Voltaire is hardly a humanist. He has little regard for all "outworn things"; like Pococurante, he is capable of saying that the reading of Homer bores him and that Virgil is often frigid. Not that he despises ancient works in themselves, but they were good for their period, and each period has its own needs. He is resolutely modern, to the point where he would cheerfully sacrifice old monuments to the needs of sanitation and city-planning. And it is from the same point of view that he judges primitive traditions and beliefs; no man has had as few scruples as he about profanation of and respect for the ancient as such. To examine by oneself and without prejudice, for him this principle admits of no exception.

Humanism can also be a meditation on the experiences of our race. Here Voltaire fits in, and he scorns no document; not that like a Montaigne he doubles all his remarks with zestfully collected references, but he is a historian by temperament. His epic, his tragedies, his philosophic articles are steeped in history. Throughout his life he researched, annotated, commented, and with a seriousness which one would not expect of a poet, or of a polemicist. His wisdom has a historical basis. The same men whom he disdained as a fighter for modernism, he studies as a moralist, and uses their example to compose his immense picture of the "manners and the spirit of nations." But his meditation always leads to the present; past experiences are those of pioneers and are enriching less through their success than through their gropings.

This brings us to a final form of humanism, which is the fructification of a heritage that is truly human, and the love of the truly human as something fragile and perfectible. That form of humanism is ardently cultivated by Voltaire, and it is what constitutes the profound unity of his constructive thought. From one end of his production to the other there is but one concern: man; but one reality: man. He chastised and maltreated man in every possible way, but he chastised him as one does when one loves, with the desperate impatience and sarcasm of a father molding a rebellious child. Despite everything, he never ceased to have confidence in man: from so many satirical pages there emerges, not a morose dejection, but a stubborn reason for acting and for persevering. Contrary to La Rochefoucauld, very different even from La Bruyère who quickly grows weary, Voltaire stirs up as he criticizes, builds as he destroys.

What, exactly, did he build, then, and what remains today of his work? Before everything else he built a morality meant to replace the one whose débris he was scattering. The latter had, to his way of thinking, two invalidating defects: it was attached to dogmas, and rational discussion of those dogmas threatened to discredit it by contagion; it exalted suspect values such as authority through tradition, conformity with obligatory adherence. So Voltaire will attempt to separate morality from dogma, in order not to tie the fate of a necessary practice to the fortuitous vicissitudes of perishable beliefs. He will also attempt to eliminate its automatic character, at least for the minority capable of rising to the superior morality, which involves free, carefully pondered consent.

It follows that Voltaire's morality has two aspects, the one utilitarian and the other liberal. Moral utilitarianism has already been evidenced in most of our remarks on society, and one may say that here morality most often blends with politics. Very different from both Montaigne and Pascal, who lose interest in the problem out of scepticism, Voltaire introduces himself into the movement of the wheelworks which make the world go as it goes, and he has hopes of accomplishing something there, and he thinks that if there is a morality, it can exist only there. This decision is at bottom very Baconian and imparts a sure effectiveness to patient experimentation; and yet, on the other hand, he is not opposed to a certain aspect of Christianity, since he highlights mutual aid in society, animated by mutual love.

The *Poème sur la loi naturelle* tends to prove the psychological reality of a universal morality by means of a body of spontaneous principles common to all men. As for the *Discours sur l'homme,* they end with a depiction of "true virtue"; Jesus is seen refusing to answer Pilate, who asked him: "What is truth?," but responding before the disciple who inquired about man's duty: "Aimez Dieu, lui dit-il, mais aimez les mortels." [" 'Love God,' he said to him, 'but love mortals.' "]

True virtue, then, is called *beneficence.* And it is once again Jesus whom we meet in that beautiful meditation on the graves of all the victims of persecution, Jesus who occupies the place of honor among the sages, Numa Pompilius, Pythagoras, Zoroaster, Socrates, and who utters the same maxim: "Love God with all your heart, and your neighbor as yourself, for that is the sum and substance of man" (*Dictionnaire,* article *Religion*).

The concluding clause is worthy of note: for that is the sum and substance of man. Voltaire thereby indicates to us that the basis of morality is less an imperative imposed from without than the result of an objective investigation of the human condition. Once everything has been carefully weighed, we discover that our task is to organize life as best we can; and for that social harmony is indispensable: a profound justification of tolerance. So, in short, this attitude is an experimental and, as it were, scientific effort to establish morality as a natural fact. But since the analysis of this morality does not lie within the capabilities of all minds, Voltaire supports a minimum of religion for the masses, that *Socinianism* which he thought he found in the ministers of Geneva and which, disencumbered of all dogma, preserved a Christianity reduced to the great themes for the guidance of conscience, popularly to the "rewarding and punishing God." Such is the utilitarianism that inspires all the exoteric works.

In parallel he builds a moral liberalism which is practicable only among initiates, but which fashions the masterpiece of civilized life. The members of the élite are doubtless not exempted from social service; on the contrary, it is from them that the impetus comes, it is through them that the common people must become acquainted with their duties. But this service is not their supreme goal; their aim is the cultivation of the self with a view to realizing the harmonious man. Thus morality finally joins aesthetics.

The principle of this superior morality is taste, definable as the intuitive discernment of that which is fitting (*quid deceat*). It is no longer through social necessity, then, through solidarity, or even through love that the *philosophe* does good: he does it through *propriety*. A key word in which one must be very careful not to see an artifice; propriety designates the natural relationships which exist among things, but a clear understanding of which is accessible only to highly skilled minds. Propriety is a nuanced realism, and taste is its refined and at the same time spontaneous instrument.

Whence the unity of the literary and the philosophic production: the man of taste is he whose sensibility immediately intuits what art, what poetry, what spirit befit his time; and he is also the thinker whose wisdom knows the attitude and the obligation which suit man in his milieu, in his country, in his human condition. So much so that in Voltaire everything finally becomes inseparable: the man, the life, the work in its manifold aspects, everything is perpetual creation, ceaseless adaptation, and, in sum, an example on the move, much more than a stereotyped lesson or a production for eternity. And it is perhaps in this way that he has given us the finest proof of humanism, expressing the plenitude of his age and showing other ages with what sincerity and what concern for social perfection man can realize the ideal he bears in his nature and, within the limits of his power, control his destiny.

Chronology of Important Dates

1694	Birth in Paris on Nov. 21(?) of François Marie Arouet, later known as Voltaire.
1704	Admission to the Jesuit collège, Louis-le-Grand, in Paris.
1711	Arouet leaves Louis-le-Grand, begins to study law.
1713	Travels to The Hague as the Marquis de Châteauneuf's secretary; becomes infatuated with a girl named Pimpette; is dismissed and sent back to Paris.
1714	Resumes the study of law.
1715	Death of Louis XIV; Regency of Philippe d'Orléans.
1716	Is exiled to Sully-sur-Loire for works attacking the Regent.
1717-18	Is imprisoned in the Bastille for eleven months for a satire against the Regent, probably composed by someone else.
1718	His tragedy *Œdipe* a great success. Renames himself Monsieur de Voltaire.
1722	"Épître à Uranie." Quarrel with the poet Jean Baptiste Rousseau.
1723	Publication of the epic poem *La Ligue* (which later becomes *La Henriade*). Death of the Regent; beginning of Louis XV's personal reign.
1725	Quarrels with the Chevalier de Rohan; Voltaire beaten by Rohan's lackeys.
1726	Is imprisoned in the Bastille as a consequence of the quarrel, then exiled to England.
1727	Attends Newton's funeral.
1728	*La Henriade.*
1728-29	Returns to France (date uncertain).

1730 "Ode sur la mort de Mlle Lecouvreur" protesting the Church's refusal to permit the actress's burial in holy ground. *Brutus.*

1731 *Histoire de Charles XII.*

1732 *Zaïre.*

1733 His poem *Le Temple du goût* provokes antagonism for its criticism of writers regarded by many as above criticism. Begins his cohabitation with the Marquise du Châtelet.

1734 *Adélaïde du Guesclin.* The *Lettres philosophiques* published in Paris; Voltaire forced to flee to Lorraine; at Cirey with Madame du Châtelet. *Traité de métaphysique.*

1735 Is allowed to return to Paris. *La Mort de César.*

1736 *Alzire.* Composition of "Le Mondain"; Voltaire forced to flee to the Netherlands.

1737 Completion of *Discours en vers sur l'homme.*

1738 *Éléments de la philosophie de Newton.* Voltaire and Madame du Châtelet compete for the prize offered by the Académie des sciences with dissertations on the nature of fire; neither wins.

1739 First chapters of *Siècle de Louis XIV* appear and are seized by the police.

1740 First meeting with Frederick II of Prussia.

1741 *Mahomet* performed at Lille.

1742 *Mahomet,* performed in Paris, arouses religious opposition and is forced to close. *Ce qu'on ne fait pas et ce qu'on pourrait faire.*

1743 *Mérope.*

1744 *Courte réponse aux longs discours d'un docteur allemand.*

1745 Is appointed Historiographer of France. *La Princesse de Navarre. Le Temple de la gloire.* "Le Poème de Fontenoy." Dedicates *Mahomet* to the Pope.

1746 Is elected to the Académie française. Named Gentleman of the Chamber. *Le Monde comme il va.*

1747 *Zadig.* Flees to Sceaux following an indiscreet remark at Court.

1748 *Sémiramis.*

1749 Death of Madame du Châtelet.

1750 *Oreste.* Goes to Prussia; Frederick appoints him Chamberlain to the King. Beginning of business dispute with Hirschell.

1751 *Siècle de Louis XIV.*

1752 Quarrels with Maupertuis; *Diatribe du docteur Akakia.* "Poème sur la loi naturelle." *Micromégas* (revision of a tale dating back to 1739).

1753 Definitive rupture with Frederick; Voltaire leaves, is detained and humiliated at Frankfort.

1754 Arrives in Geneva.

1755 Purchases Les Délices in Geneva. *L'Orphelin de la Chine.* Lisbon earthquake; "Poème sur le désastre de Lisbonne."

1756 Seven Years' War breaks out. *Essai sur les mœurs.* D'Alembert at Les Délices; works on article "Genève" for the *Encyclopédie.*

1757 Furor in Geneva over the article "Genève"; Voltaire accused of collaboration with D'Alembert. Resumes relations with Frederick by correspondence.

1758 Purchases Ferney. Composition of *Candide.*

1759 Publication of *Candide. Histoire d'un bon bramin. Tancrède. Relation de la maladie, de la confession, de la mort du jésuite Berthier.*

1760 Breaks with Jean Jacques Rousseau. Adopts the great-grand-niece of Corneille. Comes to the aid of the Crassy brothers.

1761 *Lettres sur la Nouvelle Héloïse.* "Épître à Mme. Denis sur l'agriculture."

1762 *Extrait du Testament de Meslier. Sermon des cinquante.* Execution of Jean Calas; Voltaire begins campaign to rehabilitate his memory.

1763 *Siècle de Louis XV. Traité sur la tolérance.*

1764 *Olympie. Discours aux Welches. Commentaire sur Corneille. Dictionnaire philosophique portatif. Sentiment des citoyens.* The Sirvens forced to flee.

1765 Memory of Calas rehabilitated. *Philosophie de l'histoire. Questions sur les miracles.*

1766 Execution of the Chevalier de La Barre. Execution of Count de Lally. *Relation de la mort du chevalier de La Barre. Avis au public sur les parricides imputés aux Calas et aux Sirven. Le Philosophe ignorant. Commentaire sur le livre des délits et des peines.*

1767 *Questions de Zapata. Examen important de milord Bolingbroke. L'Ingénu. La Défense de mon oncle. Le Dîner du comte de Boulainvilliers.*

1768 Voltaire evicts Madame Denis. *La Princesse de Babylone. L'Homme aux quarante écus.*

1769 Madame Denis returns to Ferney. *Les Lettres d'Amabed. Dieu et les hommes. Les Guèbres. L'A, B, C.*

1770 Execution of Montbailli. Refutation of d'Holbach's *Système de la nature* (an atheistic work).

1771 Vindication of the Sirvens. *La Méprise d'Arras.*

1772 *Questions sur l'Encyclopédie* (9 volumes). *Il faut prendre un parti.* "Épître à Horace."

1773 *Lois de Minos. Fragment sur le procès criminel de Montbailli;* rehabilitation of Montbailli's memory.

1774 Death of Louis XV, succeeded by Louis XVI. *Le Taureau blanc. Sophonisbe.*

1775 *Le Cri du sang innocent. Histoire de Jenni, ou l'âthée et le sage.* Voltaire persuades Turgot to free the county of Gex from the tax-farming system in exchange for a single annual contribution. *Les Oreilles du comte de Chesterfield et le chapelain Goudman.*

1776 *La Bible enfin expliquée. Prix de la justice et de l'humanité.*

1777 *Dialogues d'Évhémère.*

1778 Voltaire returns to Paris for the first time since 1750. Performance of *Irène;* glorification of Voltaire. Rehabilitation of Count de Lally's memory. Final illness and death (May 30).

Notes on the Editor and Contributors

WILLIAM F. BOTTIGLIA, editor of this anthology, teaches at the Massachusetts Institute of Technology. His principal work on Voltaire is *Voltaire's "Candide": Analysis of a Classic.*

THEODORE BESTERMAN is Director of the Institut et Musée Voltaire in Geneva. He has done more than any other single individual in the present generation to stimulate interest in and research on Voltaire. In the past decade and a half he has edited *Voltaire's Notebooks* (2 vols.), the *Lettres d'amour de Voltaire à sa nièce, Voltaire's Correspondence* (107 vols.), and *Studies on Voltaire and the Eighteenth Century,* a continuing series which now totals 51 volumes.

J. H. BRUMFITT, who teaches at the University of St. Andrews, is a specialist in Voltaire's historical writings. He is the author of *Voltaire Historian,* the editor of *La Philosophie de l'histoire,* and the translator and editor of *The Age of Louis XIV and Other Selected Writings.*

PETER GAY, a historian who teaches at Columbia University, has published a full-length study of Voltaire's political views, and has also translated and edited Voltaire's *Candide* and his *Philosophical Dictionary.*

GUSTAVE LANSON died in 1934. He was, among other things, the greatest all-around Voltaire scholar. His *Voltaire* remains a model of intelligent coverage, penetration, succinctness, and balanced judgment. He also published an excellent edition of the *Lettres philosophiques* and a study of Voltaire's style in *L'Art de la prose.*

RAYMOND NAVES died during the Second World War. His sound learning and keen insight are apparent in such volumes as *Le Goût de Voltaire, Voltaire et l'Encyclopédie,* and *Voltaire: L'Homme et l'œuvre.*

RENÉ POMEAU, of the University of Toulouse, is by far the finest French scholar of our time to concentrate on Voltaire. His most important works are *La Religion de Voltaire, Voltaire par lui-même,* and critical editions of *Candide, Le Taureau blanc,* and Voltaire's historical works.

NORMAN L. TORREY, Professor Emeritus at Columbia University, and IRA O. WADE, Professor Emeritus at Princeton University, are members, along with George R. Havens, Professor Emeritus at the Ohio State University, of the remarkable triumvirate which has dominated Voltaire scholarship in the United States during the past generation. Professor Torrey's two major studies are *Voltaire and the English Deists* and *The Spirit of Voltaire.* Professor Wade has published important editions of the "Épître à Uranie" and *Micromégas,* and important studies on *Candide* and on Voltaire's intellectual activity at Cirey.

Selected Bibliography

Works by Voltaire

COLLECTIONS

The Age of Louis XIV and Other Selected Writings. Transl. and ed. J. H. Brumfitt. New York: Twayne Publishers, Inc., 1963.

"Candide" and Other Writings. Ed. Haskell M. Block. New York: Random House, Inc., 1956.

"Candide," "Zadig," and Selected Stories. Transl. Donald M. Frame. Bloomington: Indiana University Press, 1961.

Choix de contes. Ed. Frederick C. Green. Cambridge: Cambridge University Press, 1951.

Contes et romans. Ed. Philippe Van Tiegham. Paris: Roches, 1930. 4 vols.

Dialogues et anecdotes philosophiques. Ed. Raymond Naves. Paris: Garnier, 1940.

Living Thoughts Presented by André Maurois. New York: Longmans, Green, & Co., Ltd., 1939.

Mélanges. Ed. Jacques van den Heuvel. Preface by Emmanuel Berl. Paris: Gallimard, 1961.

Œuvres choisies. Ed. Louis Flandrin. 6th ed. Paris: Hatier, 1930.

Œuvres complètes. Ed. Louis Moland. Paris: Garnier, 1877-1885. 52 vols.

Œuvres historiques. Ed. René Pomeau. Paris: Gallimard, 1957.

Politique de Voltaire. Ed. René Pomeau. Paris: Colin, 1963.

The Portable Voltaire. Ed. Ben Ray Redman. New York: The Viking Press, Inc., 1957.

Select Letters of Voltaire. Transl. and ed. Theodore Besterman. London: Thomas Nelson & Sons, Ltd., 1963.

Voltaire and the Enlightenment: Selections from Voltaire. Transl. Norman L. Torrey. New York: Appleton-Century-Crofts, Inc., 1931.

Voltaire's Correspondence. Ed. Theodore Besterman. Genève: Institut et Musée Voltaire, 1953-1965. 107 vols.

The Works of Voltaire. Transl. and ed. Tobias Smollett and others. Paris: Du Mont, 1901. 42 vols.

INDIVIDUAL WORKS

The Age of Louis XIV. Transl. Martin P. Pollack. Everyman's Library. London: J. M. Dent & Sons, Ltd., 1951.

L'Apologie du luxe au 18e siècle et le Mondain de Voltaire: Étude critique sur le Mondain et ses sources. Ed. André Morize. Paris: Didier, 1909.

Candide, ou l'Optimisme. Ed. George R. Havens. New York: Holt, Rinehart & Winston, Inc., 1934.

Candide ou l'Optimisme. Ed. André Morize. Paris: Hachette, 1913; Droz, 1931; Didier, 1957.

Candide ou l'Optimisme. Ed. René Pomeau. Paris: Nizet, 1959.

Dictionnaire philosophique. Eds. Julien Benda and Raymond Naves. Paris: Garnier, 1935-1936. 2 vols.

"The 'Épître à Uranie.' " Ed. Ira O. Wade. *PMLA,* XLVIII (December, 1932), 1066-1112.

Essai sur les mœurs et l'esprit des nations et sur les principaux faits de l'histoire depuis Charlemagne jusqu'à Louis XIII. Ed. René Pomeau. Paris: Garnier, 1963. 2 vols.

L'Ingénu. Ed. William R. Jones. Genève: Droz, 1957; Paris: Minard, 1957.

Lettres philosophiques. Ed. Gustave Lanson. 2nd ed. Paris: Hachette, 1915-1917. 2 vols.

Lettres philosophiques. Ed. Raymond Naves. Paris: Garnier, 1938.

Philosophical Dictionary. Transl. and ed. Peter Gay. Preface by André Maurois. New York: Basic Books, Inc., Publishers, 1962. 2 vols.

Philosophical Letters. Transl., with an Introduction, by Ernest Dilworth. Indianapolis: The Bobbs-Merrill Co. Inc., 1961.

La Philosophie de l'histoire. Ed. J. H. Brumfitt. *Studies on Voltaire and the Eighteenth Century* (ed. Theodore Besterman). Genève: Institut et Musée Voltaire, 1963. Vol. XXVIII.

The Philosophy of History. Preface by Thomas Kiernan. New York: Philosophical Library, Inc., 1965.

Poème sur la loi naturelle. Ed. Francis J. Crowley. Berkeley: University of California Press, 1938.

Sémiramis, tragédie. Ed. Jean-Jacques Olivier. Paris: Droz, 1946.

Siècle de Louis XIV. Ed. Émile Bourgeois. 5th ed. Paris: Hachette, 1906.

Le Taureau blanc. Ed. René Pomeau. Paris: Nizet, 1957.

Le Temple du goût. Ed. E. Carcassonne. Paris: Droz, 1938.

Traité de métaphysique (1734). Ed. H. Temple Patterson. Manchester: Manchester University Press, 1937.

Voltaire's "Candide" (A Bilingual Edition). Transl. and ed. Peter Gay. New York: St. Martin's Press, Inc., 1963.

Voltaire's "Micromégas": A Study in the Fusion of Science, Myth, and Art. Ed. Ira O. Wade. Princeton: Princeton University Press, 1950.

Voltaire's Notebooks. Ed. Theodore Besterman. Genève: Institut et Musée Voltaire, 1952. 2 vols.

Zadig ou la Destinée. Ed. Georges Ascoli. Paris: Hachette, 1929. 2 vols.

Works on Voltaire

Aldington, Richard. *Voltaire.* London: Routledge & Kegan Paul, Ltd., 1925; New York: E. P. Dutton & Co., Inc., 1925.

Barber, William H. *Voltaire: "Candide."* London: Edward Arnold (Publishers), Ltd., 1960.

Bellessort, André. *Essai sur Voltaire.* Paris: Perrin, 1925.

Bottiglia, William F. *Voltaire's "Candide": Analysis of a Classic.* 2nd ed. *Studies on Voltaire and the Eighteenth Century* (ed. Theodore Besterman). Genève: Institut et Musée Voltaire, 1964. Vol. VIIA.

Brailsford, Henry N. *Voltaire.* New York: Holt, Rinehart & Winston, Inc., 1935; London: Butterworth & Co. (Publishers), Ltd., 1935.

Brumfitt, John H. *Voltaire Historian.* Oxford: Oxford University Press, 1958.

Carré, Jean-Raoul. *Consistance de Voltaire le philosophe.* Paris: Boivin, 1938.

Carré, Jean-Raoul. *Réflexions sur l'Anti-Pascal de Voltaire.* Paris: Alcan, 1935.

Caussy, Fernand. *Voltaire seigneur de village.* Paris: Hachette, 1912.

Conlan, P. M. *Voltaire's Literary Career from 1728 to 1750. Studies on Voltaire and the Eighteenth Century* (ed. Theodore Besterman). Genève: Institut et Musée Voltaire, 1960. Vol. XIV.

Crocker, Lester G. "Voltaire's Struggle for Humanism." *Studies on Voltaire and the Eighteenth Century* (ed. Theodore Besterman). Genève: Institut et Musée Voltaire, 1957. Vol. IV, pp. 137-69.

Desnoiresterres, Gustave. *Voltaire et la société française au XVIII*[e] *siècle.* 2nd ed. Paris: Didier, 1867-1876. 8 vols.

Diaz, Furio. *Voltaire storico.* Torino: Einaudi, 1959.

Gay, Peter. *Voltaire's Politics.* Princeton: Princeton University Press, 1959.

Lancaster, Henry Carrington. *French Tragedy in the Time of Louis XV and Voltaire, 1715-1774.* Baltimore: Johns Hopkins Press, 1950. 2 vols.

Lanson, Gustave. *L'Art de la prose.* 13th ed. Paris: Fayard, n.d. (Preface, 1908).

———. *Voltaire.* Ed. René Pomeau. Paris: Hachette, 1960.

———. *Voltaire.* Transl. Robert A. Wagoner. New York: John Wiley & Sons, Inc., 1966.

———. "Voltaire et les *Lettres philosophiques:* Comment Voltaire faisait un livre." *La Revue de Paris,* IV (August 1, 1908), 505-33.

Lion, Henri. *Les Tragédies et les théories dramatiques de Voltaire.* Paris: Hachette, 1895.

Maestro, Marcello T. *Voltaire and Beccaria as Reformers of Criminal Law.* New York: Columbia University Press, 1942.

Maurois, André. *Voltaire.* Transl. Hamish Miles. New York: Appleton-Century, Inc., 1938.

McGhee, Dorothy M. *Voltairian Narrative Devices as Considered in the Author's Contes Philosophiques.* Menasha, Wis.: George Banta Publishing Company, Inc., 1933.

Mitford, Nancy. *Voltaire in Love.* London: Hamish Hamilton, Ltd., 1957; New York: Harper & Row, Publishers, 1957.

Morley, John. *Voltaire.* London: Macmillan & Co., Ltd., 1913.

Naves, Raymond. *Le Goût de Voltaire.* Paris: Garnier, 1938.

———. *Voltaire et l'Encyclopédie.* Paris: Éditions des presses modernes, 1938.

Naves, Raymond. *Voltaire: L'Homme et l'œuvre.* Paris: Boivin, 1942.

Pellissier, Georges. *Voltaire philosophe.* Paris: Colin, 1908.

Pomeau, René. *La Religion de Voltaire.* Paris: Nizet, 1956.

———. *Voltaire par lui-même.* Paris: Éditions du seuil, 1955.

Topazio, Virgil W. *Voltaire: A Critical Study of His Major Works.* New York: Random House, Inc., 1967.

Torrey, Norman L. *The Spirit of Voltaire.* New York: Columbia University Press, 1938; Oxford: The Marston Press, 1963.

———. *Voltaire and the English Deists.* New Haven: Yale University Press, 1930.

Voltaire's "Candide" and the Critics. Ed. Milton P. Foster. Belmont, Calif.: Wadsworth Publishing Company, Inc., 1962.

Wade, Ira O. *The Search for a New Voltaire. Transactions of the American Philosophical Society,* XLVIII (July 1958), n.s.

———. *Studies on Voltaire.* Princeton: Princeton University Press, 1947.

———. *Voltaire and "Candide": A Study in the Fusion of History, Art, and Philosophy.* Princeton: Princeton University Press, 1959.

———. *Voltaire and Mme du Châtelet: An Essay on the Intellectual Activity at Cirey.* Princeton: Princeton University Press, 1941.

Waldinger, Renée. *Voltaire and Reform in the Light of the French Revolution.* Genève: Droz, 1959; Paris: Minard, 1959.